KING P-234

Cornerstone of an Industry™

By Frank Holmes

KING P-234

Published by

LOFT
Enterprises, LLC
2767 Jeep Road
Abilene, KS 67410

Cover Design
Sandy Cochran
Fort Collins, Colorado

Cover Art
Orren Mixer

Design, Typography, and Production
Sandy Cochran Graphic Design
Fort Collins, Colorado

Copy Editor
Dan Streeter
Hurst, Texas

Printing
Friesens Corporation
Altona, Manitoba, Canada

First Printing: November 2004

Softcover

ISBN 0-9714998-5-3

Printed in Canada

DEDICATION

This book is dedicated to Loyce Lee Holmes

...Wife...Partner...Best Friend...

"You are my reason for reason."

INTRODUCTION

I'm just guessing now, but I'll bet 90 percent of horse owners can't tell you their horses' registration numbers. Yet, when anyone thinks of King, they automatically put his registration number with his name: P-234.

The "P" signifies that King was permanently registered, as opposed to "tentatively" registered, which was a category back in the 1940s. But "Permanent" was a good label to put on King, because he has had a permanent and lasting influence on the American Quarter Horse Association.

When AQHA started inducting horses into the American Quarter Horse Hall of Fame in 1989, King went in the first year. In the minds of the Hall of Fame committee members, there was never any doubt.

Even back then, King's influence had been felt in all facets of the industry for more than 50 years. He is not known today as a racehorse sire, but a daughter, Squaw H, burned up the tracks in the late 1940s, running second to world champion Shue Fly in one race, and setting a world record for mares in another. And most people don't remember that Tonto Bars Hank, champion running stallion and winner of the 1960 All American Futurity, traced close-up to King. And almost no one knows that former world champion and all-time leading race sire First Down

Dash is a sixth-generation descendant.

Yes, King sired speed and quickness. But in most cases, those two attributes were not aimed at the racetrack. They went in other directions, those being the ranches and the arenas.

As kids growing up in West Texas in the late '50s and early '60s, trying to learn to rope calves, my friends and I were duly impressed when someone showed up at the roping riding a horse that was "by an own son of King." And why not? Some of the best horses that ever backed into a roping box trace their lineage to King, and have for half a century. In 2003, every AQHA/PRCA Horse of the Year—and that includes calf roping, steer roping, heading and heeling, steer wrestling and barrel racing—had King in its pedigree.

Yep … speed and quickness.

And how about cow sense? Back in 1962, the National Cutting Horse Association started a little cutting that would grow to become the largest and richest event of its kind, the NCHA Futurity. A grandson of King won that first one, and 41 years later, the 2003 Futurity winner traced to King on both the top and bottom—as did the 2003 NCHA world champion.

King and his descendants have left a mark on the American Quarter Horse breed that continues to reverberate throughout the industry. It's been 72 years since he was foaled, 46 since he died, and still he's talked about as though he was royalty.

But, of course—he was King.

Jim Jennings

Jim Jennings
Executive Director of Publications
American Quarter Horse Association

ACKNOWLEDGMENTS

From the very beginning, this volume was designed to be the first installment of a three-book set on the life and times of King, Leo and Three Bars. And what better trio of stallions to bind together in one set than these three legendary sires?

However, two things became apparent right off the bat.

First, even though I had felt I had a rudimentary knowledge of King P-234 and his impact on the Quarter Horse breed, I was overwhelmed at the sheer magnitude of his influence. Dating back to before AQHA was founded and continuing on through more than a half century of evolution and improvement, King's influence upon literally every segment of the Quarter Horse world is profound.

Second, I was quick to realize that the King line was far too expansive to package in just one book. Consequently, in this initial effort I have focused mainly on King's background, his life and the lives of some of his more prominent first-generation get.

A second volume, to be titled, *King P-234, Vol. 2…The Lines of Succession*, is in the works. Separate books on Leo and Three Bars are still planned and will follow, in that order.

As always, this book is the result of a joint effort. My byline might be under the title, but that's about all the farther I'd get were it not for the help of a small army of people. I take this opportunity to recognize and thank those who contributed to the cause.

First and foremost, heartfelt thanks to George and Sue Hearst of Paso Robles, California, for their support. Without it, this book would not be resting in your hands right now.

The American Quarter Horse Association in Amarillo, Texas, also deserves to be recognized. Jim Jennings' crew at the *Quarter Horse Journal*, particularly Tawanna Walker and Sarah Smiddy, helped me locate scores of the great photos that appear on the following pages. Carly Sarrels in the AQHA customer service department provided me with reams of King-related production records.

The American Quarter Horse Heritage Center & Museum also provided an incredible amount of support. Crystal Phares and Gene Storlie patiently granted me access to their rich treasure trove of documents and photos.

Ross Hecox and Alan Gold at the National Cutting Horse Association in Fort Worth, Texas, also pitched in by arranging for me to rifle through their photographic files, and Carol Trimmer at the National Reining Horse Association in Oklahoma City, Oklahoma, searched through that association's photo files and forwarded along the last few reining shots that I felt I needed.

Finally, numerous people who had or have direct connections to the horses that appear in the book dug into their family photo albums and passed along even more priceless images.

Once again, *Paint Horse Journal* senior editor Dan Streeter of Hurst, Texas, served as my copy editor, and Sandy Cochran of Fort Collins, Colorado, was the book's sole designer and graphic artist.

I owe a special debt of gratitude to Bob Lapp of Eau Claire, Wisconsin. Bob is a true equine historian and one of the most meticulous researchers that I've ever known. With each book I write, Bob seems to have an expanded role. In this case, he provided invaluable research and penned the "King and the Saddlebred Controversy" treatise that appears near the end of the book. He also assembled all the data for Appendix A— "All the King's Men"

Finally, thanks to the entire LOFT crew for their support and encouragement.

I've said this before and I'll say it again: If it weren't for all of the help I received along the way, this book would still be on the drawing board and I'd still be looking for a pencil.

Frank Holmes

TABLE OF CONTENTS

Chapter 1

FERTILE GROUND

William Fleming, a frontier Indian fighter and Civil War veteran, founded the all-important "Billy" line of Quarter Horses.
Courtesy American Quarter Horse Heritage Center & Museum

It was a land of heroes and horses… a land in which the hoofbeat of the Spanish Andalusian, the Comanche war pony and the Western mustang still echoed… a land forged under the flags of six nations and conquered on the back of a horse.

It was South Texas, circa 1865.

The Civil War had just ended, and ex-Confederate soldiers by the thousands were returning home. Survivors of every ilk, intent on leaving the horrors and devastation of the conflict behind them, were also migrating west.

Many members of both factions traveled on horseback. In doing so, they introduced new strains of Chickasaw, Brimmer, Tiger and Kentucky Whip blood to what was already a fertile equine breeding ground.

Late in his life, Fleming sold his horses to Fred Matthies of Sequin, Texas. Here's a great turn-of-the-century shot of the two men, taken on the Matthies ranch.
Courtesy American Quarter Horse Heritage Center & Museum

Paul Murray, a 1906 stallion, was by Joe Murray and out of a Fleming mare. Of solid "Old Billy" blood, he served for years as a Matthies herd sire. **Courtesy American Quarter Horse Heritage Center & Museum**

Will Shely of Alfred, Texas, was yet another early South Texas breeder who incorporated the blood of the Billy horses in his foundation herd.

Courtesy American Quarter Horse Heritage Center & Museum

What better region, then, to serve as the cradle of the American Quarter Horse; what better locale in which to plant the seeds that would, six and a half decades in the future, bear fruit in the form of a four-legged King.

Any in-depth analysis of the foundations of the South Texas Quarter Horse must begin with a look at William Fleming of Belmont.

Fleming was born in Georgia on November 18, 1830. After migrating to the Lone Star State as a young man, he joined the Texas Rangers and saw considerable action as a frontier Indian fighter.

When the War Between the States broke out, he joined the Confederate Army and served under its flag for four years. He was wounded several times, and his left arm and hand were deformed as a result.

Fleming, who never married, spent most of his life on his small ranch 60 miles east of San Antonio. He made his living breeding and selling horses, and his brand was the ace of clubs. In his old age, he sold all of his horses to Fred Matthies of Sequin, Texas. Unable to live without them, he moved onto the Matthies ranch and lived there until his death on April 30, 1911.[1]

Fleming's most famous stallion, known first as Billy and then as Old Billy, was named after him.

Billy was an 1860 stallion, sired by Shiloh and out of Ram Cat by Steel Dust. He was thought to have been foaled in the vicinity of Belmont, Texas[2], and his first-known owner was further surmised to have been a local "black-dirt" farmer.

Like Fleming, the farmer fought for the Confederacy. Before leaving home, he chained Billy to a tree to keep him from running away or being stolen. The man's wife fed and watered Billy, but the young stallion was in sad shape by the time the war was over.

In 1865, William Fleming returned from the war and settled near Belmont. Shortly thereafter, he discovered Billy and bought him. The neglected colt's hooves were so long that they had to be sawed off before they could be trimmed. When the chain was removed from Billy's neck, it revealed a scar that he carried for the rest of his life.

Fleming gave $500 for Billy, a small fortune at the time. Over the course of the next two decades, the dark bay Quarter Horse, who stood 14.3 hands tall and weighed 1,000 pounds, established a line of horses so renowned that they came to be known simply as "Billy" horses.[3]

While owned by Fleming, Billy sired a number of top sons, including Martin's Cold Deck, the sire of Dan Tucker and grandsire of Peter McCue.

Peter McCue, of course, stands as one of the greatest Quarter Horse progenitors of all time.

[1] Robert M. Denhardt, *The Quarter Running Horse*, p. 162.
[2] Helen Michaelis, "The Great Little Horse Billy," *The Western Livestock Journal,* May, 1941.
[3] Robert M. Denhardt, *The Quarter Running Horse*, p. 150-151.

His descendants are far too numerous to list here. Suffice it to say that among their numbers were such foundation horses as Wimpy P-1, Chief P-5, Colonel P-8, Whiskaway P-16, Little Richard P-17, Tomate Laureles P-19, Old Sorrel P-209 and Peppy P-212.

It is doubtful, however, if Old Billy would have had as broad an impact on the Quarter Horse breed had it not been for one remarkable mare. That mare, Paisana, must go down in history as the single most influential Quarter Horse matron of all time.

Paisana was thought to have been foaled in 1854 and died in 1888. Her sire was Bailes' Brown Dick and her dam was Belton Queen.

Although Paisana's breeder has been listed as Webb Ross of Scott County, Kentucky, it is more likely that she was bred by Oliver and Bailes of Seguin, Texas. They owned both her sire and dam, and it is a matter of record that Fleming purchased Paisana from them.

Noted Quarter Horse historian Robert Denhardt was able to document that Paisana had 20 foals between 1856 and 1886. Seventeen of these were sired by Billy or one of his sons. These offspring were: Anthony, Artie, Fleming's Red Rover, Jenny Oliver, Dora, Cuadro, Chunky Bill, John Crowder, Alice, Pine Knot, Old Joe, Old Yellow Wolf, Pancho, Joe Collins, Sweet Lip, Whalebone and Little Blaze.

Several of these individuals went on to become key sires and dams in their own right, with their offspring furnishing the seed stock for many of the pioneer Quarter Horse breeding programs that were to follow.

To illustrate the genetic impact of Paisana, consider the fact that, of the first 20 horses to be registered by the American Quarter Horse Association, 12 trace back to her. They are: Rialto P-2, Joe Bailey P-4, Columbus P-7, Colonel P-8, Old Jim P-10, Sheik P-11, Cowboy P-12, Waggoner's Rainy Day P-13, Old Red Bird P-14, Brown Possum P-15, Yellow Boy P-18 and Pancho P-20.

In addition, the following foundation Quarter Horse sires trace back to the venerable producer: Old Fred, Yellow Jacket, Old Joe Bailey, Little Joe, King (Possum), Zantanon, Jim

Little Rondo, an 1895 stallion by Sykes Rondo and out of a Sykes mare, was one of the first stallions utilized by Shely. **Courtesy American Quarter Horse Heritage Center & Museum**

Traveler, the famous "mystery stallion," was the last and most renowned of the Shely herd sires. **Courtesy American Quarter Horse Heritage Center & Museum**

Ned, Concho Colonel, Red Dog P-55, Silvertone, Chubby, Joe Reed II, Blackburn, Pretty Boy, Lucky Blanton and Driftwood.

And, finally, King P-234 traces to Paisana once on the top side of his pedigree and twice on the bottom side.

Taking just the above horses and their descendants into consideration, the case touting Paisana as the most influential Quarter Horse producer of all time is easily made, and even more easily defended.

William Fleming, then, through his creation of the Billy horses, was one of the premier horse breeders of his day. Following close on his heels were such South Texas horsemen as Dow and Will Shely of Alfred, and George Clegg and Ott Adams of Alice.

The mention of all four of these legendary breeders in the same breath necessitates the establishment of a very critical point.

The South Texas horse climate that these men, and scores of others like them, grew up in was one of speed. As far as horse breeding was concerned, Fleming, the Shelys, Clegg and Adams all bred first for speed, then for working ability, and finally (if ever) for looks.

Horse racing was an integral part of the South Texas culture. Played out on a regular basis on fairground racetracks and rural dirt roads throughout the region, it afforded men of all social and economic classes the opportunity for sport and recreation. More importantly, it offered each and every one of them the winner-take-all chance for substantial financial gain.

In the decades to come, this potent South Texas foundation of speed would be taken over by a fresh set of horse breeders and improved upon to create a new class of rope, rodeo and ranch horses. Thus, the impact that the South Texas horse culture of the late 1800s and early 1900s had on the post-Civil War evolution of the Quarter Horse breed can never be overstated. It was that profound.

But let us return to the past.

In 1890, a new century was rapidly approaching and the United States was again embroiled in a military conflict. Known as the Spanish-American War and fought to the ringing battle cry of "Remember the Maine," this clash lasted a mere four months. Still, it was enough to propel Teddy Roosevelt up San Juan Hill and into the White House.

George Clegg (left) of Alice, Texas, had a profound affect on the evolution of the South Texas Quarter Horse. The AQHA Hall of Fame horseman is shown here with lifelong friend John Dial of Goliad, Texas.

Courtesy Quarter Horse Journal

Little Joe, a 1904 stallion by Traveler and out of Jenny, was bred by Clegg. Shown here with owner Ott Adams of Alice, Texas, Little Joe did much to spread the blood of the Billy line throughout South Texas.

Courtesy American Quarter Horse Heritage Center & Museum

Back home in South Texas, life, liberty and the pursuit of fast horses went on as it always had, and it was now time for the Shely brothers to enjoy their moment in the sun.

Dow and Will Shely began breeding horses on their Palo Hueco Ranch in the early 1890s.

Blue Eyes, an 1890 line-bred Billy stallion by Sykes Rondo and out of May Magnum, was their first noteworthy racehorse and sire. Later, they acquired John Crowder, an 1878 chestnut stallion by Old Billy and out of Paisana, to cross on their Blue Eyes daughters. It was an especially good nick, and produced such noted runners as Mamie Crowder and Lady S.

In or around 1903, the Shelys purchased the legendary mystery horse, Traveler, to serve as their third and final herd sire. As has often been chronicled, Traveler was a stallion of unknown breeding who arrived in Texas sometime in the 1890s. Used as a scraper-pulling workhorse for a time, he went on to gain immortality as a racehorse and sire.

The Shely brothers were Traveler's last owners, and he sired his two greatest sons, Little Joe

King (Possum), a 1905 full brother to Little Joe, was also bred by George Clegg. A renowned early-day runner, he established a stronghold of Billy-bred horses throughout Arizona and the Far West.

Courtesy Quarter Horse Journal

and King (Possum), for them. Both stallions were out of the mare known as Jenny.

Unlike Traveler, Jenny's breeding was firmly established and represented some of the most potent Billy blood of the day. Sired by Sykes Rondo and out of May Magnum, she was a full sister to the Shelys' first herd sire, Blue Eyes.

Sykes Rondo was an 1887 sorrel stallion by McCoy Billy by Billy, and out of Grasshopper by Cold Deck. May Magnum was an 1882 bay mare by Anthony by Old Billy and out of Belle Nellie by Fanning's Tiger.

In his reference volume, *Foundation Dams of the American Quarter Horse*, Robert Denhardt calls May Magnum one of the all-time great South Texas mares. She was the dam of four colts and six fillies, all sired by Sykes Rondo.

Of these, two of the colts—Blue Eyes and

Yellow Jacket, a 1908 dun stallion by Little Rondo and out of Barbee Dun, was a noted racehorse who saw action against both Little Joe and King (Possum). He is shown here in 1912 with O. G. Parke Jr. in the irons.

Courtesy Quarter Horse Journal

Dogie Beasley—and four of the fillies—Jenny, Mamie Sykes, Nettie Harrison and Baby Ruth—went on to make significant contributions as breeding animals. Jenny, the dam of Little Joe and King (Possum), was the most prolific.

And the South Texas Quarter Horse continued to evolve and improve.

Just as the Shely breeding program had prospered through the use of Fleming-bred horses, so did the subsequent programs of George Clegg and Ott Adams through the use of Shely-bred stock.

George Clegg began his horse breeding program in the early 1900s with Lane's Little Rondo, a son of Sykes Rondo. In 1905, he purchased Hickory Bill, a son of Peter McCue. Hickory Bill, who had been bred by Samuel Watkins of Petersburg, Illinois, went on to sire Old Sorrel, the foundation stallion of the King Ranch of Kingsville, Texas.

In 1905, Clegg also purchased a yearling stallion named Little Joe from the Shelys. As noted earlier, Little Joe was sired by Traveler and out of Jenny.

In Little Joe, Clegg was sure he saw a promising runner. He paid the Shelys $250 for the undersized colt and shipped him by rail to his ranch near Alice.

Clegg's plans to turn his new acquisition into a racehorse were reportedly met with a healthy dose of skepticism from both family and friends. That changed as soon as the colt began his 2-year-old racing campaign.

By this time, Little Joe had grown into a nice-looking bay that stood 14.2 hands high and weighed 1,050 pounds in racing shape. He had a star and one white rear pastern.

The exact number of races he ran has been lost to the ravages of time and poor record-keeping, but by Clegg's own account, the

Ott Adams, "the little man from Alice," parlayed a wealth of intuitive ability and the blood of the Billy and Little Joe horses into an AQHA Hall of Fame horse breeding career.

Courtesy Quarter Horse Journal

stallion raced from his 2-year-old through his 6-year-old year.[4]

Little Joe was known as a hard-mouthed, hard-headed competitor who met and defeated such top runners as Texas Chief, the famous son of Traveler; Carrie Nation, one of the best daughters of Peter McCue; and Lady S., the Shely-bred daughter of John Crowder. He was also reported to have bested his formidable brother King (Possum) in several training races.

In his prime, the Clegg-trained racehorse was hand-timed to have run 440 yards in 22 seconds flat, from a 20-foot score. He was defeated only twice.

---

[4] Garford Wilkinson, "George Clegg—Pioneer Breeder…," *Quarter Horse Journal*, Jan. 1959, p. 31.

Grano de Oro, a 1925 stallion by Little Joe and out of Della Moore, had a modest impact on the breed as a broodmare sire.   **Courtesy American Quarter Horse Heritage Center & Museum**

Joe Moore, a 1927 full brother to Grano de Oro and Ott Adams' choice to succeed his famous sire, had a much broader and longer-lasting influence on the breed.   **Courtesy Quarter Horse Journal**

Joe's first setback came in 1908, in a four-horse field that included Ace of Hearts, the top sprinting son of Sykes Rondo. After false-starting twice—and sprinting the full 440-yard race distance both times—Little Joe got off to a regulation break and was bested by Ace of Hearts by a nose. Clegg tried on numerous occasions to get a rematch from "Ace's" owners, but to no avail.

Joe's second defeat came as an aged horse, and then only after he had received an ankle injury while in polo training. Matched against the future Waggoner Ranch sire Yellow Jacket at Kyle, Texas, he was beaten and subsequently retired.

In 1910, with Hickory Bill firmly entrenched as his main herd sire, George Clegg sold Little Joe to his friend and neighbor Ott Adams.

Born in 1869 on a ranch in Llano County, Texas, Ott Adams was several years older than George Clegg. A scant five feet in height, Adams had relocated to Alice, Texas, as a young man because he had heard the best horses were being raised there. Although he was built like a jockey, Adams never cared to train or campaign racehorses. He just wanted to breed them.

In 1904, to kick off his program, the resolute Texan paid a visit to the nearby Shely brothers' ranch. There, he was shown three Traveler colts that were for sale, including Texas Chief and Little Joe.

Adams opted for the more reasonably priced Texas Chief. In time, however, he became dissatisfied with him, claiming that he had too much size due to his part-draft horse dam, and traded him back to the Shelys for Captain Joe, another Traveler son. Captain Joe also failed to satisfy Adams, so he sold him and purchased Little Joe as a 6-year-old from George Clegg.

Lady of the Lake, a 1926 mare by Little Joe and out of Silver Queen, was bred by Ott Adams. Eventually acquired by the King Ranch of Kingsville, Texas, she is shown here after winning grand champion halter honors at a 1937 Kingsville horse show. **Courtesy American Quarter Horse Heritage Center & Museum**

Ada Jones, a 1918 mare by Little Joe and out of Mamie Crowder, was not particularly good-looking but played an intriguing role in the perpetuation of the "Billy" horse.

Courtesy American Quarter Horse Heritage Center & Museum

In 1912, Dow and Will Shely dispersed their breeding herd. Adams was quick to seize the opportunity to add some top mares to his program. Among those were Mamie Crowder, Julia Crowder, Moselle and Little Kitty.

Bred to Little Joe, "Mamie" and "Julia" proved to be exceptional producers and laid the foundation for what became one of the most storied speed-breeding programs in Quarter Horse history.

The Ott Adams-Little Joe partnership blossomed and continued for 16 years. Initially breeding his Traveler son to his Sykes Rondo- and John Crowder-bred mares, Adams eventually expanded his program to include some Hickory Bill and Horace H (TB) mares, as well.

Woven Web (TB), a 1943 mare by Bold Venture and out of Bruja, was a three-time Champion Quarter Running Horse. Despite her Thoroughbred papers, the rugged mare was actually an Ada Jones/Little Joe/Billy-bred Quarter Horse.

Courtesy American Quarter Horse Heritage Center & Museum

The results of his efforts began making a name for themselves throughout South Texas as both race and breeding animals, and a new generation of local horsemen such as John Dial of Goliad, John Almond of Corpus Christi, and Robert Kleberg Jr. of the King Ranch began to build their own programs with horses of Adams breeding.

Indicative of the profound effect that the Ott Adams–Little Joe program had on the South Texas scene was the mare Ada Jones.

A 1918 chestnut (roan) mare by Little Joe and out of Mamie Crowder, Ada Jones traced six times to Old Billy and three times to Piasana. Bred by Adams, she was sold to John Dial of Goliad, Texas.

Dial successfully raced "Ada" and then sold her and her daughter Chicaro's Hallie, a 1930 roan mare by Chicaro (TB), to the King Ranch. Billy blood notwithstanding, Chicaro's Hallie was registered as a Thoroughbred in The American Stud Book with her dam being given as Lady Eloise (TB).[5]

Bred to the King Ranch stallion Livery (TB) in 1935, Chicaro's Hallie produced Bruja. Bred in turn to such King Ranch icons as Depth Charge (TB) and Bold Venture (TB), Bruja pro-duced Encantadora, a 5 furlong world record holder; Haunted, a 4½ furlong world record holder; and Woven Web, a 2½ furlong world record holder.

Woven Web, who like her two sisters was a bona-fide Ada Jones descendant, was also campaigned on the straightaway tracks under the name of "Miss Princess." In addition to being a 350- and 440-yard world record holder, she was the 1946-47, 1947 and 1948 Champion Quarter Running Horse.

The blood of the Billy horses was potent indeed, and served to inject raw speed when-ever and wherever it was employed.

By the time 1916 rolled around, America stood yet again on the brink of war. Three years earlier, World War I had erupted in Europe. The United States entered the fray in 1917. Of the more than 1 million troops it sent overseas, 100,000 would never return.

In spite of the impending conflict, it was business as usual for Ott Adams and Little Joe. As South Texas luminaries, the two were in their prime.

The stage was now set for the production of a racing wonder and royal sire.

---

[5] Robert M. Denhardt, *Foundation Dams of the American Quarter Horse*, p. 110.

Encantadora (TB), a 1948 mare by Depth Charge and out of Bruja, was a five furlong world record holder. Like her famous half-sister, Woven Web, the registered Thoroughbred mare was in reality an "Old Billy" Quarter Horse.

***Courtesy* Quarter Horse Journal**

Chapter 2

THE MEXICAN MAN O' WAR

Zantanon, a line-bred "Billy" descendant, earned fame as both a race horse and sire.
Courtesy American Quarter Horse Heritage Center & Museum

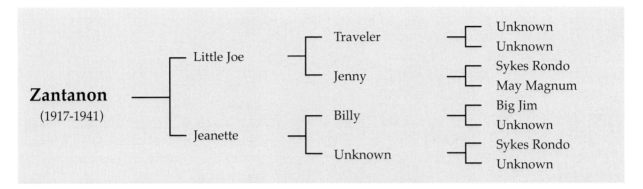

					Unknown
		Traveler			Unknown
	Little Joe				Sykes Rondo
		Jenny			May Magnum
Zantanon					Big Jim
(1917-1941)		Billy			Unknown
	Jeanette				Sykes Rondo
		Unknown			Unknown

Ott Adams, "the little man from Alice," was a racehorse man, pure and simple.

"I'm raising running horses," he once remarked. "A man can't make a living raising cow horses; you don't get enough money for them.

"I've learned from my experience and from the experience of others, that good bloodlines will not only produce speed but will produce good rodeo and cow horses. When you have speedy bloodlines on both sides, you won't have to worry about conformation; it will take care of itself."[1]

As one of the Quarter Horse breed's most storied "short-horse" aficionados, Adams knew what he was talking about. After all, he had been privileged to have either owned or personally known such legendary stallions as Traveler, Hickory Bill, Old Sorrel, Little Joe and Joe Moore.

A horseman once asked Adams to name the best stallion he had ever seen. The venerable breeder's reply was quick and to the point: "Sykes Rondo."

And why not?

South Texas was "Billy" country, and Sykes Rondo—a top ranch and race mount—was one of the best representatives of that line.

In 1916, Adams bred Little Joe—a Sykes Rondo grandson—to Jeanette—a double-bred Sykes Rondo granddaughter. This line-bred cross resulted in a 1917 sorrel colt that became

arguably his sire's greatest son, Zantanon, "El Mexicano Hombre de Guerra," the Mexican Man O' War.

Although Zantanon and Man O' War were foaled the same year, 1917, they were not foaled on the same date. Zantanon was foaled on either March 27 or 28, and Man O' War on March 29. Still, both became legends in their respective breeds and there were enough similarities in their lives to invite comparison.

Man O' War, or "Big Red" as he came to be known, was foaled in the lap of luxury and raced on the finest tracks in the eastern United States. Competing during that giddy, self-indulgent age known as the Roaring '20s, he

Although raced under the harshest of conditions, Zantanon proved to be a durable champion.
Courtesy American Quarter Horse Heritage Center & Museum

[1] "Ott Adams…Quarter Horse Breeder," *Horse Lover's*, February/March 1953, pp. 38-39.

Cuatro de Julio (Fourth of July), a 1936 chestnut stallion by Zantanon and out of Blackie, was a race and performance Register of Merit sire. **Courtesy Quarter Horse Journal**

Huge sums of money were known to have changed hands every time the sorrel stallion crossed the finish line.

In February of 1918, though, Zantanon was just one of several year-ling colts residing on a sleepy little ranch in South Texas. The youngster's name, by the way, came about as a result of an incident that happened early in his life.

Several visitors to the Adams ranch were admiring the foals. The sorrel colt bit one of the onlookers rather severely on the elbow. "Es santo non," ("He's no saint,") the victim remarked. The name, anglicized, stuck.[2]

For the country-at-large, the spring of 1918 was one in which both good news and bad news loomed on the horizon. The good news was that nine months hence, on November 18, 1918, the armistice would be signed ending World War I and bringing the American doughboys home.

The bad news was that both Europe and the United States would soon be locked in a life and death struggle of another sort—with one of the most deadly flu epidemics of all time.

Worldwide, the Spanish Influenza pandemic of 1918 killed at least 21 million people—well over twice the number of combat deaths in all the war. It first appeared in the United States in the spring of 1918. By the end of November, 600,000 Americans had died.

The virus proved to be exceptionally viru-lent, turning people black and blue and killing them in a matter of hours. In October alone, 195,000 Americans died. Society began to break down. People would not leave their homes for fear of contracting the disease. Industry came to a standstill and homeless children roamed the cities.[3]

won 20 of 21 starts, earned $249,465 and attracted a legion of loyal fans.

Zantanon came from more humble begin-nings and raced under more austere condi-tions.

Foaled on Ott Adams' small spread on the outskirts of Alice, Texas, Zantanon competed on the dirt roads and makeshift tracks of Northern Mexico. Although the purses he ran for were, for the most part, modest, his small group of backers was also very loyal. They followed their champion, or "campéon," wherever he went and backed up their unwa-vering belief in him with cold, hard cash.

[2] Robert M. Denhardt, "Zantanon—Mexico's Man O' War," *Western Horseman*, June 1962, p. 57.
[3] Frank Holmes, "Wire to Wire—the Walter Merrick Story," pp. 16-17

The epidemic wrought as much havoc in the rural areas of the Southwest as it did in the industrial regions of the Northeast. No part of the country was immune to its threat.

As daunting as the flu menace was, however, it was not enough to prevent Erasmus Flores of Nuevo Laredo, Mexico, from journeying to the Ott Adams ranch in February of 1918 in search of race prospects.

The young horseman wound up purchasing three head, including Zantanon. Eventually, the youngsters were placed in race training. Flores' uncle, Don Eutiquio Flores, saw Zantanon as the most promising of the trio and bought him.

The elder Flores raced Zantanon until the stallion was 14 years old. As a result of Zantanon's winnings, which totaled $40,000,

Bob Cuatro, a 1957 bay stallion by Cuatro de Julio and out of Leota W, was the 1963 Arizona All-Around Performance Champion. The ROM qualifier is shown here with well-known trainer John Hoyt in the saddle.

Courtesy Quarter Horse Journal

Flores became a wealthy man with a ranch and several buildings in town.

In his last race, Zantanon was matched against Coneza, a swift young daughter of Ace of Hearts. Ace of Hearts was one of the only two horses to ever defeat Little Joe, Zantanon's sire, and Coneza had twice bested Pancho Villa, Zantanon's full brother.

Zantanon proved too wily a campaigner for the youthful mare to handle, however. He scored perfectly, broke on top and led all the way to the wire.

In 1931, when Zantanon became too old to race, he was sold to Manuel (Meme)

Benavides Volpe of Laredo, Texas, for $500.

Born in Old Mexico in 1893, Volpe had immigrated to the Laredo area at the age of 10. An ambitious young man with an entrepreneurial bent, he took an inheritance he received in 1919 and converted it into a five-section ranch west of town.

Oil was discovered on the ranch and Volpe, who had long harbored a love of fast horses, used part of the ensuing royalties to get into the racehorse business.

First, he purchased Camaron, a Shely-bred stallion by Texas Chief and out of Mamie Crowder. Next, he assembled a set of the best

San Siemon, a 1934 chestnut stallion by Zantanon and out of Panita by King (Possum), was bred by Manuel Benavides Volpe of Laredo, Texas. Sold to Bert Benear of Tulsa, Oklahoma, the Little Joe grandson did more than his share to spread the fame of the Zantanon line.

Courtesy Quarter Horse Journal

speed-bred broodmares that money could buy. Finally, with both sides of the genetic equation in place, he began breeding race-horses in earnest and campaigning them throughout the Southwest.

Valentino, by Camaron and out of Jeanette by Harmon Baker, was one of the first of the Volpe-bred horses to make a name for himself. Just as the promising young racehorse and sire was coming into his own, though, an opportunity arose that placed him on the proverbial back burner.

Zantanon came up for sale and Volpe, who was very familiar with the ex-racehorse, was quick to act.

"My father's greatest desire was to beat Zantanon," Volpe said. "He and Flores matched horses many times, at least eight or 10, but Zantanon won every time.

"Soon, my father learned to dislike the horse that had outrun him so many times,

and when I bought Zantanon, he knew I had obtained one of the greatest old horses that ever lived but he would never admit it."[4]

By age, Zantanon was in the prime of his life when he was returned to the land of his birth. By condition, he was old and worn out.

In an article appearing in the May 1947 issue of *The Ranchman*, Volpe reminisced about the legendary stallion's "south of the border" racing career and the toll it exacted on him.

"First of all," he said, "I must tell you [Zantanon] was starved to death all his life. When I bought him in Mexico at 14 years of age, he was so weak and poor and full of ticks that he could hardly walk. He made the Mexicans who raced him rich, and their method of training was very hard on the horse.

"They would walk him on hard gravel streets from downtown to the track, four

[4] Unknown author, "Zantanon – The Man O' War of Mexico," *The Quarter Horse*, Aug 1948.

Little Sue, a 1929 sorrel mare by Sam Watkins and out of Sorrel Perez, was bred by George Clegg, of Alice, Texas. Acquired by Bert Benear and bred to San Siemon, the ex-rodeo mount had a profound impact on the breed.

Courtesy Quarter Horse Journal

Black Hawk, a 1937 black stallion by San Siemon and out of Little Sue, was bred by Bert Benear. Sold to King Merritt of Federal, Wyoming, he helped establish the Zantanon line in the Rocky Mountain region.
Courtesy American Quarter Horse Heritage Center & Museum

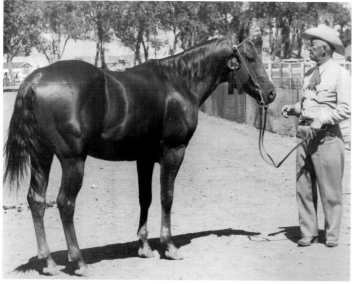

Frog W, a 1946 sorrel stallion by Black Hawk and out of Mae West P-56, was bred by Alexandria Casement of Sterling, Colorado. Sold to C. G. and Milo Whitcomb, also of Sterling, the good-looking stallion earned fame, first as a performer and then as a top sire.
Photo by James Cathey, courtesy Milo Whitcomb

good miles. Then they would trot him, and gallop him, and jog him at the track until his sweat would dry out. Then they would walk him back home the same four miles. They would not cool him, but instead would tie him under a tree and let him stay tied until four o'clock in the afternoon. Then they would saddle him up again and walk him on the hard gravel streets until dark.

"They fed him at night on oats and corn for grain and corn fodder for roughage. By that time, he was so tired he would not eat as he should. By the day of the race, he was so poor you could count each and every one of his ribs. By that time, of course, he had no pep but was absolutely dead on his feet. Yet in that condition and with his owner's son weighing 140 pounds and a surcingle (as we did not know the race saddles at that time down here), he could run 300 yards in 15⅗th seconds [from a] walking start. I really believe that he was a phenomenon to run at that speed with the weight he carried in his condition.

"In my opinion, Zantanon was the fastest horse I have ever seen, and I have seen Lady of the Lake, his half-sister; I have seen Punkin; and I have seen Shue Fly. I still consider Zantanon faster than all of them up to 300 yards for sure and maybe up to a quarter.

"John Armstrong, one of the best horsemen and the best rider that I know, said of Zantanon, 'He had won his races on his breeding only, as the condition of the horse is such that most any other horse in such condition would not catch a cow.' "[5]

After being purchased by Volpe, Zantanon's life took a decided turn for the better. Groomed and well fed

[5] "Zantanon," *The Ranchman*, May, 1947, p. 32.

for the first time in years, the aged horse was also accorded his first real opportunity as a breeding stallion. He responded by becoming one of the greatest sires of his day.

During the next nine years, Zantanon did not stand to outside mares. He was used, instead, on a small, select band of Volpe-owned mares. Among their number were direct daughters of Harmon Baker, Little Joe, Captain Joe, Joe Abb and Paul Ell.

Zantanon's first Texas foal crop arrived in 1932 and included King. His last foal crop hit the ground in 1940 and included Ed Echols. Sandwiched in between these two renowned

stallions were a number of other top-notch sons and daughters.

It must be noted here that—like Fleming, the Shely brothers, and Clegg and Adams—Volpe's contributions to the early-day Quarter Horse breed were of monumental import. Unlike the men who preceded him, however, Volpe has never been given his just due.

Through his discerning use of Zantanon alone, he afforded the Quarter Horse breed some of its greatest foundation stallions. These horses—when sold to pioneer breeders in Texas, Oklahoma, Colorado, New Mexico,

Here's Whitcomb's Frogette, a 1950 sorrel mare by Frog W and out of Whit's Sue. Bred by the Whitcomb family, "Frogette" was one of the Rocky Mountain region's first AQHA Champion show horses.

Photo by James Cathey, courtesy Milo Whitcomb

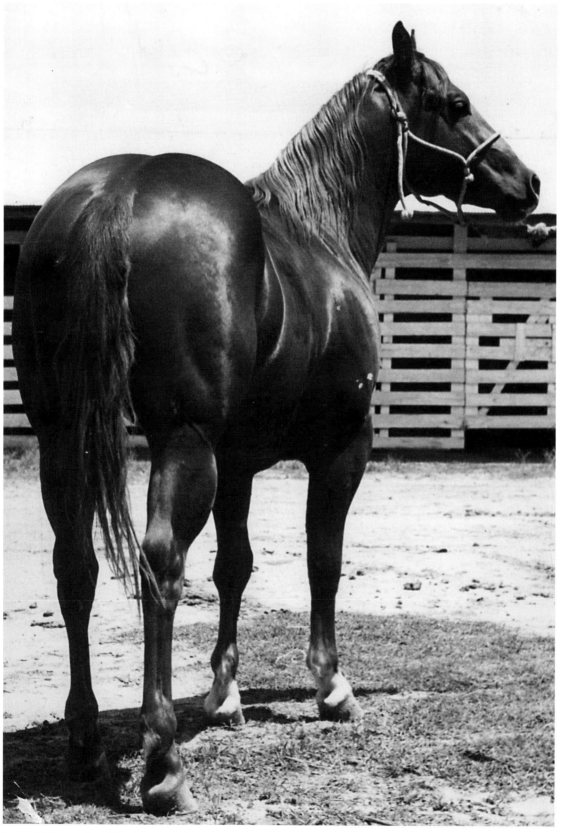

Leo San, a 1949 sorrel stallion by Leo and out of San Sue Darks by San Siemon, was bred by H. H. Darks of Wetumka, Oklahoma. A top sire in his own right, he bequeathed the breed several equally potent sons.

Courtesy **Quarter Horse Journal**

Arizona and California—played critical roles in improving the breed and propagating it throughout the land.

Simply put, Manuel Benavides Volpe was a pioneer Quarter Horse breeder of the highest order and his official recognition as such is long overdue.

Of Zantanon's Volpe-bred sons, King, San Siemon and Ed Echols were the most influential. King will be dealt with in detail in a subsequent chapter.

San Siemon, a 1934 stallion out of Panita, was owned by Bert Benear of Bartlesville, Oklahoma. Benear was one of the new wave of Quarter Horse breeders who took up where the South Texas breeders had left off. More interested in rodeo and show horses than he was in racehorses, he took animals purchased directly from George Clegg, Ott Adams and Manuel Volpe in the mid- to late 1930s and used them to breed a host of early-day rodeo and show greats.

When Benear bred San Siemon, who he had purchased from Volpe, to Little Sue, who had been bred by Clegg, he came up with a golden cross that resulted in such superior individuals as Black Hawk, Joe Barrett, Sue Hunt and San Sue Darks.

When these four horses—some of which were shown and some of which were not—were placed in production, they spawned the lines that would one day produce AQHA Super Horse Sweet And Innocent, NRHA reining icon Continental King, and NCHA cutting greats Peppy San and Mr San Peppy.

San Siemon never enjoyed the notoriety that King and Ed Echols did. Nor did he put the numbers on the board—in terms of AQHA-registered offspring—that his two famous half-brothers did. If he had, there is no telling how influential a sire he might have become.

Peppy San, a 1959 sorrel stallion by Leo San and out of Peppy Belle, was bred by G. B. Howell of Seagoville, Texas. The 1967 NCHA Open World Champion Cutting Horse, he is also an AQHA and NCHA Hall of Fame horse.

Courtesy Quarter Horse Journal

Ed Echols, a 1940 stallion by Zantanon and out of Dorothy E (TB), benefited from both notoriety and numbers. Purchased from Volpe by W.D. "Dink" Parker of Tucson, Arizona, for $1,500, he was subsequently owned by Ray Sence of Burbank, California; Jack Clifford of Kelseyville, California; and B.F. Phillips of Frisco, Texas.

Mr San Peppy, a 1968 sorrel full brother to Peppy San, was also bred by Howell. The 1974 and 1976 NCHA Open World Champion Cutting Horse, he, too, is an NCHA Hall of Fame Horse.

Courtesy Quarter Horse Journal

Named after a famous early-day Arizona rodeo cowboy and Pima County sheriff, the half-Thoroughbred stud proved equally adept in siring speed, working ability and conformation.

Among his AAA-rated racing get were Ed Heller, Little Smoke Echols, Dusky Parker, Parker's Trouble, Dark Intruder and Echols Baby.

Among his top arena performers were Echo Reed, Superior Calf Roping and 1964 AQHA High-Point Calf Roping Horse; Mike Echols, 1964 AQHA High-Point Reining Stallion; Bert Echo, Superior Cutting; Echo Ed, Superior Reining; and Gin Echols, Superior Cutting.

Among his top all-around get were AQHA Champions Hula Girl P, Cherry Echols, Annie Echols, Zantan Echols, Bert Echo, Echo Brett and Echo Ed.

And, as had been the case with San Siemon, the blood of Ed Echols proved potent for generations to come and resulted in such race, show and cutting stalwarts as Arizonan, 1955 Champion Quarter Running Gelding; Big Step, sire of 18 AQHA Champions; Tanquery Gin, sire of NCHA earners of more than $2 million; Par Three, Superior halter horse and sire of 10 AQHA Champions; and Zan Parr Bar, three-time AQHA world champion, three-time AQHA high-point award winner, and sire of 40 AQHA world champions and 43 AQHA high-point award winners.

In addition to King, San Siemon and Ed Echols, several other Zantanon sons made noteworthy contributions to the breed.

Zandy, a 1934 stallion out of a mare by the Strait Horse, was a Register of Merit performance horse and the foundation sire of the well-known Haythorn Ranch of Ogallala, Nebraska. Chico, a 1936 full brother to San Siemon, was a grand champion halter horse and the foundation sire of the F.E. Weimer Quarter Horse program in Council Hill, Oklahoma.

Still other Zantanon sons, such as Sonny Kimble, Jack Salinas, Cuate, El Bandido, El Rey H, Cuatro de Julio, Dock and Zantanon Jr, made solid contributions, as well.

Zantanon was foaled 23 years before the formation of AQHA, and died one year after its inception. As a result, only 33 of his get found their way into the registry. Sixteen of these were stallions, and the remaining 17 were mares.

Zantanon daughters proved to be excellent producers. Several of them—such as Maria Elena, Gondola H, Little Potato and Uncle's Pet—were at their best when crossed back on the Zantanon–King lines.

Getting back to the patriarch of the family, in or around 1936, Manuel Volpe decided to disperse his horses. Zantanon and the majority of his broodmare band were sold to Byrne

Ed Echols, a 1940 chestnut stallion by Zantanon and out of Dorothy E, was bred by Manuel Benavides Volpe of Laredo, Texas. Sold to W. D. "Dink" Parker of Sonoita, Arizona, he went on to become a leading foundation sire.

Photo by James Cathey, courtesy Quarter Horse Journal

Ed Heller, a 1947 sorrel stallion by Ed Echols and out of Glass Eyes, was bred by Dink Parker. One of the Southwest's first AAA-rated racehorses, he was a three-time stakes winner and a seven-time track record holder.

Courtesy Quarter Horse Journal

Here's Annie Echols, a 1952 sorrel mare by Ed Echols and out of Orphan Annie. A grand champion halter horse with 40 points to her credit, she was also a AAA, AQHA Champion and Superior halter producer.

Courtesy Quarter Horse Journal

Gin Echols, a 1954 chestnut mare by Ed Echols and out of Gin Squirt (TB), was bred by Ray Sence of Burbank, California. Sold to B. F. Phillips, Jr. of Frisco, Texas, she went on to earn a Superior cutting award.

Courtesy Quarter Horse Journal

James of Encinal, Texas. Unable to fill the void left by the colorful stallion's departure, Volpe bought him back within a year.

By 1941, Zantanon's health was failing. As a result, Volpe sent him to the home of Alonzo Taylor, a friend who lived near Hebbronville, Texas. Taylor planned to take the stallion to Dr. J.K. Northway, the famed King Ranch veterinarian, for treatment. However, Zantanon died shortly after arriving at Taylor's, before any treatment could be prescribed.

For a stallion who spent the first half of his life in relative obscurity, and who was not—for all practical purposes—utilized as a breeding animal until he was 14 years old, the horse known as the Mexican Man O' War had a far-reaching and positive impact on the Quarter Horse breed.

Zantanon might not have been a saint, but he was absolutely a sire.

Mike Echols, a 1960 bay stallion by Ed Echols and out of Poco Dotty, was an AQHA Champion and the 1964 High-Point Reining Stallion. Through his NRHA Hall of Fame daughter Glenda Echols, he has continued to exert a positive influence on the reining horse industry.

Courtesy Quarter Horse Journal

Chapter 3

A KING IS BORN

King P-234 – Cornerstone of an Industry. This classic photo of the mahogany bay stallion was taken in Rocksprings, Texas.
Courtesy Quarter Horse Journal

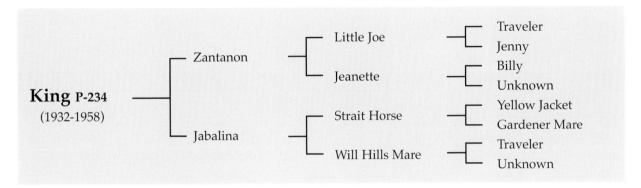

King P-234
(1932-1958)

- Zantanon
  - Little Joe
    - Traveler
    - Jenny
  - Jeanette
    - Billy
    - Unknown
- Jabalina
  - Strait Horse
    - Yellow Jacket
    - Gardener Mare
  - Will Hills Mare
    - Traveler
    - Unknown

As the 1920s drew to a close, Zantanon neared the end of his racing career and approached the beginning of his breeding career. The country-at-large was also in a state of transition. The Roaring '20s had jitterbugged its way to an end, and a new, more somber decade loomed on the horizon.

On October 29, 1929—or "Black Tuesday," as it came to be known—Wall Street came crashing down and the country was sent spiraling into the worst economic depression in history. More than 5,000 banks failed. Millions of bank patrons lost their life savings, the American economy ground to a halt and 15 million people found themselves out of work.

In the Midwest, the national woes were compounded by years of severe drought and the effects of poor farming practices. Much of this area came to be known simply as the Dust Bowl.

It was into this volatile setting that a horse sired by Zantanon and out of Jabalina, and who was destined for true greatness, was born.

As detailed in the previous chapter, Zantanon was the product of South Texas "Billy" horse breeding. Jabalina was steeped in the blood of the South Texas "short horse," as well.

AQHA records show Jabalina to be an unregistered mare by the Strait Horse and out of a bay mare of unknown breeding. Another account lists her as being a 1925 brown mare by the Strait Horse by Yellow Jacket,

bred by Fred Binkley of Encinal, Texas. Yet another lists her dam as a Will Hill mare by Traveler. Given the fact that William Hill was a Binkley neighbor and a noted stockman, this last version is conceivable.

The Strait Horse was a 1918 dun stallion sired by Yellow Jacket and out of a Gardner Quarter mare. He was bred by O.G. Parke of

Jess Hankins – Rancher, pioneer Quarter Horse breeder, 13th President of the American Quarter Horse Association and AQHA Hall of Fame horseman. **Courtesy Quarter Horse Journal**

Byrne James of Encinal, Texas, was King's third owner. He is shown here with Band Play, another of his foundation stallions.

Courtesy J. Frank Daugherty

Kyle, Texas, and owned by Yancey C. Strait of Big Wells, Texas.[1] The Gardner Quarter mare is further surmised to have been sired by Traveler. Again, with Traveler having been owned for a number of years by the Gardner brothers of San Angelo, Texas, this speculation is plausible.

Yellow Jacket was a 1908 dun stallion by Little Rondo and out of Barbee's Dun by Lock's Rondo. He was bred by Jim Barbee of Kyle, Texas, and later owned by John Parke, also of Kyle; W.T. Waggoner of Fort Worth, Texas; and J. Lee Bivins of Amarillo, Texas.[2]

Through his double infusion of Rondo blood, Yellow Jacket traced twice to Old Billy and once to the redoubtable Paisana.

At some point in the late 1920s, Manuel Benavides Volpe acquired Jabalina—who was also known as the hog-backed, or hump-backed, mare. The circumstances surrounding the acquisition were, to say the least, unusual.

"My good friend, Fred Binkley of Encinal, Texas," Volpe said, "waged Jabalina against one of my fat heifers, that his expectant wife would bear him a baby boy. As it turned out,

the child was a girl, and Jabalina became mine."[3]

In 1931, Volpe bred Jabalina to Zantanon for the first time. That breeding bore fruit on June 25, 1932,[4] in the form of a mahogany bay colt who was known for the first few years of his life simply as "Buttons."

By his own account, Volpe made the Zantanon and Jabalina cross three more times. The resulting foals were Jack Salinas, a 1934 chestnut stallion; El Rey H, a 1935 sorrel stallion; and Gondola H, a 1936 chestnut mare.[5]

AQHA records credit Jabalina with being the dam of three additional horses: Queen, by Valentino; Pluma, by Valentino; and Little Jabalina, a 1936 chestnut mare by Zantanon.

Volpe's breeding records, recorded in Spanish, offer the following clarification: "Binkley's big brown mare foaled 15 September, 1930; had a dark bay filly sired by Valentino. Small brown Binkley mare foaled 22 May, 1931; brown filly by Valentino."[6]

Given the fact that Valentino has but two AQHA-identified get—Queen and Pluma—it seems safe to theorize that they are the two Valentino fillies that appear in Volpe's breeding book.

Furthermore, given the exacting descriptions of the two fillies' dams that appear in the same journal, it is apparent that Volpe owned not one, but two Binkley mares. Jabalina was probably one of the two, but which one is purely a matter of conjecture.

Finally, as far as Little Jabalina is concerned, AQHA records list Volpe as her breeder. His breeding records, however, do not substantiate that claim.

Of the four known Zantanon-Jabalina full siblings, only Buttons went on to achieve any measurable level of fame.

[1] Robert M. Denhardt, *Foundation Sires of the American Quarter Horse*, p. 208
[2] Robert M. Denhardt, *Foundation Sires of the American Quarter Horse*, p. 237
[3] M. Benavides Volpe, letter to *The Cattleman*, May, 1958, pp. 104-107
[4] M. Benavides Volpe, letter to *The Cattleman*, May, 1958, pp. 104-107
[5] M. Benavides Volpe, letter to *The Cattleman*, May, 1958, pp. 104-107
[6] Garford Wilkinson, "M. Benavides Volpe," *Quarter Horse Journal*, Aug. 1962, p. 19

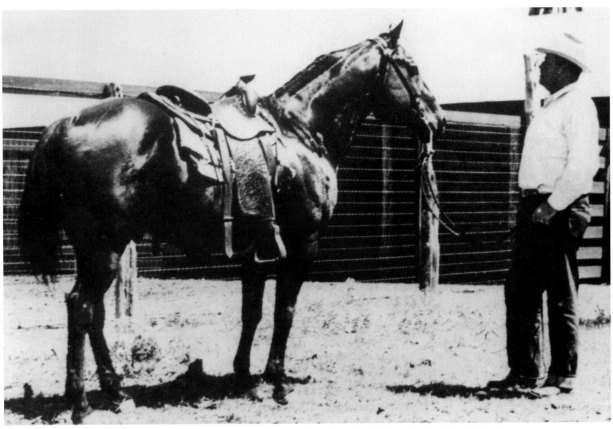

Jess Hankins of Rocksprings, Texas, bought King as a 5-year-old on July 5, 1937.   **Courtesy Quarter Horse Journal**

To begin with, he was sold by his breeder prior to being weaned. Charles Alexander of Laredo, Texas, was the buyer and the price was $150. Alexander was reputed to have successfully raced Buttons two or three times as a "rough-broke young horse."[7]

Whether these contests did, in fact, occur, and whether they were backyard training events or organized sprints, has never been fully documented.

In late 1933 or early 1934, Buttons came to the attention of Byrne James of Encinal, Texas. James, who was a rancher and professional baseball player, reportedly got his first glimpse of the young stallion as he was being led down a dusty Laredo street by a Mexican handler. Impressed by the colt, he immediately conspired to own him.

Again, varying accounts of this pivotal point in Buttons' life have appeared in print over the years. Several were garnered through first-hand interviews with James, but even these fail to lay certain key points of confusion to rest.

In one account, James said: "I fell in love with the colt and trailed him and the boy to Charlie Alexander's place. I bought [him] on the spot for $325. His name was Buttons. I bought [him] in 1931. He was a long yearling, so Charlie Alexander couldn't have raced him, because [he] was too young, and unbroke. I'm the one that broke him. [He] was 3 years old when I left him [and] went back to New York to play with the Giants. Don't tell me I've forgotten the year, because it's the year [1933] we beat Washington and won the World Series."[8]

In a subsequent story, however, James contradicts himself, saying, "I bought [Buttons] as a young horse from Benavides Volpe and

[7] Nelson C. Nye, *Champions of the Quarter Tracks—Squaw H*, p. 176.
[8] Lyn Jank, "The Horse That Would be King," *Eastern/Western Quarter Horse Journal*, June 1988, p. 16.

The Hankins family headquarters was located on the River Ranch, six miles south of town.

Courtesy Quarter Horse Journal

we broke him on the ranch. The year that [Buttons] was a 3-year-old, in 1935, I was playing baseball for the Giants."[9]

Whenever the transaction took place, and however old Buttons was at the time, it is a matter of record that James did buy him, that he did train him for calf roping, and that he did change the horse's name. Or, more accurately, his wife did.

Mrs. James, who was quite enamored with the young stallion's rich, "gold-flecked" bay color and regal bearing, decided that Buttons was just not a masculine-enough moniker. She settled, instead, on the name by which the stallion would be known for the rest of his life: King.

By the mid-1930s, Byrne James and King were regular fixtures at local "ranch roping" contests. The Texas stockman was impressed enough with his young stallion that he paid a visit to the Volpe Ranch and successfully negotiated the purchase of Zantanon and 40 mares. Among those mares was the hog-backed Jabalina.

The cards were stacked against the production of any more full siblings to King, though. Shortly after Jabalina was turned out to pasture on the James Ranch, she waded into a stock pond, got tangled up in some submerged wire and drowned.

As detailed earlier, in the spring of 1935, James was called up to play ball for the New

[9] Byrne James, "My Life with Quarter Horses," *Western Horseman*, Sept. 1979, p. 26.

York Giants. King was loaned to W. O. "Win" DuBose of Uvalde, Texas, with the understanding that he would stand the stallion to outside mares on a share basis. The stud fee was set at $10 and James' share of the proceeds amounted to $100.[10]

At the conclusion of the baseball season, James returned home to Encinal. By this time, DuBose had decided that he would like to be King's next owner. He offered $500 for the young stallion, and James accepted.

Like James, Win DuBose was a calf roper and he continued to use King for that purpose. He also used him for steer-necking, a South Texas-based sport in which a steer is roped and then led up to a forked tree or post to which it can be tied and eventually gathered up.

"Once I had King in Uvalde," DuBose said, "I got serious about roping. We hauled about to everywhere, but there's one haul that sticks out in my mind more than any of the others.

"In those days, we hauled in open trailers and all I'd do with King was leave his bridle on and sic him into the trailer, and he'd ride free like that with the wind in his face. Once, when we were on our way to a rodeo, this truck with canvas flapping everywhere passed us, and that scared my horse. The feel of King squatting down and getting ready to jump came all the way into me in the driver's seat, and I put on the brakes easy-like.

"King jumped as I was coming to a standstill. He shattered everything there was on the front end of the trailer. It was long-tongued, so he had a ways to go, but he made it to the top of my car, knocking out my rear windshield on the way and denting the roof to heck and gone. Then he jumped

Situated in the South Texas region known as the Edwards Plateau, the ranch was ideally suited for the raising of cattle, sheep and Angora goats.

Courtesy Quarter Horse Journal

onto the hood and landed like a cat, hunkered down on all four feet.

"He sprung off, wheeled around and nickered at me, then trotted on up the road. I ran and got him and put him back in what was left of the trailer. We went on to the roping, and I won it."[11]

Over the next several years, DuBose and two of his friends—Johnny Stevens and Lester Gilleland—hauled King to numerous South Texas roping contests. According to Gilleland, who passed the information on to fellow King enthusiast T. C. Stoner of Uvalde, Texas, all three men felt they were well-mounted.

[10] Byrne James, "My Life with Quarter Horses," *Western Horseman*, Sept. 1979, p. 26.
[11] Lyn Jank, "The Horse That Would be King," *Eastern/Western Quarter Horse Journal*, June 1958, p. 18.

In addition to being noted Quarter Horse breeders, Jess and Olga Hankins were also avid big game hunters. Here the couple is in the mid-1960s, at home in their spacious, trophy-laden living room.

Courtesy **Quarter Horse Journal**

"Lester Gilleland was a personal friend of mine," Stoner said. "And we were both big fans of King, so we spent many hours reminiscing about him.

"Lester told me that King was a good match-roping horse for several reasons. First off, he was consistent. He'd give you a good run every time out of the box. No matter how slow or fast the calf was, King would rate it and pick it up at around the same spot in the arena. No matter what the draw, he'd put you in a position to win.

"And then, if you drew a big or rank calf, all you had to do as you were stepping off King to tie the calf was to touch him on the neck. If you did that, he'd screw his ol' tail in the ground and set down hard. He'd take a lot of the fight out of the calf before you even got to it.

"Lester told me it got to the point that no one wanted to match Win and him in a roping. He said, one time, they matched a roping up north someplace, around Kerrville or Fredericksburg. When they got there and it was time to put up the money, the boys who were going to rope against them took one look at King and said, 'We didn't know you boys were the ones who had that bay stud. If you're going to use him, we ain't gonna match you. You can ride any other horse and

Jess Hankins and King P-234, shown here in front of the Hankins' River Ranch home, created a Quarter Horse dynasty. **Courtesy Quarter Horse Journal**

4 3

we'll go ahead and rope. But if you're going to use that bay stud, the deal is off.' "

By the time 1937 rolled around, King's reputation as both a top roping mount and a promising young sire was on the rise. As a result, he came to the attention of the man who became his fifth, and final, owner.

That man was Jess L. Hankins.

The Hankins family was not native to the Lone Star State. James Lowell Hankins, patriarch of the clan, was a farmer from Pine Bluff, Arkansas. In 1912, with a wife, three sons and a daughter to provide for, he relocated from the southeast corner of "The Natural State" to the Eastland County region of Texas, midway between Fort Worth and Abilene. Several years later, he moved again, this time to a ranch situated in Terry County, southwest of Lubbock.

Soon after arriving in West Texas, Hankins sent his eldest son, Jess—who was born April 23, 1905—to attend San Antonio Academy in San Antonio, Texas. One year later, Jess transferred to the Baptist Academy in San Marcos, Texas.

Shortly after arriving in San Marcos, Jess was introduced to fellow student Olga

Burney, the daughter of Mr. and Mrs. Leo Burney of Rocksprings, Texas. From the onset, it was apparent that the two young students had much in common.

To begin with, both came from solid ranching backgrounds and shared a love of animals, the great outdoors and sports. Jess was a standout basketball, football and track competitor and the captain of both his football team and military squad. Olga, two years Jess's junior, was an outstanding basketball player, and was editor-in-chief of the annual and president of the Home Economics Club. Jess was named the best all-around boy in his graduating class and Olga was named the best all-around girl of her class.

The pair seemed made for each other, and after a courtship that lasted several years, they were married on July 24, 1925.

Jess initially took his bride back to Texas and his parents' ranch. Shortly thereafter, his father purchased another ranch in Taylor County and moved his family to Abilene. Jess and Olga remained on the Terry County ranch for several years, in an isolated existence fraught with hard work and loneliness.

In the spring of 1926, the young couple

King's broodmare band was comprised mainly of mares of "Old Billy," Zantanon and Little Joe blood.

***Courtesy* Quarter Horse Journal**

King's consistency as a sire was readily apparent in the get-of-sire competition that was popular in the registry's early years. Here, a trio of King get win the get-of-sire class at the 1953 Houston Livestock Exposition.

***Courtesy* Quarter Horse Journal**

paid a visit to her parents' ranch near Rocksprings. Jess liked the milder climate, diverse agricultural opportunities and abundance of wild game, and eventually purchased four sections of grazing land 10 miles west of town and the couple moved there.

In the mid-1930s, J. L. Hankins traveled down from Abilene to see Jess and Olga. Impressed with the lay of the land, the elder Hankins staked his son and daughter-in-law to a second ranch. In 1936, Jess and Olga decided their new property, called the River Ranch and situated six miles south of town, would serve as an excellent headquarters and relocated to it.[12]

Having been farm- and ranch-raised, Jess Hankins was no stranger to animal husbandry. The region of South Texas that he

and his young bride had chosen for their new home proved to be rich in livestock ranching opportunities.

Rocksprings, the seat of Edwards County, is situated 100 miles west of San Antonio on the banks of Hackberry Creek. The town was so named because of the natural springs bubbling forth from the rocks. The surrounding Edwards Plateau region is rough and hilly land, well suited for raising cattle, sheep and mohair-producing Angora goats.

By this time, the late 1920s to early 1930s, it was also a land well stocked with good horseflesh. The descendants of the Billy horses that had been so successfully bred in South Texas had begun to find their way into the South Central, North Central and far western portions of the state.

[12] Garford Wilkinson, "Jess Hankins—13th President of AQHA," *Quarter Horse Journal*, April 1964, pp. 22-24.

At the 1950 Southwestern Livestock Exposition and Fat Stock Show in Fort Worth, Texas, the Hankins-owned brood-mare Miss Taylor won the produce-of-dam class. From the left, the winning horses and their handlers are Cactus King and Britt Fulps, and Poco Bueno and Jess Hankins.

Courtesy Quarter Horse Journal

By 1936, Jess and Olga and their two daughters—Olga Fay and Jessie Lea—were settled into the life of long hours and hard work that was considered the everyday fare of "The Dirty '30s."

The hard economic times and persistent drought that held most of the American West in its steely grip wreaked havoc on the Rocksprings region, as well. Faced with the double specter of starving livestock and non-existent markets, many farmers and ranchers were forced to shoot their own animals. Land holdings of every size and description were lost to bank and tax lien foreclosures. Able-bodied men begged for the chance to trade a full day's labor for the going wage of 50 cents.

It was a time and place in which only the strong survived. Already well adapted to the rigors of isolation and hard work, Jess and Olga were among those hardy souls who not only persevered, but eventually prospered.

Jess was one of the first ranchers in his area to recognize the value of diversification. On the livestock front, he raised cattle, sheep and goats. To supplement his ranching income, he acquired a meat market and a Jeep dealership.

In support of his livestock operations, Jess also maintained a string of ranch mounts.

Among their number was an above-average mare of Thoroughbred and Quarter Horse breeding. One day, Jess mentioned to one of his ranch hands that he would consider breeding the mare if he could find a good enough stallion. The hand told Jess that Win DuBose had a rope horse that might fit the bill, so Jess loaded his mare in a trailer and made the 75-mile trek south to Uvalde.

Years later, he recalled the incident.

"Before we even stopped the truck," he said, "I knew I had found the horse to whom I wanted to breed my mare, and I also knew that someday I was going to own that stallion. I thought then, and still think, he was the most magnificent stallion I had ever seen."[13]

Jess immediately made DuBose an offer to buy King. The offer was just as promptly turned down. Hankins did, however, get his mare bred to DuBose's stallion, a mating that resulted in Ginger H, a 1938 chestnut mare.

Noteworthy for being the first of what became hundreds of Hankins-bred King get, Ginger H went on to produce eight foals. When bred to Joe Bailey P-4, she produced Little Ginger H, a 1943 sorrel mare. Little Ginger H, when bred back to King, produced Scharbauer's King, a 1949 black stallion and a top sire in his own right.[14]

Back in Rocksprings, Jess Hankins was not ready to give up on the notion of owning King. As spring gave way to summer, he continued to negotiate with DuBose on a purchase price that both men could live with. Finally, Hankins offered $800 for King and DuBose accepted—with one stipulation. The

[13] Franklin Reynolds, "King P-234," *The Cattleman*, Sept. 1957, p. 56.
[14] Appendix A, p. 236.

By the mid- to late 1950s, King was one of the most popular Quarter Horses in the world. Here a Mexican contingent poses with the famous stallion after being accorded a tour of his home.

***Courtesy* Quarter Horse Journal**

Uvalde rancher wished to compete in calf roping at several upcoming rodeos. The last two of these were scheduled for the 4th of July, an afternoon performance in Comfort, Texas, and an evening event in Kerrville. DuBose agreed to deliver King to Hankins at the conclusion of the second contest.

True to his word, DuBose pulled into Rocksprings at two o'clock on the morning of July 5, 1937, with King in tow.

"Jess was waiting on a corner," DuBose said. "Wasn't anyone around except me and him and the horse. We transferred King from my trailer to Jess's, and I watched them drive off. Years afterward, when King got so famous, I knew just how piddling $800 was for such a horse."[15]

DuBose's acceptance of Hankins' offer—piddling or not—caught the young Rocksprings rancher off guard. Having just purchased a truckload of calves, he was without the necessary funds to complete the transaction.

Jess first approached his father about a loan. The elder Hankins was reluctant to help, expressing his concern over the outrageously steep price. Jess then turned to his younger brother, Lowell, for aid. Lowell had never seen King, but he was familiar with Win DuBose. He reasoned that if DuBose thought highly of the stallion, then he was probably good enough to take a chance on. He loaned his big brother the money, and the deal was finalized.

But only weeks after arriving on the Hankins ranch, King threw a scare into his new owner.

"I hadn't had King but a few weeks, and a damn rattlesnake bit him on the head," Hankins said. "[It] swelled up 'bout as big as a barrel. We didn't have any vets or anything—just had to kind of let Nature take care of most of it. It scared me to death, but he got over it all right."[16]

At the time Jess Hankins bought King for $800, the median price for a new car was $675. To start recouping some of what amounted to a major investment, the stallion's stud fee for the remainder of the 1937 breeding season was set at $15. In 1938, it was raised to $25, and in 1939, to $50. By 1940, King's stud free was an unheard-of $100 and Hankins was reported to have had to turn down 80 mares.

The astronomical jump in the bay stallion's service fees was probably due, at least in part, to the fact that there was a movement afoot that stood an excellent chance of making every Quarter Horse in the land a much more valuable commodity.

In March of 1939, Robert M. Denhardt, a young Texas A & M college professor, published an article in *Western Horseman* magazine titled, "The Quarter Horse, Then and Now." That article was a rallying point for a group of people who were interested in forming a Steel Dust—or Quarter Horse—registry.

That same month, Denhardt met with several breeders in Fort Worth during the Southwestern Livestock Exposition and Fat Stock Show in an attempt to gauge the interest in a registry. One year later, on March 14, 1940, J. Goodwin and Anne Hall Goodwin hosted a supper in their Fort Worth home to further discuss the matter.

The following evening, 75 people met at the Fort Worth Club. Stock subscriptions were taken, a constitution and by-laws were adopted, 20 directors were appointed and the American Quarter Horse Association was born.[17]

Although he had been invited to attend the inaugural AQHA meeting, Jess Hankins was unable to do so because of illness. He was subsequently asked to purchase stock in the fledgling association and promptly did so.

For better or worse, the new registry was very much a product of the Texas "Bulldog" Quarter Horse scene. While it is true that such prominent out-of-state horsemen as J. E. Browning of Willcox, Arizona; Albert Mitchell

[15] Lyn Jank, "The Horse That Would be King," *Eastern/Western Quarter Horse Journal*, June 1988, p. 18.
[16] Richard Chamberlain, "King P-234," *Quarter Horse Journal*, May 1964;
[17] Don Hedgpeth, *They Rode Good Horses*, p. 3.

of Albert, New Mexico; Jack Casement of Whitewater, Colorado; and Marshall Peavy of Clark, Colorado; were among the association's founding fathers, it was, by and large, a Lone Star State endeavor.

And in Texas, the Billy horse still ruled; so much so that, of the first 100 horses to be AQHA-approved, 96 traced to the Civil War-era stallion.

In Rocksprings, Jess Hankins had a line-bred Billy stallion that he wished to get registered with the new association. Through luck or fate, the stallion was inspected, accepted and assigned a number that was easy to remember. So easy that, in time, it simply became an extension of the horse's name—King P-234.

It was a name and number destined to be known throughout the land because, just as

the American Quarter Horse Association would take hold, flourish and spread to every corner of the country, so, too, would the King P-234 family of horses multiply and be dispersed nationwide.

Throughout modern horse breeding history, promising young sires have benefited by being bred to mares that "nick" with them. These nicks, or "golden crosses," resulted in the production of superior individuals that quickly established the line as an "up and comer."

Early on in his life, King P-234 was the beneficiary of not one, but two such crosses. The first of these occurred, quite appropriately, when two members of Hankins Quarter Horse royalty were united.

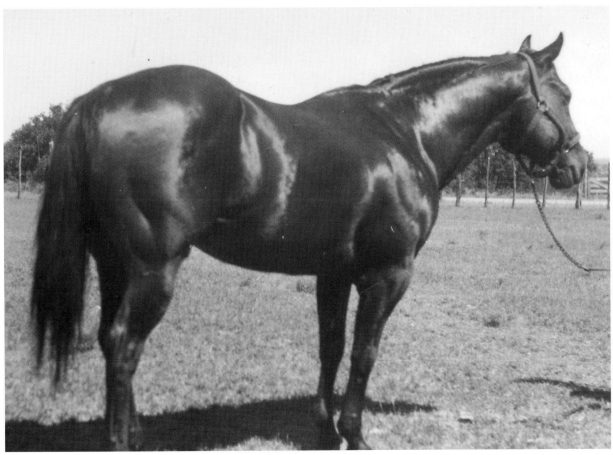

Here's a newly discovered shot of King. Judging by his excellent shape and nice-looking neck, it was probably taken at some point during his abbreviated show career.

Courtesy American Quarter Horse Heritage Center & Museum

Chapter 4

THE FIRST FAMILY

Queen H, a 1936 sorrel mare by Dan and out of a Nail Quarter mare, provided the distaff power for the first great King cross.
Courtesy Quarter Horse Journal

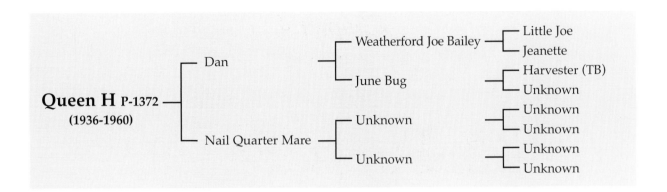

Queen H P-1372
(1936-1960)
- Dan
  - Weatherford Joe Bailey
    - Little Joe
    - Jeanette
  - June Bug
    - Harvester (TB)
    - Unknown
- Nail Quarter Mare
  - Unknown
    - Unknown
    - Unknown
  - Unknown
    - Unknown
    - Unknown

The decade of the 1940s dawned upon a country that had once again learned to hope. Beginning in the mid- to late 1930s, the economic chaos of the previous 10 years had been replaced with a New Deal blueprint for stability and growth.

During that same time period, a racehorse named Seabiscuit emerged as a symbol of the newfound hope that coursed through the land. When the undersized, overachieving Seabiscuit took on and trounced the mighty War Admiral in a 1938 match race, the entire

Here is a rare, never-before-published, shot of King P-234 in his prime. Although the exact date and location of this shot are unknown, the show ribbon affixed to King's halter narrows the date down to 1941 or 1942.
Courtesy American Quarter Horse Heritage Center & Museum

Duchess H, a 1940 bay mare by King and out of Queen H, was the earliest representative of "El Primero Dorado Cruz" – the first golden cross.

Courtesy American Quarter Horse Heritage Center & Museum

nation shared in the victory.

A bold new wind blew across the land.

In Europe and the Far East, the winds of change were also on the move. What they whispered of was not rebirth and prosperity, however. They were the winds of war and they spoke instead of death and destruction.

On September 1, 1939, Nazi Germany invaded Poland, and a new word, "blitzkrieg" or "lightning war," found its way into the world's vocabulary. By the summer of 1940, the German army had attacked and conquered Denmark, Norway, the Netherlands, Belgium, and France. On July 10, the Battle of Britain was joined.

Squaw H, a 1941 full sister to Duchess H, was the individual most responsible for King,s early rise to prominence as a sire. The speedy-looking mare is seen here in racing shape with AQHA Hall of Fame horsewoman Helen Michaelis of Eagle Pass, Texas.

Courtesy American Quarter Horse Heritage Center & Museum

In the United States, the Isolationist Movement that advocated nonintervention in other countries' affairs attempted to insulate the country from the horrors of what was transpiring overseas. Life in this country was good and getting better all the time. And in Rocksprings, Texas, a certain Jess Hankins-owned bay stallion was quickly establishing himself as one of the top Quarter Horses in all the land.

At the time AQHA was formed in the spring of 1940, King was an 8-year-old. One of the first orders of business for the new association was the creation of organized horse shows. Although King was an aged horse, Jess Hankins felt compelled to test the waters with him in sanctioned competition and showed him at halter five times.

On July 4, 1941, King placed second to Dexter P-193 in the aged stallion

Shown first at halter, Squaw H was a multiple grand champion.
Courtesy Quarter Horse Journal

Sent to the track by breeder J. O. Hankins of Rocksprings, Texas (left), Squaw H became a record-setting racehorse.
Courtesy Quarter Horse Journal

Retired from racing and bred to her sire, Squaw H produced Squaw King, a 1956 chestnut stallion.

Courtesy Quarter Horse Journal

competition at Stamford, Texas; on October 2, 1941, he was named the champion aged stallion at Abilene, Texas; and on October 26, 1941, he placed second to Little Joe Jr. P-430 in the aged stallion class at Eagle Pass, Texas.

In March of 1942, King placed second to Red Jacket P-255 at the Southwestern Livestock Exposition and Fat Stock Show in Fort Worth, Texas. Later that same year, he put the wraps on his brief halter career by being named the grand champion stallion at a show in San Angelo, Texas.

King was also entered in several performance competitions.

At the 1941 Abilene show, he was named the champion stock horse. At the 1942 Southwestern Livestock Exposition, he won a reining go-round, placed second in the reining finals, and second in the cutting.

From the very beginning, however, it was apparent that King's true calling was not as a show horse, but rather as a sire.

Even prior to the formation of AQHA, King P-234 had put a number of get on the ground that went on to make solid contributions as performers and/or breeding animals. Among them were two sons—King April and King Gotch—and two mares—Clyde Sis and Dipsydoodle Milligan. These four individuals were joined in short order by three additional sons of note: King Joe, Cuellar and Jess Hankins.

Together, these horses secured King a solid rating as a top regional sire. What was needed now was a second, better set of horses to propel King into the national limelight.

In the spring of 1941, a small bay filly was born that would set that ball in motion. Bred by J.O. Hankins of Rocksprings, the filly was the first of several full siblings to result from "El Primero Dorado Cruz," the first golden cross.

J.O., born on November 22, 1917, was the third and youngest of the Hankins boys. Like his brothers before him, he opted early on for a farming and ranching lifestyle.

To begin with, J.O. farmed with his father, J.L. Hankins, in the Abilene, Texas, area. In 1935, at the age of 18, he bought a ranch 20 miles northeast of Rocksprings. For several years, he and his wife, the former Velma Clark, continued to maintain an Abilene residence and commute back and forth to the Rocksprings ranch. In the late 1930s, the young couple relocated to the southern location.

In time, their branch of the Hankins family tree would grow to include four children: Sheila, Kay, J. L. and Clark.

In the winter of 1939, J.O. decided to follow the lead of his oldest brother and get into the Quarter Horse business. In the hunt for a young broodmare prospect, he and his father attended an Abilene auction.

J.O. was bidding on a young mare when a local farmer named Hay—who knew the elder Hankins—approached him and said that he had a nice filly he would like to sell. His asking price was $100, a pretty steep amount at the time.

J.O.'s interest was aroused though, so he said that he would look the filly over the next time he was in town. A month later, the younger Hankins drove up from Rocksprings, collected his father and continued on to the Hay farm.

Once there, the Hankins duo was treated to the sight of a 3-year-old, blaze-faced mare of exceptional quality. Still, $100 was a lot of money to give for a Depression-era horse, so J.O. told Hay that he would think the matter over and get back to him within a couple of days.

At that point, J.O.'s father spoke up and told Hay that he could consider the filly sold, that if his son didn't take her, he would.

"After my dad said he would take her," J.O. later recalled, "I knew I had to have her. My dad wouldn't give $100 for a horse unless it was a good one."[1]

"Queen," the object of the Hankins's' interest, was a 1936 sorrel mare by Dan and out of a Nail Quarter mare. Dan was, in turn, a 1920 sorrel stallion by Weatherford Joe Bailey and out of June Bug by Harvester (TB).[2]

---

[1] Nelson C. Nye, "Hankins' Mare," *Quarter Horse Journal*, Nov. 1949, p. 10.
[2] Robert M. Denhardt, *Foundation Sires of the American Quarter Horse*, p. 83.

Sold to B. A. Skipper Jr. of Longview, Texas, Squaw King displayed great potential as a cutting horse. Skipper's death in a 1962 airplane crash, ended the talented stallion's budding show career.

Courtesy **Quarter Horse Journal**

Weatherford Joe Bailey, like so many other good horses of that day, was a line-bred descendant of Old Billy and Piasana. The Nail Quarter Mare was of unknown breeding.

Queen, who was subsequently registered with AQHA as Queen H, was in foal to a Percheron stallion at the time of her purchase. She gave birth to her half-draft foal on April 19, 1939, and was bred to King P-234 eight days later. On April 24, 1940, she foaled a bay filly that was—to say the least—something of a disappointment.

"[She was] the ugliest thing I had ever seen," J.O. said. "I was ashamed for anyone to see the dang thing and offered to take $75 for her. But nobody wanted her. Later on, when she had filled out a little, you wouldn't hardly have known her.

"In July, I took her to a colt show in Kerrville and she placed first in her class. The following July, I took her to Stamford, and although only a yearling, she was named Grand Champion Mare. I called her Duchess H."[3]

Queen H was re-bred to King in 1940 and gave birth to a second sorrel filly on April 19, 1941. J.O. named her Squaw H, after Coke Roberds' famed Peter McCue daughter, "Old Squaw," and immediately began preparing her for a show and racing career.

As was the case with every aspect of American life during the early to mid-1940s, however, the development of the Quarter Horse breed in general, and the King family of horses in particular, was subject to the ever-widening impact of the war.

On December 7, 1941, the Japanese launched a sneak attack on the U.S. Pacific fleet at Pearl Harbor. President Roosevelt successfully lobbied Congress to declare war on Japan. Germany and Italy promptly declared

[3] Nelson C. Nye, *Champions of the Quarter Track—Squaw H*, p. 174-5.

El Greco, a 1940 chestnut stallion by King and out of Old Sugar, was one of the first Hankins-bred horses to be import-ed to the West Coast. Purchased by pioneer breeders Channing and Kathy Peake of Lompoc, California, El Greco went on to become a champion show horse and sire. **Courtesy American Quarter Horse Heritage Center & Museum**

war on the United States, and Roosevelt and Congress reciprocated by declaring war on them.

The Age of Isolationism was over.

Unemployment disappeared as most of the able-bodied men were drafted and sent overseas. Women were actively recruited to the workforce and "Rosie the Riveter" became one of the country's most popular pinup girls. Automobile production ceased in 1942, and rationing of food supplies began in 1943. Home garden plots, known as Victory Gardens supplied 40 percent of the nation's vegetables.

Despite the material and emotional hardships that they endured throughout the war years, the American people went about their day-to-day lives as best as they could.

Booger H, a 1942 sorrel stallion by King and out of Queen H, topped the 1945 Hankins Brothers horse sale. Sold to Perry Cotton of Visalia, California, he was initially groomed as a show horse.
Courtesy Quarter Horse Journal

After being purchased from Cotton by the Peakes, the stallion was successfully campaigned as a racehorse.
Courtesy Quarter Horse Journal

Boomer Isle, a 1958 sorrel gelding by Booger H and out of Honey Bug, was an AQHA Champion. He is shown here with Bob Hollister in the saddle after earning honors as the 1963 Pacific Northwest Quarter Horse Association All-Around Champion Horse. **Photo by Shirley Dickerson, courtesy Quarter Horse Journal**

For J.O. Hankins, that meant raising cattle, sheep and children—and racing horses. In Squaw H, his second homebred King foal, J.O. found that he had the perfect vehicle for speed.

As luck would have it, Squaw H's appearance on the straightaway coincided with emergence of Quarter Horse racing as an organized sport.

In the early 1940s, a group of Tucson, Arizona, horsemen formed the Southern Arizona Horse Breeders Association (SAHBA). Shortly thereafter, they began racing horses at a local track owned by R.C. "Bob" Locke of Hacienda Moltacqua. When the Locke ranch was sold in 1943, J. Rukins

Jelks of nearby Rillito offered the use of his training track.

This second track—located on the banks of the Rillito River northwest of Tucson—was the birthplace of modern-day Quarter Horse racing.

Under the direction of Melville Haskell, an American Quarter Horse Hall of Fame inductee, and Van Smelker, who later became head of the AQHA Performance Department, SAHBA experimented with weighted handicaps, futurities, derbies and stakes races, and photo-electric timers. Beginning with the 1940-41 racing season, the group also named yearly racing champions, known as

Cue Stick, a 1960 chestnut gelding by Booger H and out of Cue 13, was an AQHA Champion and Superior Western pleasure horse. Here he is after being named the grand champion gelding at a 1966 Covina, California, show.

Photo by Danny Santell, courtesy Quarter Horse Journal

Champion Quarter Running Horses.

In early 1945, the American Quarter Racing Association (AQRA) was born. Not a blood registry per se, AQRA's main purpose was to identify horses for racing and devise a uniform method by which their performances could be graded.[4]

Short-horse racing enthusiasts throughout the West were quick to respond to the Arizona initiatives and such world famous sprinters as Shue Fly, Joe Reed II, Piggin String, Hard Twist, Queenie and Miss Panama flocked to Rillito to compete against each other.

Squaw H raced there, as well, but not until she was deemed ready.

"I broke her to the saddle right here on the ranch," J.O. said. "My wife first rode her

bareback while I led her around. Then I rode her about the ranch for about two months before I started training her to run. For that purpose, I took her to Jess Barker at Sonora 20 days before the Eagle Pass meet that year [1943]."[5]

At Eagle Pass, Texas, Squaw H was raced twice and recorded one win and one second. The following spring, she made two starts at Cowboy Park in El Paso, Texas. After winning her first race there, she was matched in a second contest against a field that included Shue Fly—the reigning Champion Quarter Running Mare. Shue Fly won the 340-yard sprint, with Squaw H finishing second by a half-length.

After the El Paso meet, Squaw H was trailered home to the Hankins ranch and turned

[4] Frank Holmes, *Wire to Wire—the Walter Merrick Story*, p. 85
[5] Nelson C. Nye, *Champions of the Quarter Tracks—Squaw H*, p. 176

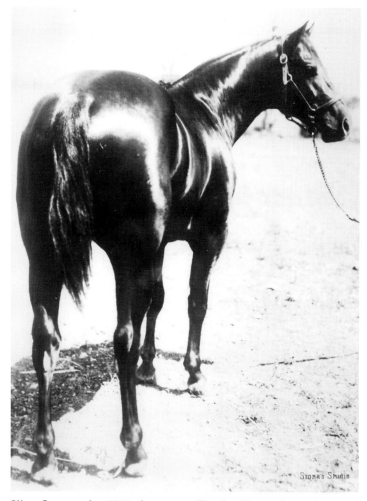

King Command, a 1955 chestnut stallion by King and out of Crickett McCue, was an early-day J.O. Hankins herd sire.

Courtesy Quarter Horse Journal

was 440 yards. At the finish line, it was Squaw H by a nose over a deep field of horses that included Chovasco (Maggie), Punkin, Queenie and Jimmy.

In the 1945 World's Championship Quarter, held at Rillito, Squaw H finished second by a head to Queenie—the 1945-46 Champion Quarter Running Horse. Shown at halter in the big Tucson Livestock Show, the race-fit mare was named the grand champion model cow horse mare.

In seven racing seasons—1943 through 1949—Squaw H made 19 official starts. Competing at distances ranging from 220 to 440 yards, she notched seven firsts, eight seconds and two thirds. In her last race, run in March of 1949, "Squaw" won the 250-yard Tucson Speed Stakes over Leota W, Miss Panama and Wagon N. Her time of :13.6 established a new world's record for mares and was only one-tenth of a second off the overall world's record.

Although Squaw H was not the first of the King horses to achieve success as a performer, she was without a doubt the first to attain superstar status. She was also unique in several other ways.

To begin with, she was a dyed-in-the-wool Billy horse who, without the benefit of any Thoroughbred blood, met and defeated the top "hot-blooded" racehorses of her era.

Secondly, she was a Quarter Horse with classic "bulldog" conformation who also managed to qualify as one of the breed's first AAA-rated sprinters.

Finally, and more important in the over-all scheme of things, Squaw's stellar show and racing achievements focused national attention on the King P-234 family of horses in general, and the King/Queen H golden cross in particular.

And that cross was just firing up.

Hank H, a 1942 sorrel stallion, was the family's next addition. One of the best-looking

out on pasture for several months. Taken back up in early fall, she was sent to Blain Speers for conditioning.

One month later, Speers entered the mare in the Quarter Mile Championship at the 1944 New Mexico State Fair in Albuquerque. Pitted against the formidable Shue Fly and equally dangerous Queenie, she managed to eke out a third-place finish.

From Albuquerque, Speers hauled Squaw H to the Eagle Pass fall meet. Matched against the good Flying Bob daughter Rosedale in a 350-yard affair, she won it handily. Then, on October 29, 1944, the Hankins mare ran what is generally conceded to have been her best race. The occasion was the Eagle Pass Derby, and the distance

King horses of all time, Hank H went on to achieve success as a show horse, racehorse and sire. He will be profiled in a subsequent chapter.

Flapper H, a 1944 chestnut mare, came next. Unlike her three older siblings, "Flapper" was not shown or raced. Used primarily as a broodmare, she was the dam of Hard Twist II, a Register of Merit racehorse; and Flapper's Breeze, an AQHA Champion.

By the mid-1940s, the Hankins brothers were well on their way to becoming highly successful Quarter Horse breeders, and the world was just as far along in surviving its latest conflict.

On June 6, 1944—D-Day—the Allies stormed Normandy Beach and began the invasion of Europe. Eleven months later, Germany surrendered unconditionally.

President Roosevelt did not live to see the end of the war. On April 12, 1945, he died of a massive cerebral hemorrhage, and Harry S. Truman was sworn into office.

Commander King, a 1958 bay stallion by King Command and out of Bay Reba, was a top J.O. Hankins-bred, Duchess H/Queen H descendant. **Courtesy Quarter Horse Journal**

Sold to James Kemp of Dallas, Texas, Commander King went on to become an AQHA Champion, Superior cutting horse and the NCHA earner of $1,578.

Courtesy Quarter Horse Journal

On August 6, 1945, Truman authorized the first atomic bomb to be dropped on Hiroshima, Japan. Three days later, a second bomb was dropped on Nagasaki. Japan officially surrendered on September 2, 1945, and World War II was over.

In Rocksprings, the King P-234/Queen H combine continued to churn out champions. Booger H, a 1945 chestnut stallion, was the fifth to be foaled.

By the late 1940s, King and the Hankins brothers had turned Rocksprings, into something of a Quarter Horse mecca. With wartime gas rationing a thing of the past, horsemen from throughout the land flocked to the Texas Hill Country in search of King-bred horseflesh.

The Californians were among the first to tap into the Hankins-bred mother lode.

In late 1941 or early 1942, Channing and Kathy Peake, Lompoc, California, imported El Greco to the Golden State. A 1940 chestnut stallion by King and out of Old Sugar, El Greco was the champion aged stallion at the 1945 Pomona, California, show. This event was the first AQHA-approved horse show ever held in California.

In 1945, in response to the growing demand for their horses, the Hankins brothers began holding their own auction sales. The third such auction took place on October 25, 1948, when the brothers offered 32 head of "Little Joe-bred" horses.

Booger H, then a 3-year-old, was the high-selling horse at $1,500; Dan Traveler, a weanling colt by Joe Traveler and out of Flapper H, was the second-highest-selling horse at $1,100; and Little Duchess H, a 2-year-old mare by King and out of Duchess H, was the third-highest-seller at $900.

Booger H was purchased by Perry Cotton of Visalia, California, and promptly re-sold to Katy and Channing Peake of Lompoc, California. The Peakes, who by this time also

Joe Hank, a 1954 bay stallion by King and out of Queen H, was first golden cross's sole AQHA Champion performer.
Courtesy Quarter Horse Journal

owned the legendary Driftwood, would go on to campaign Booger H as a racehorse. From 23 official starts, the chestnut stallion recorded eight wins, seven seconds, five thirds and a AA race rating.

After his racing career was over, "Booger" was sold back to Cotton and retired to stud. Used lightly as a breeding animal, he was the sire of two AAA racehorses—Ocean Mist and King Booge—and four AQHA Champions—Jericho Lark, Booda Bar, Boomer Isle and Cue Stick.

After Queen H foaled Booger H, it was six years before she was re-bred to King. In the interim, she was bred to Joe Traveler, Joe Moore, Hygro (TB) and Balmy L. These breedings resulted in four additional race Register of Merit qualifiers: Pale Face H, Miss Della Moore, Hygro Jr and Queen Cheta.

Between 1951 and 1955, Queen was bred to King four times. These breedings resulted in

Queen H was, at the time of her death in 1960, one of the breed's leading producers of race ROMs.

Courtesy **Quarter Horse Journal**

Your Highness, a 1952 chestnut mare; Joe Hank, a 1954 bay stallion; Queen Dawn, a 1955 bay mare; and King's Queen Ann, a 1956 black mare.

Your Highness was sent to the track, where she became her dam's eighth race Register of Merit qualifier. Retired to the broodmare band, she became a AAA race producer.

Joe Hank was groomed for a show career and, in 1964, became the only one of the full siblings to earn an AQHA Championship. Retired to stud, he became an AQHA Champion and Superior Performance Horse sire, as well.

Queen Dawn was also conditioned for a show career and earned 11 halter points. Retired to the broodmare band, she, too, became a AAA race producer.

King's Queen Ann, the last of the King/Queen H family, was not shown. Retired to the broodmare band, she produced one AQHA point earner and two NCHA money earners.

In the fall of 1960, Queen H, the original "King Maker," gave birth to her last foal. Several days later, on October 2, she quietly lay down and died. The foal, a chestnut colt sired by King Command, was named Queen's Last and raised with the help of a nursing bottle and several milk goats.

Queen H's death signaled the end of a crucial early chapter in the King P-234 story. Together, the sorrel, blaze-faced mare and the mahogany bay stallion forged one of the American Quarter Horse Association's first golden crosses.

In retrospect, it might also have been one of its very best.

Chapter 5

A Clean Sweep

L H Quarter Moon, a 1950 black gelding by King and out of Miss Alice, was a classic example of the quality produced by "El Segundo Dorado Cruz," the second golden cross.

Photo by James Cathey, courtesy Quarter Horse Journal

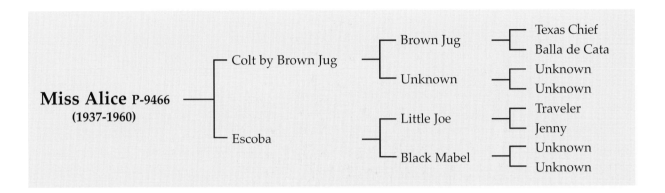

					Texas Chief
		Brown Jug			Balla de Cata
	Colt by Brown Jug				Unknown
		Unknown			Unknown
Miss Alice P-9466					
(1937-1960)					Traveler
		Little Joe			Jenny
	Escoba				Unknown
		Black Mabel			Unknown

In the spring of 1942, AQHA was in its third calendar year of existence, the King/Queen H cross was producing its third foal, and the Hankins family was set to contribute its third member to the Quarter Horse cause.

Lowell Hankins, born October 10, 1911, was the middle Hankins boy. In the late 1920s, Lowell's father, J. L. Hankins, staked him to a small Rocksprings, Texas, ranch. After graduating from high school in Abilene, Texas, in 1929, Lowell took up residence at the ranch.

Quickly deciding that the life of a young bachelor was not all it was cut out to be, Lowell returned to Abilene to marry his high school sweetheart, the former Sarah Boutwell. Back home in Rocksprings, the young couple set about raising cattle, sheep, goats and a pair of girls, Lorelei (pronounced "Laura Lee") and Louise.

As noted earlier, in 1937 Lowell Hankins loaned his older brother the $800 he needed to buy King P-234. It was only natural, then, that Lowell should decide at some point to try to capitalize on the stallion's burgeoning popularity.

That point came in the spring of 1941, in the form of a timely visit to the nearby L. B. Wardlaw ranch.

"I was at this fellow's place," Lowell said, "and I saw a filly by King that I sure did want. I figured that the best way to buy the filly would be to just bump into the man up in town some day.

"Well, it wasn't very long before this happened. I had gone to town and ran into this fellow and some more men standing on the corner talking. I kinda joined in, and before long the conversation turned to horses, so I said, 'Yeah, there's a feller that's got a little ole filly and there's no telling what he would want for her.'

"The man realized what filly I was talking about and said, 'Well, I wouldn't take less than $150 for her.' Right then, I told him that I just believed I would buy her. He went to backing up and said, 'Now wait a minute. I

Barney Blue, a 1944 chestnut stallion by King and out of Miss Alice, was one of the first Lowell Hankins-bred King offspring. **Courtesy Quarter Horse Journal**

Diamond Bob, a 1946 sorrel stallion by Flying Bob and out of Escoba, was also bred by Lowell Hankins. The 1949 Champion Quarter Running Stallion, he spent years as a Hankins herd sire.

Courtesy **Quarter Horse Journal**

don't want to get a lot of feed in her after I wean her.' I just told him to call me when he weaned her. She turned out to be a real good mare."[1]

After taking possession of the filly, a 1941 sorrel by King and out of Schuhart, Lowell registered her with AQHA as L H Princess. Once raised and placed into production, "Princess" was the dam of two race Register of Merit earners—Cowboy King and L H Balmy Princess—and one halter point earner—Balmy King.

L H Balmy Princess, a 1950 sorrel mare by Balmy L P-387, was the most accomplished of the three. Turned over to Blain Speers for race training as a 2-year-old, she became a AAA-rated stakes-placed winner of three races.

Retired to the Lowell Hankins broodmare band, she was the dam of four top race hors-es: Hankins Bar, S.I. 100; Hankins Deck, S.I. 95; Go Miss Hankins, S.I. 92; and Go Mr Hankins, S.I. 91.

The L H Princess/L H Balmy Princess mare line, then, was Lowell Hankins' first. The Palano line came next, courtesy of older brother Jess.

In the summer of 1941, Jess Hankins made a trip to South Texas in search of broodmares to breed to King. He happened upon Palano, a 1933 sorrel mare by Leonel and out of a granddaughter of Texas Chief, and bought her for Lowell.

Lowell registered the mare with AQHA and bred her to King. Winnetka, a 1943 bay mare was the resulting foal. Re-bred to King, Palano foaled L H Susie, a 1944 sorrel mare who became a top producer.

[1] Jim Jennings, "Lowell Hankins," *Quarter Horse Journal*, May 1973, p. 81

By the fall of 1942, the Lowell Hankins program was well on its way. It was now time for mare line three to make its appearance. That it did so at all was less a matter of choice and more a matter of chance.

"Jess and I went back down to where we got Palano and found three more mares," Lowell said. "The three mares were Miss Alice, her sister, and the mother of the two, an old mare called Escoba.

"We bought all three mares, but then had to make a decision as to who got what mare. So, Jess put three cards in a hat to draw out, and on one of them was written, 'You are stung.'

That was the old mare and, sure enough, I got her.

"She was a daughter of Little Joe, out of a mare called Black Mabel. We knew Miss Alice was by a son of Brown Jug, but that's all we could find out."[3]

After Lowell got Escoba home, Jess told him that Miss Alice was in foal to a Paint Horse. Jess didn't want anything to do with spotted horses, so he traded the Escoba daughter to Lowell.

If it could be said that L H Princess and Palano put Lowell Hankins in the horse business on the ground floor, then Escoba and

[3] Jim Jennings, "Lowell Hankins," *Quarter Horse Journal*, May 1973, p. 81

King P-234, shown here in a circa 1950s ranch shot, was the sire of 11 of Miss Alice's 14 foals.
Courtesy American Quarter Horse Heritage Center & Museum

L H Chock, a 1944 stallion by King and out of Miss Alice, is listed on AQHA records as being a sorrel in color." He was actually a "chocolate-colored" chestnut, hence his name.

***Courtesy* Quarter Horse Journal**

While owned by the Waggoner Ranch, Vernon, Texas, L H Chock sired King Jacket, 1952 smutty-colored palomino out of Lady Beaver by Beaver Creek. Sold to Dr. C. F. Steinhauser, River Falls, Wisconsin, King Jacket went on to become a top show horse and sire.

***Courtesy* Quarter Horse Journal**

Miss Alice propelled him into the penthouse.

Escoba, Spanish for "broom," had been a top race mare in her youth. She was reputed to have come by her name because she swept the track clean of competitors when she ran.

Despite the fact that Escoba was 18 when he acquired her, Lowell immediately set about raising foals with her. Bred three times to King, she produced Barney Blue, a 1944 chestnut stallion; L H Goodnuff, a 1947 bay stallion; and Maybeso Joe, a 1949 black gelding.

In 1945, Lowell bred Escoba to Flying Bob. With Escoba being an ex-race mare and the Louisiana-bred Flying Bob one of the top race sires of his day, Lowell had his sights set on raising a runner.

Diamond Bob, a 1946 chestnut stallion, was the resulting foal and he proved to be everything his breeder had hoped for. Trained by Blain Speers and campaigned on the track from 1948 through 1951, Diamond Bob was the 1949 Champion Quarter Stallion. In addition, he was one of only a handful of horses to ever outrun the legendary Maddon's Bright Eyes twice. Retired to stud, he sired six AAA racehorses.

When he got "stuck" with Escoba, Lowell Hankins got a world champion race producer. When he traded for Escoba's daughter, Miss Alice, he got "El Segundo Dorado Cruz," the second golden cross.

As noted earlier, Miss Alice, a 1937 black mare, was of somewhat ambiguous breeding on the top side of her pedigree. While the Hankins's were able to determine that she was sired by a son of Brown Jug, they were unable to establish the exact identity of the horse.

Brown Jug was by Jim Ned by Pancho, and thus a direct descendant of Old Billy and Piasana. So, while the precise connection to the two Fleming greats might have been unclear, the fact that it was there was good enough for Lowell Hankins.

In 1942, Miss Alice foaled a black

and white tobiano Paint filly. That same year, Lowell took her to be bred to King.

Lorelei Hankins, Lowell's oldest daughter, was a dyed-in-the-wool tomboy who grew up with her father's horses. She remembers Miss Alice and her first foal quite clearly.

"Miss Alice was not a pretty mare," she recalled. "She was a tall, kind of raw-boned horse; not a show horse, but definitely the kind you'd like to ride. Her first foal for daddy, the black and white Paint filly, was beautiful. Daddy sold her to some people in California. I think he always regretted the fact that he didn't keep her."

L H Lady B, a 1943 black mare, was the result of the first King/Miss Alice mating. The dam of 12 foals, she produced two racing Register of Merit earners and three performance Register of Merit earners.

L H Chock, a 1944 "chocolate-colored" chestnut stallion, came next. Sold as a young horse to the Waggoner Ranch of Vernon, Texas, he was loaned for several breeding seasons to Willie Evans, the famed black horseman from Tatum, Oklahoma.

Returned to the Waggoner Ranch, L H Chock was used as a herd sire for several additional seasons. During this time, his most significant accomplishment was to sire King Jacket, a 1952 palomino stallion out of Lady Blackburn IV. As a show horse, "Jacket" earned 13 halter and 23 performance points. Retired to stud, he sired 10 AQHA Champions.

Given the fact that Jess Hankins had initially traded Miss Alice away because she was in foal to a spotted horse, it is ironic that King Jacket, her grandson, would one day make a significant contribution to the Paint Horse industry.

In 1966, King Jacket was bred to Bar's Cherry by Little Bartender. Jacket Bar's, a

King's Joe Boy, a 1946 black stallion by King and out of Miss Alice, was an AQHA Champion, an NCHA earner of $2,084 and a top sire.

Courtesy Quarter Horse Journal

Eve Pearce, 1951 bay mare by King's Joe Boy and out of Rocky Pearce by King, was an AQHA Champion and a Superior halter horse.

Courtesy Quarter Horse Journal

1967 red roan cropout overo stallion, was the resulting foal. An APHA Champion, Jacket Bar's was also a five-time national champion in halter, cutting and Western pleasure.

L H Chock made further contributions to the Waggoner Ranch horse program as the maternal grandsire of six AQHA Champions, including Poco Enterprise. "Enterprise," in turn, made a major contribution to the

Quarter Horse breed as the maternal grandsire of National Reining Horse Association (NRHA) hall of fame inductee Be Aech Enterprise.

In the spring of 1945, World War II was almost over, 16 million military personnel were poised to return home, and 76 million "Baby Boomers" were waiting to be born.

The American Quarter Horse Association was undergoing some growing pains of its own.

As noted earlier, in February of 1945, a group of speed-conscious breeders had formed the American Quarter Racing Association (AQRA) in Tucson, Arizona. While that association's main purpose was the development of the Quarter racing industry, it was still seen by many as a challenge to AQHA's authority.

In December of 1945, a third group of breeders who had chafed under AQHA's direction and restrictive registration policies, broke away and formed a rival Quarter Horse registry. Headquartered in Alice, Texas, and known as the National Quarter Horse Breeder's Association (NQHBA), it was championed by such prominent horsemen as George Clegg and Ott Adams.

For several years, the animosity between the three groups grew until it threatened the very sanctity of the breed.

The Quarter Horse industry was in dire need of a conciliator, and it found one in Albert K. Mitchell of Albert, New Mexico. Elected to an unprecedented three straight terms as AQHA president, from 1945 through 1947, Mitchell moved the association headquarters to Amarillo, hired a full-time executive secretary and set the ball in motion for a December 1949 merger of the three groups.

There was yet another equine-related association formed during this time that impacted the Quarter Horse industry in general and

AQHA in particular. This one, however, was of a more positive nature.

In May of 1946, the National Cutting Horse Association (NCHA) came into being. Headquartered in Fort Worth, Texas, its primary goals were the establishment and promotion of organized cutting competition and the standardization of cutting contest rules.

As a result of AQRA and NCHA initiatives, both racing and cutting horses now had well-organized venues through which they could compete. AQHA had no choice but to offer the remaining segments of the industry the same type of opportunity.

In March of 1950, the AQHA Executive Committee approved a national point system and established the Register of Merit, AQHA Champion and Honor Roll (year-end high-point) awards. In the fall of 1952, the first seven AQHA Champions were named.

The Quarter Horse industry was on the move, and, as had been the pattern in the past, the South Texas "Billy" horse continued to adjust and keep pace.

Leading the charge were the King horses. Once known primarily for their ability as roping and bulldogging mounts, the family now gained fame as cutting and show horses.

King's Joe Boy, a 1946 black stallion by King and out of Miss Alice, was one of the first to excel under the new guidelines.

Sold to Jack Mehrens of Richmond, Texas, and prepared for the show ring as both a halter and performance horse, "Joe Boy" qualified for his AQHA Champion award in mid-1953. At the time of the award, he was credited with 14 grand championships and numerous cutting and reining wins at venues in places such as Houston and Fort Worth, Texas, and Baton Rouge, Louisiana.

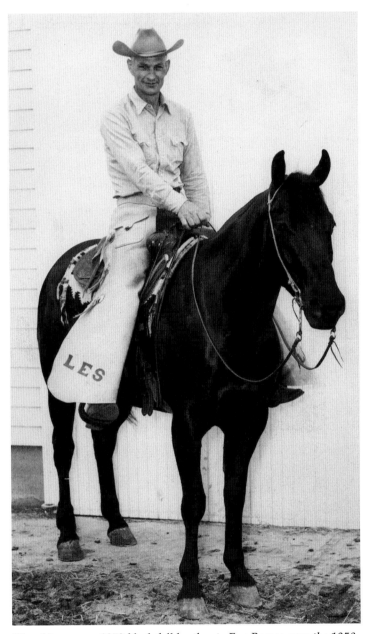

King Vaquero, a 1953 black full brother to Eve Pearce, was the 1958 High Point Western Riding Horse and Working Cowhorse, the 1960 High Point Western Pleasure Gelding, an AQHA Champion and the earner of 109.5 performance points.

Courtesy Quarter Horse Journal

Retired to stud, he sired five AQHA Champions: B M Sporty Gal, J M Tuffy, Eve Pearce, King Vaquero and Joe Peg. In addition, King Vaquero was the 1958 high-point Western riding horse and high-point working cow horse gelding, and the 1960 high-point Western pleasure gelding.

Meanwhile, back home in Rocksprings, Texas, the King/Miss Alice cross continued

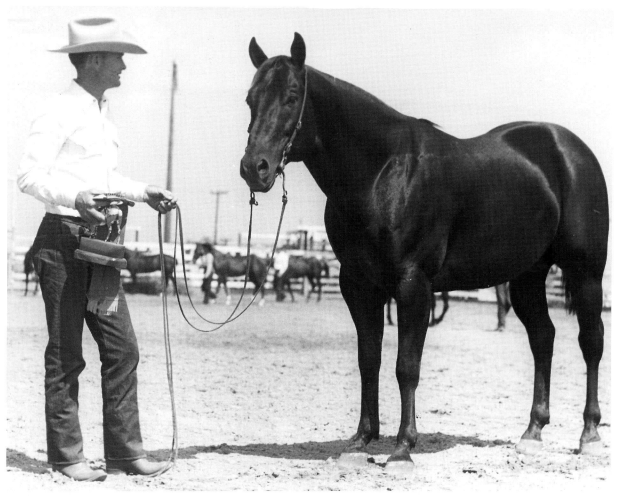

Black Gold King, a 1949 black stallion by King and out of Miss Alice, did much to enhance his sire and dam's reputations. An AQHA Champion and the NCHA earner of $2,137, he went on to sire five AQHA Champions.

Courtesy Quarter Horse Journal

in its cookie cutter production of champions. Black Jug, a 1947 black stallion, and Alice Hankins, a 1948 bay mare, were next in line.

Black Jug was the sire of 189 foals and one performance Register of Merit qualifier.

Alice Hankins was the dam of 15 foals and two point earners. When bred to El Bandido, a son of Zantanon, she foaled Bay Bandit, a 1954 bay stallion.

Sold to Ralph and Dorothy Russell of McKinney, Texas, "Bandit" sired one AQHA Champion—Kay Bandit—and four Superior performance horses—Bay Bandit Josie, Bandit Cooper, Cooper Bandit and Bandit's Dandy Man.

With the Russell family deeply involved in the Paint Horse movement of the early 1960s,

Bay Bandit also sired a number of top spotted horses, including Bandit's Pinto, the first registered Paint Horse, and APHA Champions Bandit's Squaw and Bueno Bandit.

El Segundo Dorado Cruz was in full stride.

Black Gold King, a 1949 black stallion, and L H Quarter Moon, a 1950 black gelding, were the sixth and seventh King/Miss Alice family additions.

Initially sold to Raymond Early of Wharton, Texas, and shown at halter, reining and cutting, "Black Gold" earned his AQHA Champion award in 1957. That same year, Early sold his entire herd of 49 horses, including Black Gold King and 17 of his foals, to J. B. Ferguson, also of Wharton.

Retired to stud, Black Gold sired five AQHA Champions—Early's Doll, Gold Billy, Gold Coyote, Black Mabeline and Poco Duke—and three AQHA Superior cutting horses—Bitsy King, Mackay Alice and Gold Coyote.

The Lowell Hankins-bred stallion had just reached his prime as one of the more popular halter and cutting horse sires of the day when he died prior to the 1960 breeding season.

The cross that had produced Black Gold King was still very much alive, however, and geared to produce yet another champion family member. This was L H Quarter Moon, a 1950 black gelding.

Sold first to B. F. Phillips of Frisco, Texas, and then to J. P. Davidson of Albuquerque, New Mexico, "Quarter Moon" went on to become one of the top show geldings of his era.

Shown at halter, he stood grand champion in Denver, Colorado; and Fort Worth, San Antonio, Houston and Dallas, Texas; and earned 121 points. Shown in cutting, reining and calf roping, he earned 39 performance points. In 1954, he became the third of the King/Miss Alice foals to earn an AQHA Champion award and the only one to earn a Superior halter award.

Next up for the King/Miss Alice production line was King's Little Man, a 1951 black stallion. An NCHA money earner, he sired nine foals but no performers.

In 1951, Lowell Hankins chose to breed Miss Alice to Diamond Bob, his world champion running horse. The cross resulted in Jenny Belle, a 1952 brown mare.

For the next three years, though, it was business as usual. That meant three more King/Miss Alice foals: Lady Jeanette, a 1954 sorrel mare; Queen Alice, a 1955 sorrel mare; and King Lowell, a 1957 black stallion. None of this trio was shown.

Lady Jeanette was the dam of 10 foals, including King Two Eye, the earner of 97 performance points. Queen Alice was the dam of 16 foals, but none of them were point earners.

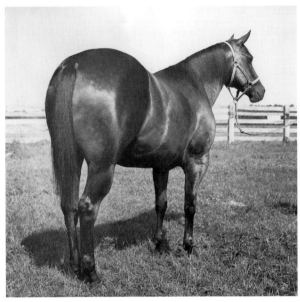

Early's Doll, a 1953 brown mare by Black Gold King and out of Little Doll, qualified for her AQHA Championship in 1960.

Courtesy Quarter Horse Journal

Gold Coyote, a 1960 grullo stallion by Black Gold King and out of Ever Bright, was an AQHA Champion and Superior cutting horse. He is shown here with Jim Reno in the saddle after winning the 1964 San Antonio Junior Cutting Horse Futurity.

Courtesy Quarter Horse Journal

L H Quarter Moon, a 1950 black gelding by King and out of Miss Alice, was an AQHA Champion, a Superior halter horse and the earner of 121 halter points.

Photo by James Cathey, courtesy Quarter Horse Journal

King Lowell, the 11th and final member of the second golden cross, spent his entire life as a Lowell Hankins herd sire. He is credited with 197 get, including two Superior Western pleasure horses: April Molly and Foxey King.

In 1958, Miss Alice was bred to King Breeze by King. Chief Breeze, a 1959 black stallion, was the resulting foal. In 1968, he became his dam's fourth AQHA Champion. At the time, this accomplishment made Miss Alice the industry's leading show-producing dam.

In 1960, at the age of 23, Lowell Hankins' renowned "tradin' mare" gave birth to her 14th and final foal. This was Alice King Bars, a sorrel mare by King Bars.

Mackay Alice, a 1955 bay mare by Black Gold King and out of Willa Girl, was one of her era's top performers. In AQHA competition, she was a Superior cutting horse and earner of 297 performance points. In NCHA competition, she earned $21,315 and finished in third place among the World Champion Cutting Horses of 1966.

Courtesy Quarter Horse Journal

Miss Alice passed away shortly thereafter.

Just as the King/Queen H golden cross propelled the Hankins sire into the forefront of a newly created racing industry, so did the King/Miss Alice golden cross catapult him into the lead position in a newly created cutting and show industry.

From beginning to end, the King/Miss Alice cross was a true "black type" affair. It helped establish the standard for the breed's first two-way halter and cutting champions, and then laid down the gauntlet to the rest of the industry to match or better it.

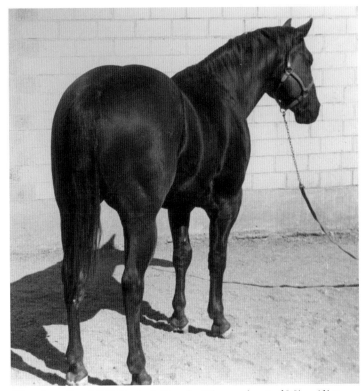

King Lowell, a 1957 black stallion by King and out of Miss Alice, was the 11th and final member of the second gold cross. He spent his entire life as a Lowell Hankins herd sire.

Courtesy Quarter Horse Journal

Chief Breeze, a 1959 black stallion by King Breeze and out of Miss Alice, was his famous dam's 4th and final AQHA Champion. He is shown here with Jack Mehrens after earning champion stallion honors at the 1964 Houston Livestock Show. **Photo by Jim Keeland, courtesy Quarter Horse Journal**

Chapter 6

THE FROST FACTOR

J. M. Frost III, Houston, Texas – shown here on Red Bud L – was one of the first Quarter Horse breeders to build a program almost exclusively on the blood of King.

Photo by James Cathey, courtesy Quarter Horse Journal

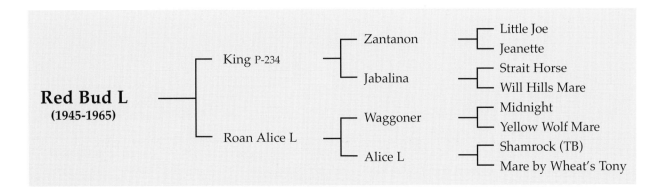

```
                                        ┌─ Zantanon ──┬─ Little Joe
                    ┌─ King P-234 ──────┤             └─ Jeanette
                    │                   └─ Jabalina ──┬─ Strait Horse
Red Bud L ──────────┤                                 └─ Will Hills Mare
(1945-1965)         │                   ┌─ Waggoner ──┬─ Midnight
                    └─ Roan Alice L ────┤             └─ Yellow Wolf Mare
                                        └─ Alice L ───┬─ Shamrock (TB)
                                                      └─ Mare by Wheat's Tony
```

Up to this point, the King P-234 story, at least the post-AQHA part of it, had been written largely by the Hankins clan.

King had been discovered, registered and promoted by Jess Hankins, the King/Queen H. cross had been orchestrated by J. O. Hankins, and the King/Miss Alice cross had been carried out by Lowell Hankins.

These efforts had succeeded in establishing King as one of the industry's up-and-coming sires. What was needed now was for someone outside of the Hankins family, someone with a solid set of credentials, to take the line and add to its luster.

J. M. Frost III of Houston, Texas, an ambitious young oilman-turned-rancher, proved to be just what the doctor ordered.

"My people came from Tennessee," Frost said. "They moved to Texas and settled in the Richmond area of Fort Bend County. In the late 1880s, John Miles Frost, my grandfather, got into the 'rice canal' business and helped build the miles of irrigation systems that were used in the Richmond area rice fields.

"My family was always 'cow-minded,' though, so we eventually branched out into cattle ranching. Then, when the cattle business broke us, we got into the oil lease business. We did better with that; so well, in fact, that we were eventually able to get back into the cattle business."

In addition to rice, cattle and oil, the Frosts also delved for a short while into another form of livestock production.

"During World War I," Frost said, "my father, Jaybird Miles Frost Jr., decided there was money to be made supplying mules to the U.S. Army. So, he went out and bought 200 mares at $1.75 a head. Then he bought 33 jackasses and began raising mules.

"When those mules got old enough, he loaned them out to local farmers for free, but with one small catch. They were unbroken. Those farmers would break the mules to work, use them for a season, and then return them. At that point, my dad would sell them. A pair of broke work mules was worth $75.

"When he got tired of that venture, he sold the jackasses and all but five or six of the mares. He received $13.75 a head for the mares that he sold."

Fiesty B King, a 1950 bay mare by King and out of Fiesty Britches, was the first of several Frost-owned King daughters to become an AQHA Champion.

Courtesy **Quarter Horse Journal**

Owned, trained and ridden by J. M. Frost III, "Fiesty" was a top cutting competitor.

Courtesy Quarter Horse Journal

In 1941, at the age of 27, J. M. Frost III ventured into the registered Brahman cattle business. He and his family purchased a small ranch southeast of Sugar Land, Texas. Originally 326 acres in size, it was added on to over the years until it encompassed 27,000 acres of owned or leased ground in three counties.

In the late 1940s, J. M. and his father decided they wanted to get into the show and performance end of the Quarter Horse business. In August of 1948, they attended the C. E. Hobgood Quarter Horse dispersal sale in Lubbock, Texas, and purchased nine head of Chubby-bred horses.

J. M. also began hauling mares to the Jess Hankins Ranch in Rocksprings, Texas, and the court of King.

In 1950, Frost's first homebred King foals hit the ground. Among their number were Fiesty B King, a bay mare out of Fiesty Britches by Chubby; King's Four Roses, a sorrel mare out of Four Roses Frost by Kavalry

Jack (TB); and Sally B King, a sorrel mare out of Sally Baker by Zeak.

Of the three, "Fiesty" proved to be the best show horse. Trained and shown by Frost at halter and in cutting and reining, she earned reserve champion mare honors at the 1953 Minnesota State Fair in St. Paul, and split first and second with Honey B Joe—also owned by Frost—in a field of 39 Junior cutting horses at the 1954 Southwestern Exposition and Fat Stock Show in Fort Worth, Texas.

In 1954, Fiesty earned her AQHA Champion award, becoming the second King daughter to do so. (Gay Widow, the first, will be profiled in a subsequent chapter.)

Even prior to hitting the show trail with Fiesty, Frost decided that he wanted to own the best daughter of King. To help him locate her, he enlisted the aid of T. C. Stoner of Uvalde, Texas.

"I had become acquainted with J. M. in the late 1940s," Stoner recalled. "In fact, I went with him to C. E. Hobgood's sale in 1948 and helped him pick out some of the mares he bought there. Later on, when J. M. told me he wanted to find and buy the best daughter of King, I knew right where to point him.

"Suel Lanning of La Pryor, Texas, was a good friend of mine," Stoner continued. "Suel had been breeding mares to King for a number of years and he had an especially nice 5-year-old daughter of the old horse that I knew could be bought.

"In June of 1950, J. M. and I paid Suel a visit. He showed us the mare, and J. M. liked her. So well, in fact, that he bought her on the spot and then went back later and bought her full sister and their dam."

The three Lanning mares acquired by Frost were Red Bud L, a 1945 roan mare by King; Little Alice L, a 1947 roan mare by King; and their dam, Roan Alice L, a 1939 roan mare by (One-Eyed) Waggoner.

At the 1954 Southwestern Exposition and Fat Stock Show, Fort Worth, Texas, the Frost-owned duo of Honey B Joe (left) and Fiesty B King split 1st and 2nd in a class of 39 junior cutting horses.

***Courtesy* Quarter Horse Journal**

Red Bud L, a 1945 roan mare by King and out of Roan Alice L, was bred by Suel Lanning of La Pryor, Texas. Shown here with Lanning as a yearling, "Red Bud" was purchased by J. M. Frost III and campaigned to her AQHA Championship.

Courtesy **Quarter Horse Journal**

By the time he acquired Red Bud L and Little Alice L, Frost had already trained and shown Fiesty B King to her AQHA Champion award. His goal for his two new mares was to qualify them for the same award.

Setting out to do so, "Red Bud" was sent to legendary trainer Matlock Rose, then training for Lester Goodson of Houston, for 30 days of cutting training. At the end of that session, Frost took over the mare's training and began campaigning her.

From the onset, Red Bud proved to be something of a challenge to ride and show.

"From the first time I got on her to the last time I ever rode her, Red Bud L was a cold-backed horse," Frost

Little Alice L, a 1947 roan full sister to Red Bud L, was also purchased by Frost and shown to AQHA Champion honors.

Courtesy **Quarter Horse Journal**

recalled. "Unless you untracked her, she'd try to buck every time you got on her. You either had to talk her out of it or ride her through it. Once you got either of those two things accomplished, she was a joy to ride.

"At the beginning of a cutting contest, she had a tendency to loaf and not pay attention. She might lose her first calf and then, after it was too late, turn in a heart-stopping performance on the second and third calves. From time to time, that kind of inconsistency made winning hard.

"On the other hand, she was very active. She was the only horse I ever rode that would literally jump backwards to keep from losing a calf."

Character flaws notwithstanding, Red Bud L compiled an outstanding show record. Shown in halter, cutting and reining, she won or placed at shows in Houston, Fort Worth, Waxahachie, Wharton, Rosenburg, Waller, Beeville, Liberty, and Odessa, Tex.; and Baton Rouge, La. In 1955, she earned her AQHA Champion award, the third of King's daughters to do so.

Red Bud L was retired to the Frost broodmare band in 1955. She went on to become one of the breed's premier producers and the dam of four AQHA Champions: Red Rueben, a 1956 bay stallion by Bay Bob; Red Bars, a 1957 sorrel mare by Three Bars (TB); Little Rayleen, a 1958 bay mare by Leon Bars; and Eyes of Texas, a 1962 brown stallion by Three Bars (TB).

Of these, Red Bars created the biggest splash in the show ring. Shown 42 times at halter, she amassed 23 grand championships, seven reserve championships, 30 firsts and 126 halter points.

Among her top halter wins were being named the grand champion mare at the 1961 Dallas State Fair in Dallas, Texas, and the 1963 American Royal in Kansas City, Missouri. In early 1964, she swept the Texas

The colorful Roan Alice L daughters, Red Bud L and Little Alice L, were virtually unbeatable in produce-of-dam competition.
Photo by Jim Keeland, courtesy Quarter Horse Journal

Alice Star, a 1953 sorrel mare by Saltillo and out of Little Red Alice, was yet another example of the prepotency of the Roan Alice L line. An NCHA Hall of Fame horse, she was the 3rd place finisher among the World Champion Cutting Horses of 1962 and 1963. The NCHA earner of $35,909, she once sold at public auction for $30,500.

Courtesy Quarter Horse Journal

livestock show circuit by earning grand champion mare honors in Fort Worth, El Paso, San Antonio and Houston.

Little Alice L, Red Bud L's full sister, was trained and shown exclusively by Frost. Like her older sister, she, too, proved to be an exceptional halter and cutting horse. In 1955, she earned her AQHA Champion award, the fourth of King's daughters to do so.

As frosting on the cake, Red Bud L and Little Alice L were the first two full sisters to qualify as AQHA Champions.

"'Little Alice' didn't have quite as much action as Red Bud did," Frost said, "but she was easier to ride. I showed her right along-side the other mare and they were tough to beat. They were almost identical in size and coloring, and they sure got a lot of peoples' attention.

"In those days, not very many horsemen knew who I was by name; they just knew me as 'that fellow with those two good roan mares.'"

Spurred on by his successes with Fiesty B. King, Red Bud L and Little Alice L, Frost delved even deeper into the King line.

In 1950, he purchased Bay Bob, a 1946 bay stallion by King and out of Maud Koy, to serve as his main herd sire.

"I first saw Bay Bob in 1949," Frost said. "He was owned by Jess Koy of Eldorado, Texas. Jess had him at a show in Del Rio, Texas. Bay Bob was the grand champion stallion there, and I bought him about six months later."

Bay Bob served as a Frost Ranch herd sire for six years, from 1950 through 1955. Bred first to the Chubby mares, and later to a top set of Little Joe-bred mares, he sired five AQHA Champions—Bay Breezy Bob, Brown Marina, Nava, Sonofagun Too and Red Rueben; two Superior cutting horses—Bellmat and Gal's Bob; and one Superior reining horse—Bell Bob Jr.

Bay Breezy Bob, a 1952 bay stallion out of Breezy by Rialto P-2, was his sire's first AQHA Champion. Slated to be a Frost Ranch junior sire, he died at a relatively young age.

"I had great plans for Bay Breezy Bob," J. M. Frost III said. "He was a big, strong horse, and he had a good mama. Breezy had been a

top roping mare in her day. I bought her and three other mares, Billy Jack and Sugar Babe and Annie B, from O. C. 'Preacher' O'Quinn of Brenham, Texas.

"I had decided to start intensifying the King blood within my herd, so I took Bay Breezy Bob and line-bred him to my King mares. And it looked like it was going to work.

"I never bred Bay Breezy Bob very heavy," Frost continued. "He only sired 17 foals for me, but they were all good. Linda Bob, a 1955 sorrel mare out of Black Dogie by King,

Rose King, a 1952 brown mare by King and out of Four Roses Frost, was bred by J. M. Frost III. Trained and shown by him, she was an AQHA Champion, a Superior cutting horse and the NCHA earner of $3,402.

Courtesy Quarter Horse Journal

Bay Bob, a 1946 bay stallion by King and out of Maud Koy, was bred by Jess Koy of Eldorado, Texas. A grand champion halter horse, he was purchased by J. M. Frost III in 1950.

Photo by Jim Keeland, courtesy Quarter Horse Journal

earned 44 halter points. Bob Britches, a 1956 bay stallion out of Fiesty Britches by Chubby, was the 1962 AQHA Honor Roll Working Cowhorse, and Carr Hop, a 1956 bay mare out of Sally B King by King, was an AQHA Champion.

"Bay Breezy Bob died prior to the 1958 breeding season. We never really pinned down what killed him. I had him insured for $3,500, the only horse I ever insured. We collected on him, but I would have rather have had the insurance company keep their money and I still have the horse."

Despite his short life, Bay Breezy Bob made yet another significant contribution to the cutting horse industry.

From his second foal crop came Lemon Squeezer, a 1956 bay stallion

Bell Mat, a 1955 bay gelding by Bay Bob and out of Sally Barker, was the 1966 High Point Cutting Gelding, a Superior cutting horse and the earner of 179 performance points. In NCHA competition, he was the ninth-place finisher among the World Champion Cutting Horses of 1966 and the earner of $21,394.

Photo by Dalco, Courtesy National Cutting Horse Association

out of Lady H King by King. Unshown himself, Lemon Squeezer was an ROM race and performance sire. In 1962, he was bred to Mildred, a gray NQHBA-registered mare who was, in reality, a faded tobiano Paint Horse.

The resulting foal was Delta, a 1963 bay and white tobiano mare who went on to become arguably the greatest Paint cutting mare of all time. In 1973, she was the NCHA World Champion Cutting Mare and Reserve World Champion Cutting Horse. In 1974, she won the NCHA World Open Finals championship in Amarillo, Texas, defeating Mr. San Peppy and eight of the current top 10 cutting horses in the process.

Retired to the broodmare band and bred to the likes of Doc O'Lena and Peppy San Badger, Delta produced several champion cutting horses. Delta Flyer, a 1982 sorrel tobiano stallion by Peppy San Badger, was the most accomplished of these. The winner of the 1986 NCHA Super Stakes, he tallied $210,902 in NCHA earnings.

Red Rueben, a 1956 bay stallion by Bay Bob and out of Red Bud L, was bred by Frost. The double-bred King grandson achieved his AQHA Championship in 1962.
Photo by Jim Keeland, courtesy Quarter Horse Journal

Throughout the late 1940s and early 1950s, Frost continued to train and show his King-bred horses and expand his Little Joe-bred broodmare band.

In 1957, he qualified yet another King daughter for her AQHA Champion award. This was Rose King, a 1952 brown mare out of Four Roses Frost by Kavalry Jack (TB). To this day, "Rose" remains an all-time favorite.

"Rose King was special to me for several reasons," Frost said. "To begin with, I bred, owned, trained and showed her. On top of the satisfaction that I got from doing all of that, she was a pure pleasure to ride and show; riding her was just like sitting on a rocking chair.

"I showed Rose at halter and she did well, but it was at cutting that she really excelled. We showed all over: Texas, Arkansas, Indiana, Pennsylvania, Florida, Tennessee, Illinois, Colorado and Ohio. And not in one- or two-horse classes. In 1957, at Baton Rouge, Louisiana, there were 56 horses in the Senior cutting class.

"By the time I retired her in 1964 she had earned 60 points and was a Superior cutting horse."

For J. M. Frost III and the Frost Brahman Ranch, the decade of the 1950s proved to be a highly successful one, marked by rapid growth and extensive show ring accomplishments.

By the late 1950s, Frost had amassed one of the most extensive Little Joe-bred broodmare bands ever assembled. In it were 21 daughters of King, 20 daughters of Royal King and seven daughters of Joe Moore. Of the 21 King mares, four were AQHA Champions and nine were AQHA honor roll, AQHA Champion and/or AAA producers.

Breezy, a 1941 brown mare by Rialto P-2 and out of Babe Watkins, was purchased by J. M. Frost III specifically to breed to Bay Bob. A top race and rope horse in her youth, she is shown here in 1950 at Eagle Pass, Texas, with. then-owners Mr. and Mrs. G. H. Carr and jockey Milo Trevino.

Courtesy Quarter Horse Journal

Bay Breezy Bob, a 1952 bay stallion by Bay Bob and out of Breezy, served as the Frost Ranch junior sire until his untimely death as a 6-year-old.

Photo by James Cathey, courtesy Quarter Horse Journal

In 1958, following the death of Bay Breezy Bob, Frost found himself with a pasture full of mares but no herd sire.

"I knew I had to find a stallion, quick-like," he said. "I had it in my mind to get a Hank Wiescamp-bred horse; one of those good-looking Skipper W horses.

"One day at a horse show, I told Don Dodge, the well-known cutting horse trainer from Sacramento, California, of my plans. 'I don't think you should do that,' he said. 'I think you should go out and get yourself a Three Bars son instead.' So that's what I did."

In the spring of 1958, Frost acquired Leon Bars, a 1954 sorrel stallion by Three Bars (TB) and out of

Here's Red Bars, a J. M. Frost III-bred mare. A 1957 sorrel mare by Three Bars (TB) and out of Red Bud L, she is shown here after being named grand champion mare at the 1961 State Fair of Texas, Dallas, Texas. That's J. M. at the beautiful mare's head and then-AQHA Executive Secretary Howard K. Linger presenting the trophy.

Photo by James Cathey, courtesy Quarter Horse Journal

Bubbles II by Joe Hancock Jr, to head his horse-breeding program. The results of that move over a 21-year period were nothing short of phenomenal. Leon Bars sired 232 foals and 102 performers.

As a racehorse sire, four of his offspring became AAA-rated runners: Some More Bars, who was out of a Joe Moore daughter; and Brodus, Bronte and Piave, who were out of King daughters.

As a show sire, Leon Bars sired 10 AQHA Champions: Acomita, Alf, Chockie, Little Rayleen, Sandra's India, Little Deedy, Shank Bars, Amerita, Miss Mesita and Call Me Royal. Sandra's India was out of a daughter of Tom Burnett; the remaining nine horses were all out of King or Royal King daughters.

In addition, Call Me Royal, a 1969 chestnut gelding out of Miss Royal Fleet by Royal King, was the 1978 AQHA World Champion Senior Reining Horse; an AQHA Youth Champion and Performance Champion; and the earner of 10 Open and Youth Superior awards.

And the Frost-bred Leon Bars/King horses were versatile, as well.

Mighty Tiny, a 1967 sorrel mare out of May King by King, was a four-time AQHA high-point hunter under saddle and working hunter horse, and the earner of three Open and Youth Superior awards.

Little Rayleen, a 1958 bay mare out of Red Bud L by King, was the 1962 AQHA High-Point Calf Roping Mare; and Sandra's India, a 1959 palomino mare out of Sandra Hancock by Tom Burnett, was a Superior reining horse.

Yet another Leon Bars mare made her mark on the Quarter Horse breed. Vila, a 1960 brown mare out of Fairy Adams by Joe

Clip Bars, a 1963 sorrel stallion by Three Bars (TB) and out of Linda King, was another top Frost-bred horse. A AAA-rated stakes-placed racehorse, he was also an AQHA Champion show horse.

Photo by Jim Keeland, courtesy Quarter Horse Journal

Leon Bars, a 1954 stallion by Three Bars (TB) and out of Bubbles II, was bred by Tom Schnaubert, Hobbs, New Mexico. Purchased by J. M. Frost III to cross on his King-bred mares, Leon Bars went on to become a leading sire.

Photo by Jim Keeland, courtesy Quarter Horse Journal

Moore, earned five halter points. Retired to the Frost broodmare band and bred to Top Deck (TB) in 1964, she produced the AAA-rated Vila Deck. Sold to Sol West III of Vanderbilt, Texas, and bred to Azure Te (TB) in 1972, Vila produced AQHA leading sire Te N' Te.

By the mid-1960s, J. M. Frost III was one of the country's foremost Quarter Horse breeders and his name was a regular fixture on virtually all of the AQHA's performance-oriented leading breeders lists. In 1965, he ranked as the third all-time leading breeder of AQHA Champions, behind only E. Paul Waggoner and H. J. Wiescamp.

By the early 1970s, Frost had begun to lose a little of his interest in show horses. He found himself, instead, more intrigued by racehorses. As a result, he held a show and cutting horse dispersal sale in the fall of 1971.

"In the 30-plus years that I'd been in the show horse business," he said, "I'd seen it change a lot. When I started showing in the mid-1940s, a lot of the breeding, training and showing chores were being handled by the people that actually owned the horses.

"By the time I got out of the business, that had all changed. The trainers had kind of taken over the show end of the deal. And that wasn't all bad. But I had always preferred to do the majority of my own training and showing. The thought of having to turn that part of it over to someone else in order to win just wasn't very appealing to me.

"And even though I'd made up my mind to quit, I couldn't stand the thought of seeing my King mares dispersed throughout the country," continued Frost, "So, prior to my sale, I called Rex Cauble of Denton, Texas, and sold my entire set of King daughters to him.

"They'd been pretty good to me, and I kind of wanted to see that they went to a good home."

The October 1971 Frost Brahman Ranch Quarter Horse dispersal sale marked the end of a most-colorful era.

J. M. Frost III—with the support of his wife Martha (Mickey) Frost and long-time friend and ranch foreman Sam Magana—took a family of horses he believed in and promoted it on a grand scale. In the process, he contributed greatly to the growth of that family and its reputation as show, cutting and breeding horses.

His efforts amounted to the "Frost Factor," and they should forever be recognized as an integral part of Quarter Horse history in general and the King P-234 story, in particular.

Little Rayleen, a 1958 bay mare by Leon Bars and out of Red Bud L, was an AQHA Champion and the 1962 High Point Calf Roping Mare.

Photo by James Cathey, courtesy Quarter Horse Journal

Te N'Te, although not King-bred, serves as a classic example of the J.M. Frost III breeding program. The famous halter stallion and sire is shown here earning champion of champion honors at the 1976 Sun Country Quarter Horse Show in Phoenix, Arizona. Appearing with Te N' Te are handler Jerry Wells, Clarence Scharbauer, Bob Kiekheffer and Don Jones.

Photo by James Cathey, courtesy Quarter Horse Journal

Chapter 7

THREE SISTERS

89'er, shown here as a yearling, was one of a trio of King daughters destined make Quarter Horse history.

***Courtesy* Quarter Horse Journal**

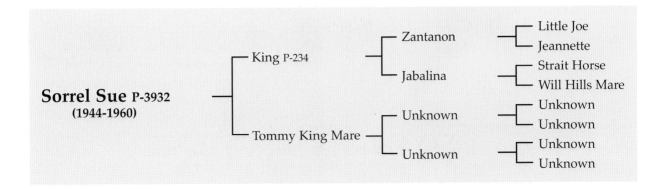

Sorrel Sue P-3932
(1944-1960)

King P-234
— Zantanon
  — Little Joe
  — Jeannette
— Jabalina
  — Strait Horse
  — Will Hills Mare

Tommy King Mare
— Unknown
  — Unknown
  — Unknown
— Unknown
  — Unknown
  — Unknown

Note: While this chapter deals in part with Bud Warren and Leo—two of the Quarter Horse industry's most enduring icons—its primary focus is on a trio of Warren-owned King daughters and what they contributed to the breed.

Whereas J. M. Frost III became associated with the King family of horses by design, Bud Warren of Perry, Oklahoma, got mixed up with it by chance. The results of both men's involvement, however, were the same—unbridled success for them and added prestige for the King name.

Originally, Bud and Reba Warren were in the dairy business, with a dried-milk plant in Perry and a cow outfit on the outskirts of town.

In the spring of 1944, Bud accompanied a neighbor to the Rocksprings, Texas, ranch of Jess Hankins. The neighbor was in the market for a young Quarter Horse stallion and Hankins had several for sale. Among the horses he showed the men was one that had been named after him.

Jess Hankins—the horse—was a 1942 chestnut stallion by King and out of Spider H by Darity (TB). A typey individual with better-than-average conformation, he was priced at $500. Warren's neighbor decided the tag was too steep and turned him down. Bud, on the other hand, found the price to be reasonable and anted up the money.

After Warren got his spur-of-the-moment purchase home, he began showing him at halter. In 1944, Jess Hankins was named the junior champion stallion at Oklahoma's Second Annual Quarter Horse Show. In 1945, he won his class at the Tri-State Fair in Amarillo, Texas.

With a promising young stallion in place, Warren reasoned that the next step was to acquire some mares. In the fall of 1944, he attended the Beall Brothers dispersal sale in Stillwater, Oklahoma, where he purchased Swamp Angel, a 1936 bay mare by Grano De Oro and out of Nancy. At the time of her purchase, the 8-year-old mare was in foal to a young, relatively unknown stallion named Leo. The result of the breeding was Leota W, a 1945 bay mare.

Jess Hankins, a 1942 chestnut stallion by King and out of Spider H, was the first Quarter Horse stallion to be owned by AQHA Hall of Fame horseman Bud Warren, Perry, Oklahoma.
Courtesy American Quarter Horse Heritage Center & Museum

Leo, a 1940 sorrel stallion by Joe Reed II and out of Little Fanny, was added to the Warren stallion battery in 1950.
Courtesy Quarter Horse Journal

Sweet Leilani W, a 1951 sorrel mare by Leo and out of Jezebell W by Jess Hankins, was a member of Bud Warren's first home-bred Leo foal crop. An AQHA Champion, she also qualified for a racing ROM.
Photo by James Cathey,
courtesy **Quarter Horse Journal**

After foaling Leota W, Swamp Angel was bred to Jess Hankins three years in a row. Jezebell W, a 1946 sorrel mare, was the most distinguished result of this cross. Destined to be one of the Warren breeding program's cornerstone mares, she founded a female line that resulted in such horses as Sweet Leilani W, AQHA Champion; Southern Sea, AAA AQHA Champion; Milk River, AQHA Supreme Champion; Little Town AQHA Supreme Champion; and Smooth Town, 1969 World Champion 3-Year-Old Stallion.

Late in 1945, Bud Warren made a second horse-hunting trek to the Hankins ranch, this time returning with three yearling King daughters. Registered with AQHA as Sorrel Sue P-3932, Betty Warren P-3933 and 89'er P-3934, this trio went on to become one of the greatest set of producers in the history of the breed.

There were several years, though, before the fillies were put into production. In the interim, Warren continued to build his herd and delve deeper into the racehorse game.

Between the mid- and late 1940s, Warren added Julie W, a 1940 brown mare by Joe Hancock; Lena Horn, a 1943 black mare by Dock and out of Julie W; and Flit, a 1945 brown mare by Leo and out of Julie W, to his budding program.

In 1947, Warren sent Leota W, his first Leo mare, to the racetrack. She responded by winning four of five starts, including the Oklahoma Futurity. In addition, she equaled the 2-year-old filly track record for 440 yards at Del Rio, Texas, and the 2-year-old world record at Tulsa, Oklahoma. Sent back to the track as a 3-year-old, Leota W won six of her eight starts.

By the late 1940s, Warren had been severely bitten by the racehorse bug. So much so that, in 1950, he bought Leota W's 10-year-old sire for $2,500.

The Bud Warren Quarter Horse breeding program was now in full swing. At its core were two stallions, Leo and Jess Hankins; three older broodmares, Swamp Angel, Julie W and Lena Horn; and the three young King daughters.

Lemac, a 1949 sorrel stallion by Leo and out of Sorrel Sue by King, provided early proof that the first of the three sisters would be a superior producer. The good-looking colt is shown here with Bud Warren after winning the yearling stallion class at the 1950 Southwestern Exposition and Fat Stock Show in Fort Worth Texas.

Courtesy Quarter Horse Journal

Jess Hankins died unexpectedly in the summer or 1951. With the remaining seven horses, Warren built a racing dynasty—literally the first family of speed. At the very heart of the dynasty were the Three Sisters: Sorrel Sue, Betty Warren and 89'er.

Sorrel Sue, a 1944 sorrel mare by King and out of a Tommy King mare, was bred for the first time as a 3-year-old.

AQHA records reveal that she was the dam of 13 foals: one by Star Deck, five by Leo, three by Leo Tag, three by Sugar Bars and one by Croton Oil.

Of the first four Leo foals, Lemac and Mac

Lee were the most accomplished.

Lemac, a 1949 sorrel stallion, won the yearling stallion class at the 1950 Southwestern Exposition and Fat Stock Show in Fort Worth, and became a Register of Merit race and performance horse. Retired to stud, he founded a family of performers that included Leo Lark, AQHA Champion; Alisa Lark, AQHA Champion and two-time Youth world champion; Rugged Lark, 1985 and 1987 Superhorse; The Lark Ascending, 1991 Superhorse; and Look Whos Larkin, 1993 Superhorse.

Mac Lee, a 1950 sorrel stallion, achieved a speed index of 95, was a Superior racehorse,

Leo Tag, a 1949 sorrel stallion by Leo and out of Tagalong, was acquired by Bud Warren in 1952 to fill in for his injured sire as a breeding stallion.

Photo by James Cathey, courtesy Quarter Horse Journal

and won the 1953 Kansas and Rocky Mountain Quarter Horse Association Derbies. Retired to stud, he sired Pearl's King Leo, AAA AQHA Champion and the 1966 AQHA high-point barrel racing horse; Lee Scotland, AAA AQHA Champion; and Mac Lee's Buck, NCHA earner of more than $41,000.

Early in 1952, Leo suffered a serious injury while breeding a mare. Leo Tag, a 1949 sorrel stallion by Leo and out of Tagalong, was brought in to finish out the season.

Warren made the Leo Tag/Sorrel Sue cross three times and was rewarded with two clear-cut winners: Burke's Gayle and Leo Scamp.

Burke's Gayle, a 1953 sorrel mare by Leo Tag and out of Sorrel Sue, was a AAA-rated racehorse.

Photo by James Cathey, courtesy Quarter Horse Journal

Mr Three Bars, a 1959 sorrel stallion by Three Bars (TB) and out of Burke's Gayle was a AAA AQHA Champion.
Photo by Darol Dickinson, *courtesy* Quarter Horse Journal

Okie Leo, a 1956 sorrel stallion by Leo and out of Sorrel Sue, was arguably the most-distinguished member of the cross. An AQHA Champion and Superior reining horse, he also became a leading sire.

Photo by Orren Mixer, courtesy Quarter Horse Journal

Burke's Gayle, a 1953 sorrel mare, was a AAA-rated racehorse. Retired to the broodmare band, she produced Mr Three Bars, AAA AQHA Champion; and Go Gayle, SI 95.

Leo Scamp, a 1954 sorrel stallion, made his presence felt in the breeding shed as the sire of four AQHA Champions: Leo Whiz, Scamp's Sandy, Scamp's Nugget and Fire Biscuit.

Leo Whiz, a 1957 chestnut stallion out of Clavel R, earned Superiors in barrel racing, cutting and reining; and Registers of Merit in racing, working cow horse, barrel racing, reining, Western pleasure, cutting, calf roping, pole bending and Western riding. In addition, he was also 1964's high-point calf roping and pole bending stallion.

Scamp's Nugget, a 1961 palomino gelding

out of Juanita Lee, earned Superiors in halter and Western pleasure, and was the 1966 Youth high-point halter gelding.

By the time the 1955 breeding season arrived, Leo had recovered enough to resume his breeding responsibilities. He was bred to Sorrel Sue for a fifth time, and that cross resulted in Okie Leo, a 1956 sorrel stallion.

Okie Leo was an AQHA Champion and a Superior reining horse. Retired to stud, he founded a performance horse dynasty that included Leonard Milligan, 1980 Superhorse; Smoke Um Okie, 1986 Superhorse; and Kim's Pica Pride, the 1977 world champion in junior calf roping.

After producing Okie Leo, Sorrel Sue was bred to Sugar Bars three times.

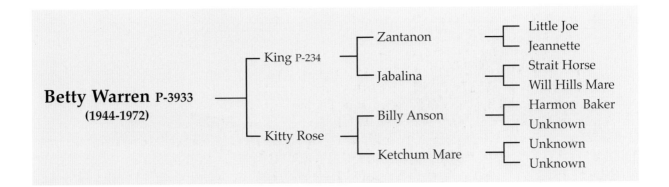

Betty Warren P-3933 (1944-1972)	King P-234	Zantanon	Little Joe
			Jeannette
		Jabalina	Strait Horse
			Will Hills Mare
	Kitty Rose	Billy Anson	Harmon Baker
			Unknown
		Ketchum Mare	Unknown
			Unknown

In 1959, she was bred to Croton Oil, Warren's top young Leo son. That cross resulted in Rinski, a 1960 sorrel stallion.

A Register of Merit racehorse and AQHA Champion, Rinski went on to sire Sooner Rinea, AQHA Champion; Mr Double Dose, AQHA Champion; Miss Barbob, AQHA Champion; and Poco Mae Day, Superior Halter.

In retrospect, the Leo/Sorrel Sue cross produced some of the fastest, best-looking and most-talented horses in the history of the breed. Certainly, it was a cross that resulted in added fame for the four principals concerned: Bud Warren, Jess Hankins, Leo and King.

And Sorrel Sue had two sisters who were still to be heard from.

Leola, a 1948 bay mare by Leo and out of Betty Warren by King, was the first horse to be produced by the second sister. A AAA AQHA Champion, Leola won the Wyoming, RMQHA and Kansas Futurities, and the RMQHA Derby.

Photo by Stewart's, courtesy Quarter Horse Journal

Jag, a 1957 bay stallion by Jaguar and out of Leola, was the first AAA AQHA Champion whose sire and dam had achieved the same dual honor.   ***Courtesy* Quarter Horse Journal**

Idaho Betty Lee, a 1949 bay mare by Leo and out of Betty Warren, was a Register of Merit racehorse.

***Courtesy* Quarter Horse Journal**

Betty Warren, a 1944 brown mare by King and out of Kitty Rose, was raced as a 2-year-old and finished second in the 1946 Oklahoma Futurity. She entered the broodmare band in 1947, and AQHA records show her to have produced 21 foals: eight by Leo, one by Leo Tag, seven by Sugar Bars and five by Croton Oil.

Of the eight Leo/Betty Warren foals, Leola, Sooner Lady, Soonerette and Idaho Betty Lee were undoubtedly the best.

Leola, a 1948 bay mare, was a AAA AQHA Champion and won the Wyoming, Rocky Mountain Quarter Horse Association and Oklahoma Futurities, as well as the Rocky Mountain Quarter Horse Association

Derby. Retired to the broodmare band, she was the dam of AAA AQHA Champion Jag.

Sooner Lady, a 1955 bay mare, achieved a speed index of 95 and won the 1957 Oklahoma Quarter Horse Exhibitors Association Futurity. Retired to the broodmare band, she was the dam of: Sugar Roll, SI 95; Bars Warren, SI 95; Sugar Bars Boy, AQHA Champion; Forthcoming, SI 100; Lancer Jet, SI 97; Sooner Easy Jet, SI 95; and Sooner Girl Greene, SI 99.

Soonerette, a 1962 bay mare, was AAA on the tracks and the dam of Mr Sooner Jet, SI 92. Idaho Betty Lee, a 1949 bay mare, was a Register of Merit racehorse and the dam of AQHA Champion and Superior Halter Horse Quincy Lee.

In addition to her three Leo daughters, Betty Warren produced one more top racehorse.

Otoe Maiden, a 1959 bay mare sired by Sugar Bars, achieved a 95 speed index and was the dam of Miss Oil Strike, SI 95; Good Measure, SI 93; and Charleo Jet, SI 91.

With her 21 foals, Betty Warren was the most prolific of the three sisters. And while her overall production record didn't quite stack up to the one established by Sorrel Sue, it still did much to advance the reputations of Leo and King.

And there was still one more sister to be reckoned with.

Slightly better-bred than her two siblings, 89'er was a 1944 bay mare by King and out of High Glee. High Glee, a 1932 brown mare by My Pardner and out of a mare by Dogie Beasley, traced to Old Billy six times and to Piasana twice. In addition to 89'er, High Glee produced a second King daughter,

Quincy Lee, a 1959 chestnut mare by Cuellar and out of Idaho Betty Lee, was an AQHA Champion and a Superior halter horse. **Photo by Darol Dickinson, courtesy Quarter Horse Journal**

Rocky Pearce, who was a noted producer in her own right.

In addition to being the best-bred of the three sisters, 89'er was also the only one given an ample opportunity to prove her worth as a performer. AQHA records reveal that she made two official starts as a 2-year-old. Both were 220-yard sprints and resulted in one first, one second and a racing Register of Merit.

Retired to the Warren broodmare band as a 4-year-old, 89'er produced 17 foals: 10 by Leo, three by Sugar Bars, two by Croton Oil and two by Jet Deck.

As would be expected, the Leo/89'er cross proved the most successful and contributed seven Register of Merit racehorses to the breed: Mr 89'er, Miss Sabre, Whimper, Leo Bob, 89er's Boy, Sooner Leo and Mora Leo.

Whimper, a 1951 bay stallion, achieved a 95 speed index and was the sire of Leo Up, SI 95, and Whimper's Gem, SI 95.

Leo Bob, a 1952 sorrel stallion, likewise achieved a 95 speed index and was a grand champion halter horse. Retired to stud, he sired Barley Riker, AQHA Champion; Chuckles Riker, AQHA Champion; and Salty Bob Snip, AQHA Champion.

Miss Sabre, a 1950 bay mare, was a Register of Merit racehorse and the dam of Leo Dial, SI 95, and Go Sabre Go, SI 92. Through her son Sabre Twist, she contributed such top sec-

Mr 89'er, a 1949 sorrel stallion by Leo and out of 89'er by King, was the first horse produced by the third sister. A Register of Merit Racehorse, Mr 89'er went on to become a top sire.

Photo by Darol Dickinson, courtesy Quarter Horse Journal

Whimper, a 1951 bay stallion by Leo and out of 89'er, achieved a AAA-rating on the track.
Photo by Ann Schlenzig, courtesy Quarter Horse Journal

ond and third generation individuals as AQHA Champion Sabre Etta and AQHA Supreme Champion Sugar Sabre.

In addition to her seven Leo performers, 89'er was the dam of four more Register of Merit racehorses: Niner, Strip Runner, Fast Stripper and 89'ers Jet.

Niner, a 1956 bay mare by Sugar Bars, achieved an 85 speed index. Retired to the Warren broodmare band, she produced Hill's Leo Bars, SI 95; Ninerette, SI 05; Wallaby, AQHA Champion, Superior Halter and the 1967 high-point halter stallion; Envoy, AQHA Champion and Superior Halter; Distinctive, SI 95; and Wallaby's Sis, AQHA Champion.

Strip Runner, a 1959 sorrel mare by Croton Oil, qualified for a 95 speed index and was the dam of Jet Runner, SI 95; Jet Landing, SI 96; and April Stripper, SI 94.

89er's Boy a 1953 sorrel stallion by Leo and out of 89'er, was a Register of Merit racehorse and the sire of ROM race and performance horses.
Courtesy Quarter Horse Journal

Wallaby, a 1964 sorrel stallion by Croton Oil and out of Niner by Sugar Bars, was one of the best of the second generation members of the Leo/89'er family. The 1967 High Point Halter Stallion, Wallaby was also an AQHA Champion and a Superior halter horse.   **Photo by Esler, courtesy Quarter Horse Journal**

Fast Stripper, a 1962 bay mare by Sugar Bars, earned an 85 speed index and was the dam of Calamity Bill, SI 94; Fast Fling, SI 98; and Grand Stripper, 1993 high-point working cow horse stallion.

A 1965 sorrel mare by Jet Deck, 89'ers Jet was her famous dam's last performer. Winner of the 1967 Midway Downs Premier Futurity and earner of a 95 speed index, she had no foals.

By the mid-1960s, 89'er reigned supreme as AQHA's all-time leading dam of ROM qualifiers with 11.

The final tally for Bud Warren's King daughters was an impressive 51 foals, 38 performers, 25 ROM racehorses, three AQHA Champions, one Superior Reining Horse and five ROM performance horses.

More important than these figures is the fact that, particularly when bred to Leo or one of his sons, the three mares were instrumental in founding one of the greatest all-around families in the history of the breed.

It was a family comprised of horses that were fleet enough to run races in AAA time, good-looking enough to win in the toughest halter competition, and athletic enough to earn national acclaim as cutting, roping and reining horses.

In many ways, the Bud Warren/Leo/King experience epitomized everything that a true Quarter Horse should be, at a level and scope that has seldom, if ever, been equaled.

In terms of what it did to enhance the King name, the program was just as profound. Thanks to the direct contributions of the Three Sisters—Sorrel Sue, Betty Warren and 89'er—the reputation of their sire as one of the breed's most potent broodmare sires was established beyond a shadow of a doubt. As a result, the King P-234 legend continued to expand and prosper.

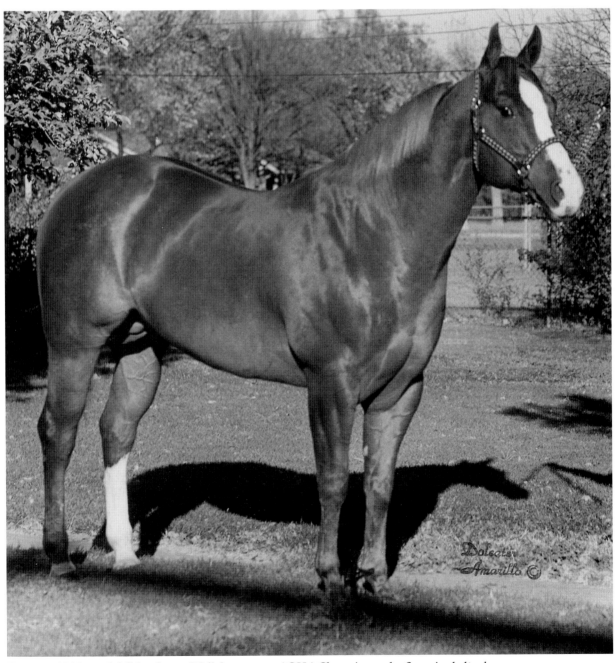

Envoy, a 1966 sorrel full brother to Wallaby, was an AQHA Champion and a Superior halter horse.
Courtesy Quarter Horse Journal

Chapter 8

THE SORREL SON

Hank H, although short-lived, would have an enduring impact on the Quarter Horse breed.
Courtesy American Quarter Horse Heritage Center & Museum

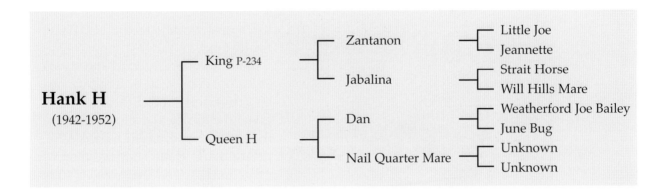

King P-234's ascension to his ranking as one of the Quarter Horse industry's all-time leading sires began in earnest in the late 1930s and early 1940s.

As previously noted, those first years saw King contribute such top young stallions as Jess Hank, King Gotch, Cuellar, Jess Hankins and Hank H to AQHA's foundation gene pool.

Of the aforementioned horses, Hank H went on to have the most enduring impact on the breed. And he did so not just as a show horse, a racehorse or a breeding animal, but as all three wrapped up in one.

Hank H was a 1942 sorrel stallion out of Queen H. Bred by J. O. Hankins of Rocksprings, Texas, he was the first son to be produced by the pairing known as El Primero Dorado Cruz.

Like his two older sisters—Duchess H and Squaw H—Hank H was endowed with a beautiful head and neck, and above-average conformation. He also came equipped with one additional trait that made it easy to pick him out in a crowd. Whereas most of the King horses were bay, brown or black in color, Hank H was bright red.

He was, in essence, The Sorrel Son.

At the beginning of his show career, Hank H was a halter horse. Shown lightly by Hankins, he placed first in the yearling stallion class at the 1943 San Angelo, Texas, show, and second in the 2-year-old stallion class at the 1944 Fort Worth Fat Stock Show.

In early 1945, "Hank" was purchased by Jack and Paul Smith of Indiahoma, Oklahoma. The two brothers were cattle ranchers and wheat farmers by vocation, who dabbled in fast horses on the side.

The fact that Squaw H had already begun to make her presence felt on the straightaway tracks was no doubt a factor in the Smiths' decision to acquire her full brother and point him toward a racing career, as well.

Hank's initial race training and conditioning was handled by Jack and Paul's father, Tom G. Smith. When it became apparent that the 3-year-old stallion was a bona fide prospect, he was turned over to George Ogle of Claypool, Oklahoma. Ogle was a renowned Oklahoma "brush track" denizen who, as a boy, had piloted the legendary Joe Hancock to a number of his greatest racing victories.

Hank began his straightaway career on July 4, 1945. Matched in a 440-yard contest at Woodward, Oklahoma, against a local favorite named Red Elk, he emerged victorious. Nine days later, he was hauled to Lawton, Oklahoma, to be pitted against Black Bottom, a prominent Waggoner Ranch-bred sprinter. Again, he came out on top.

Over the next 12 months, from mid-1945 through mid-1946, Hank H no doubt saw regular action as a runner. Due to the lack of organized record keeping, however, no further accounts of his exploits are available.

By the fall of 1946, it was decided that the blaze-faced sorrel was ready for the big time, and that meant a trip to Rillito Park in Tucson, Arizona, to lock horns with the fastest sprinters in the land.

Hank H's first start at Rillito occurred on November 17, 1946. Entered in a 330-yard sweepstakes, he won it. Later that same year, he finished second to the formidable Miss Bank in a 300-yard feature that saw her estab-

Although not quite as speedy as his famous full sister Squaw H, Hank H was a Register of Merit racehorse. Here, he defeats "Buster" in a 1946 match race at Rillito Park, Tucson, Arizona.
Courtesy American Quarter Horse Heritage Center & Museum

lish a new world's record of :17.4 at the distance.

In yet another 330-yard speed stake at Rillito, Hank was beaten by a nose by Prissy and Senor Bill, who were given the identical time of :17.4 for the sprint, equaling Miss Bank's record mark. Hank's official time was given as :17.5, and that was enough for the American Quarter Racing Association (AQRA) to award him a AA track rating.

Hank H was raced lightly over two seasons, from 1946 through 1947. His official AQHA record shows that he started six times with two wins, one second and three thirds. It further lists his speed index as 85.

By this time, the Smith Brothers' charge had matured into a well-balanced stallion who stood 14-3 hands high and weighed 1,200 pounds. In

On November 17, 1946, Hank won a 330-yard sweepstakes at Rillito Park.
Courtesy American Quarter Horse Heritage Center & Museum

1947, while in racing shape, he was shown to a third-place ribbon in the aged stallion class at the big Tucson Quarter Horse show.

At the conclusion of the 1947 Rillito race meet, Hank H was taken off the track and retired to stud.

Even prior to his exit from the racing wars, Hank had been bred to a few mares. His first two foal crops, which hit the ground in 1945 and 1947, resulted in only eight AQHA-registered get. Included among that number were three Register of Merit racehorses: Hank H Jr, Gold King Bailey and Lady Hank.

(Note: As was the case with many of the breed's foundation sires, a number of Hank H's gelded sons were never registered. They spent their lives as unpapered ranch horses and rodeo mounts.)

By 1947, Hank's reputation as one of the breed's most promising young sires was a matter of fact and his breeding opportunities increased. From his next six foal crops, born between 1948 and 1953, came a host of show and race champions. The Smith stallion's future looked bright, indeed.

Then, suddenly, everything came crashing down.

In 1952, much of the Southern and Great Plains lay helpless in the grip of a serious drought. Although not as widespread or dev-

Whitcomb's Lady Hank, a 1949 gray mare by Hank H and out of Lady Speck, was one of her sire's first Register of Merit racehorses. She is shown here with owner C. G. Whitcomb of Sterling, Colorado, after winning a race at the 1953 Colorado State Fair in Pueblo.

Courtesy Milo Whitcomb

107

Gold King Bailey, a 1945 palomino stallion by Hank H and out of Beauty Bailey, played a huge role in perpetuating the Hank H line of all-around race, show and performance horses.

Courtesy Quarter Horse Journal

astating as the Dust Bowl Drought of 1933-1940, the Six-Year Texas Drought of 1951-1956 wreaked its share of havoc.

Dust pneumonia—a drought-induced malady that coated the air passages of human and animal alike with dust and impeded breathing—was one of the plague's worst manifestations. In the fall of 1952, Hank H succumbed to it.

AQHA records reveal that Hank H sired 137 registered horses from eight foal crops.

As a sire, he was responsible for 28 race starters that earned 14 ROMs and $20,948; 18 halter competitors that earned one Superior and 132 points; and 17 arena performers that earned one AQHA Championship, eight ROMs and 77 points.

Gold Pacific, a 1958 palomino stallion by Gold King Bailey and out of South Pacific by Leo, achieved a speed index of 95.

Courtesy Quarter Horse Journal

Among his top race and show get were:

- Little Bay Lady, a 1951 bay mare out of Tom's Lady Gray—Race Register of Merit (SI 85).
- Hank's Sue, a 1951 sorrel mare out of Patsy Sue—1957 AQHA High-Point Halter Horse; Superior halter (62 points).
- Hanky Doodle, a 1951 sorrel gelding out of Osage Jessie—AQHA Champion.

Despite the fact the Hank H died in the prime of his life and sired only five full foal crops, history has proven him to be one of King P-234's most influential sons. Much of the credit for this fact belongs to three horses: Gold King Bailey, Harlan and Last Hank.

Gold King Bailey, a 1945 palomino stallion by Hank H and out of Beauty Bailey, was bred by the Smith Brothers. Sold as a yearling for $1,250 to Guy Ray Rutland of Pawhuska, Oklahoma, he developed into the same kind of triple-threat show, race and breeding horse as his sire.

Here's Pacific Bailey, a 1963 sorrel stallion by Gold Pacific and out of Nell Bert McCue. A AAA AQHA Champion, he went on to become an all-time leading race sire.

Courtesy **Quarter Horse Journal**

Harlan, a 1951 buckskin stallion by Hank H and out of Dixie Beach, would shoulder much of the responsibility for seeing that the Hank H line was carried on.

Courtesy Quarter Horse Journal

Among his top race and show get were:

- Pat Dawson, a 1954 palomino gelding out of Socks Dawson—1961 and 1962 AQHA High-Point Barrel Racing Horse; Superior barrel racing.
- Goldteen Bailey, a 1958 palomino mare out of Girl—Superior halter.
- Ell Bailey, a 1961 sorrel gelding out of Girl—AQHA Champion; Superior halter; Superior Western pleasure.
- Bucket Bailey, a 1962 buckskin stallion—SI 100, three-time stakes winner, Superior racehorse.
- Frosty Leo Hank, a 1963 buckskin stallion out of —SI 100, Superior racehorse.
- Bailey's Law, a 1965 gray stallion out of Miss Wardlaw 66—AQHA Champion, Superior Western pleasure.

Finally, Gold King Bailey sired Gold Pacific.

A 1958 palomino stallion out of South Pacific by Leo, Gold Pacific was bred by Bud Warren of Perry, Oklahoma.

Warren had taken South Pacific, who was a full sister to Rosa Leo and Croton Oil, to the court of Gold King Bailey in hopes of getting a sorrel filly. Rutland told Warren that, if the mare threw a palomino colt, he would like to trade for it. When just such a colt was born, the swap was made and the Rutland Ranch wound up with a junior stallion.

Like his sire, Gold Pacific was given the chance to prove his speed. From 10 starts, he tallied two firsts, two seconds and two thirds, and achieved a speed index of 95.

Then, he, too, passed away at an early age.

"Gold Pacific was one of the most perfect little palomino Quarter Horses you ever saw," Guy Ray Rutland said. "He did not stand tall on this earth, only being 14 hands and weighing 1,100 pounds, but he stood tall and mighty as a sire.

Shown at halter, Gold King Bailey earned honors as the grand champion palomino stallion at the National Western Stock Show in Denver, Colorado, and the Fort Worth Fat Stock Show.

Sent to the track, he earned a Race Register of Merit (SI 85).

Retired to stud, he sired 32 race ROM qualifiers, nine AQHA Champions, two Superior halter horses, three Superior performance horses and 14 ROM performance horses.

"[He] was retired to stud at 4 years old in 1962. He stood for three years, until his untimely death on July 7, 1964. He died in the night with an acute case of colic. No one knew he was sick."

Before he died, Gold Pacific managed to sire a son who did much to ensure that the Hank H line lived on.

Pacific Bailey, a 1963 sorrel stallion out of Nell Bert McCue, was bred by Rutland, who had relocated to Independence, Kansas.

Sent to the track, the Hank H great-grand-son achieved a speed index of 100, won four futurities and earned $15,073. Conditioned for the show ring, he earned 24 halter points and an AQHA Championship.

Retired to stud, he sired 2,942 foals, among them 1,435 performers, 611 Register of Merit racehorses and the earners of $2,367,727.

Jim Harlan, a 1960 bay stallion by Harlan and out of Nancy Squaw, was the 1962 High Point Halter Stallion.
**Photo by Jim Keeland,
courtesy Quarter Horse Journal**

Miss Jim 45, a 1966 red dun mare by Jim Harlan and out of Miss Paulo's 45, was the 1970 High Point Halter Horse. An AQHA Hall of Fame horse, she amassed 642 halter points.
Photo by Guy Kassal, courtesy Quarter Horse Journal

Although primarily known as a speed sire, Pacific Bailey also sired six AQHA Champions, three Superior halter horses and six Superior performance horses. Among his most accomplished show horse descendants were those bred by Marvin and Peggy Heil of Riverton, Wyoming.

Beginning in 1971, the Heils bred their top show mare. Lady Good Bar, to Pacific Bailey four times. Good Pacific, a 1972 sorrel stal-lion, and Ladies Choice, a 1974 sorrel stallion, were two of the resulting foals.

Both blaze-faced, stocking-legged stallions enjoyed successful show ring careers and then helped the Heils establish a Wyoming show horse dynasty that included such horses as Crystal Debonair, Superior halter; Chicles Choice, AQHA Champion and three-time Superior award winner; and Chicles Angle, three-time World Champion halter horse.

Hanka, a 1948 chestnut mare by Hank H and out of Hi Baby by King, was bred by the Smith Brothers of Indiahoma, Oklahoma. Sold to C. G. and Milo Whitcomb of Sterling, Colorado, she was a Register of Merit racehorse.

Courtesy Milo Whitcomb

Tonto Bars Hank, a 1958 sorrel stallion by Tonto Bars Gill and out of Hanka, was a three-time Quarter Champion Running Horse, an AQHA Champion and a top sire.
Courtesy Milo Whitcomb

By the time it was all said and done, Guy Ray Rutland's Gold King Bailey horses did more than their fair share to ensure that the Hank H line flourished.

And, just as Gold King Bailey and his descendants took the line and made it prominent in contemporary racing and halter circles, Harlan and his offspring made it shine in modern-day performance arenas.

Harlan, a 1951 buckskin stallion by Hank H and out of Dixie Beach, was bred by the Smith Brothers. Sold as a 3-year-old for $250 to Bob and Joan Robey of Edmond, Oklahoma, he went on to make a top rodeo calf roping mount and an all-time leading sire.

From 403 AQHA-registered get, he sired 17 AQHA Champions, five Superior halter horses, eight Superior performance horses and the earners of 51 ROMs and 2,996 AQHA points.

Among his top show and race get were:
- Harlene, a 1956 dun mare out of Pla Mor's Lady—Superior cutting.
- Harlady, a 1959 buckskin mare out of Lady—AQHA Champion, Superior halter.
- Jim Harlan, a 1960 bay stallion out of Nancy Squaw—1962 AQHA High-Point Halter Stallion, AQHA Champion, Superior halter.
- Slash J Harletta, a 1961 palomino mare out of Frog's Annette—AQHA Champion.
- Harlan's Tyree, a 1963 buckskin stallion out of Sandsarita—1966 AQHA High-Point

Western Pleasure Stallion; AQHA Champion; Superior halter.

• Miss Harlacue, a 1965 buckskin mare out of Oklacue—1976 AQHA High-Point Calf Roping Horse, Superior calf roping.

Like the Gold King Bailey branch of the Hank H tree, the Harlan line flourished and contributed such horses as Miss Jim 45, AQHA Hall of Fame inductee, and Firewater Flit, all-time leading barrel horse sire, to the breed.

Hank H's third-most influential son did not put up the numbers that his two better-known brothers did. Still, he made his presence felt.

Last Hank, a 1953 bay stallion out Preview W, was bred by Roy Schenk of Chickasha, Oklahoma. Sold to John Logan of Leedy, Oklahoma, Last Hank sired Plus Ten, AQHA Champion, and Logan's Miss Lue, the maternal granddam of The Invester, AQHA and NSBA Hall of Fame inductee.

In addition to Gold King Bailey, Harlan and Last Hank, there were three Hank H daughters who made especially noteworthy contributions to the cause. Their names were

Mr Scat Man, a 1965 chestnut stallion by Tonto Bars Hank and out of Horned Scat Bar by Bob's Folly, was bred by Walter Merrick of Sayre, Oklahoma. A Superior halter horse, he earned 247 halter points.

Courtesy Quarter Horse Journal

Hank Will, a 1966 chestnut stallion by Tonto Bars Hank and out of Mine Will (TB), was also bred by Merrick. An AQHA Supreme Champion, Hank Will was also the 1972 High Point Steer Roping Stallion.

Courtesy Walter Merrick

Hanka, Flying May and White Rose.

Hanka, a 1948 chestnut mare out of Hi Baby by King, was bred by the Smith Brothers. Purchased as a yearling by C. G. and Milo Whitcomb of Sterling, Colorado, the double-bred King granddaughter was a Register of Merit racehorse and a third-place finisher in the 1950 Oklahoma Futurity.

Bred to Tonto Bars Gill in 1957, she produced Tonto Bars Hank, the legendary "Flying Boxcar." The winner of 10 stakes and $133,919, Tonto Bars Hank was a three-time

AQHA Champion Quarter Running Horse, an AQHA Champion and a top sire.

From 12 foal crops, the Whitcomb's "Hank" sired 403 foals, among them 212 race starters, 95 Registers of Merit earners and the winners of $2,367,727. As a show horse sire, he was responsible for one AQHA Supreme Champion, eight AQHA Champions, six Superior halter horses and 13 Superior performance horses.

Flying May, a 1951 sorrel mare by Hank H and out of Winnie Mae by Fool's Gold, was

Hank's Sue, a 1953 sorrel mare by Hank H and out of Patsy Sue, was the 1957 High Point Halter Horse.

Courtesy Western Horseman

bred by Leo Edwards of Duncan, Oklahoma. Sold to Rebecca Lockhart of Ryan, Oklahoma, "May" produced nine point-earners, including Flying San, AQHA Champion; Leo San Siemon, Superior halter; Flying May Bug, Superior Western pleasure; and Zippo May Bars, AQHA Champion, Superior halter.

White Rose, a 1952 sorrel mare by Hank H and out of White Angel, was bred by Davis Blocker of Elk City, Oklahoma. Sold to Howard Pitzer of Ericson, Nebraska, "Rose" produced Two Eyed Rosie, AQHA Champion, Superior reining; Rosie Jack, AQHA Champion, Superior Western pleas-

Bars Bailey, a 1957 sorrel stallion by Sugar Bars and out of Beauty Bailey II by Hank H, was typical of the second generation members of the Hank H family, An AQHA Champion, Bars Bailey went on to sire six AQHA Champions.

Courtesy Quarter Horse Journal

ure; Miss Rosy Jack, 1977 AQHA World Champion Senior Heading Horse, Superior steer roping; and Jack Henry, AQHA Champion, Superior Western pleasure.

Numerous other Hank H sons and daughters proved to be excellent breeding animals, as well.

Bottom River, Capital, Hank, Hank Parrish, Hank's Baldy, Jay Hank, Midnight Hank, Whale Bone and Wolf Hank were AQHA Champion and/or AAA sires.

Anthony's Miss H, Beauty Bailey II, Ginger Marie, Hank's Bunch, Hank's Joy, Hank's Nancy, Hank's Van, Hanka Woka, Hi Honey, Miss Hank, Miss Sooner Hank, Rafter N Hanka, Sally Hank Sherry Ann and Speed Belle were AQHA Champion and/or AAA producers.

All things considered, the Hank H chapter of the King book was a colorful one.

It began as a Horatio Alger-type success story, progressed into something akin to a Greek tragedy and ended up as a Phoenix "rising from the ashes" tale.

Simply put, Hank H simply didn't live long enough to do it all by himself. But his sons and daughters—and their sons and daughters—did.

Consequently, their descendants can still be found competing and winning in almost all aspects of the Quarter Horse show and racing industries. With their deep red coats, blaze faces and high white stockings, they serve as living testimonies to the enduring prepotency of Hank H—The Sorrel Son.

Leo San Siemon, a 1959 sorrel stallion by Leo San and out of Flying May by Hank H, was bred by Rebecca Tyler of Gainesville, Texas. A Superior halter horse and earner of 85 halter points, he is shown here with George Tyler after earning grand champion stallion honors at the 1962 Houston Livestock Show.

Courtesy **Western Horseman**

Chapter 9

A CUT ABOVE

Royal King, an all-time great cutting horse and sire, is shown here with owner Earl Albin of Comanche, Texas, after being named the grand champion stallion at the 1954 Wyoming State Fair in Douglas.

Photo by James Cathey, courtesy Quarter Horse Journal

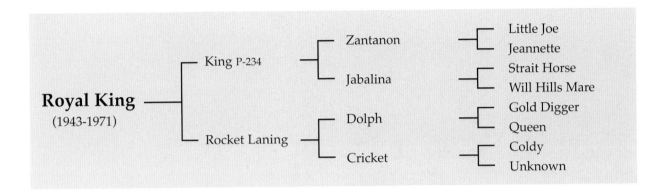

		Zantanon	—	Little Joe
	King P-234			Jeannette
		Jabalina	—	Strait Horse
Royal King				Will Hills Mare
(1943-1971)		Dolph	—	Gold Digger
	Rocket Laning			Queen
		Cricket	—	Coldy
				Unknown

While it is true that much of King P-234's initial rise to prominence as a sire was due to the racing exploits of Squaw H and her full siblings, it was not as a progenitor of speed that the Hankins stallion was destined to be most remembered.

Rather, he would be universally recognized as the founder of one of the Quarter Horse breed's most accomplished arena performance lines.

Royal King, a 1943 sorrel stallion by King and out of Rocket Laning, was the first member of the clan to make a big-time splash in the cutting arena. He was bred by Felton Smathers of Llano, Texas.

Royal King's dam, Rocket Laning, remains something of a mystery from a pedigree standpoint. Originally known just as "Rocket," she is listed in AQHA Stud Book No. 7 (1953) as a 1937 sorrel mare sired by Dolph by Gold Digger and out of Cricket by Coldy.

The theory has been advanced that the stallion Gold Digger is, in reality, Golddigger P-606, a 1937 Waggoner Ranch-bred palomino stallion by Folsom and out of a Waggoner mare. Given the fact that both Golddigger and Rocket Laning were foaled the same year, this supposition seems highly unlikely.

Another account has Dolph being sired by Cremo (who is also known as Gregg Horse) and out of Queen by Yellow Jacket. This version also lists Coldy as being sired by Yellow Jacket.

AQHA records further list Felton Smathers as Rocket Laning's breeder.

Given her name and ancestry, it is more likely that the mare was bred by L. A. Lanning of Rocksprings, Texas. Lanning owned Queen and raised several horses out of her that impacted the early AQHA registry.

This shot of Royal King was taken in the early 1940s on the Albin ranch. **Courtesy Sue Albin Magers**

Royal King was ridden to his first cutting contest win by James Boucher of Hempstead, Texas. The event occurred in 1949 in Dublin, Texas. **Courtesy Sue Albin Magers**

mare by Dogie Beasley, was the Albins' first registered stallion. A line-bred Old Billy–Paisana descendant, he made his greatest contribution to the breed as a broodmare sire.

In the fall of 1944, Earl Albin decided that it was time to hunt for a young Quarter Horse stallion to cross on the family's Dogie Boy mares.

King P-234 had not yet established himself as a nationally known sire, but he was well known on a regional level. Albin saw that the King-bred horses were being bought and sold at a premium rate, so he decided that a King son was what he needed.

After hearing about the Smathers colt, Albin invited a friend, Jack Whiteside, to accompany him on a trip south to check the youngster out. When the two men arrived at the Smathers Ranch, the yearling stallion was still running with his dam and wasn't even halter broke. Still, the quality of the 17-month-old was readily apparent and the two men pooled their resources and bought him for $250. Shortly thereafter, he was registered with AQHA as Royal King P-2392.

The partners lost little time in attempting to get their investment back.

As a 2-year-old, Royal King was bred to 17 mares. The following year, 16 of those mares had foals. Of the 14 foals that lived long enough to be registered, four went on to earn performance Registers of Merit and two, Major King and Miss Nancy Bailey, achieved superstar status.

In early 1945, Albin and Whiteside took Royal King to a San Angelo, Texas, horse show. There, they were offered $1,500 for him. Whiteside was eager to sell, but Albin was not.

"So, I just gave Jack a check for $750 and kept the horse," Albin said.[1]

The decision turned out to be a good one.

No matter how Rocket Laning was bred, or who her breeder was, it is a matter of record that Smathers was in possession of both the mare and her yearling colt by King P-234 when the pair first came to the attention of Earl Albin of Comanche, Texas.

Albin was a fourth-generation cattle rancher and horseman whose great-grandfather had settled in the outpost community of Comanche, located 95 miles southwest of Fort Worth, before the Civil War. C. M. Albin, Earl's father, was a well-known horseman who had once augmented his ranching income by buying horses for the U.S. Army.

Like the Hankins clan of Rocksprings, Texas, the Albin family entered the AQHA-registered Quarter Horse business on the ground floor. Dogie Boy P-1725, a 1932 brown stallion by My Pardner and out of a

---

[1] "Royal King," by Garford Wilkinson; *The Quarter Horse Journal;* December, 1965; page 30.

The following year, Royal King was bred to 51 mares.

A top horseman in his own right, Albin broke Royal King to ride as a 2-year-old. For the next several years, the blaze-faced sorrel's life was spent in relative obscurity as a combination breeding stallion and using horse on the ranch.

It didn't take long to realize that both the stallion and his offspring were above average as far as their dispositions and using abilities were concerned.

"Royal King is a natural cow horse," Earl Albin said, "and his colts take to cattle as naturally as they took to their mothers' teats. In training them for cutting, they show wonderful progress in from 30 to 60 days. I don't mean they're finished horses in that time, by any means, but by then they're pretty well along on the way."[2]

In the fall of 1948, when Royal King was a 5-year-old, Albin sent him to Bob Burton in Fort Worth, Texas, for cutting training. The National Cutting Horse Association (NCHA) was, by this time, two years old and growing rapidly.

After several months of work under Burton, Royal King was returned to the Albin ranch for the 1949 breeding season. In the fall of the year, James Boucher, an Albin ranch hand, took the stallion to a few cutting contests and rode him to his first win at an event held in Dublin, Texas.

By 1951, Royal King was a seasoned cutting competitor who showed enough promise to be turned over to veteran trainer Milt Bennett of Crockett, Texas. Bennett rode the now-8-year-old stallion through the late summer and early fall.

At that point, he was turned back over to Boucher for a fall campaign.

The seemingly random carousel of trainers and riders who handled

"Royal" won the senior cutting at the 1953 Southwestern Exposition and Fat Stock Show in Fort Worth, Texas, with Andy Hensley of Pecos, Texas, in the saddle. **Photo by James Cathey, courtesy Quarter Horse Journal**

In a 1953 NCHA-sanctioned cutting at the Cow Palace in San Francisco, California, Royal King and Phil Williams (right) dueled their way to a first-place tie with Skeeter and Milt Bennett. **Courtesy Sue Albin Magers**

[2] "They Called Him Traveler," by Franklin Reynolds; *The Quarter Horse Journal*, May, 1957; page 65

Rocky Red, a 1947 sorrel full brother to Royal King, was an AQHA Superior cutting horse, the NCHA earner of $16,846 and Earl Albin's regular cutting mount. When the gritty gelding pulled up lame half-way through the 1952 NCHA season, Albin switched to Royal King.

Courtesy **Quarter Horse Journal**

Royal King to this point was indicative of how his entire cutting career progressed. If nothing else, it served to illustrate that, no matter who was in the saddle, the King son could be counted on to turn in the same solid performance.

In January of 1952, Stanley Bush of Mason, Texas, showed Royal King at the National Western Livestock Show in Denver, Colorado. Matched against the top cutters in all the land, the stallion finished second. At the end of the 1952 breeding season, Kirby Walters of Pampa, Texas, hauled Royal King to contests at such far-flung locations as Midland and Olney, Texas; Albuquerque, New Mexico; San Diego, California; and St. Paul, Minnesota.

Up to this time, Earl Albin had been competing in NCHA events on Rocky Red, a gelded full brother to Royal King. When "Rocky" pulled up lame in the late summer of 1952, the 5-foot 10-inch, 225-pound Albin

At first glance, the heftily built Albin and the diminutive Royal King might have seemed to be mismatched. Despite this fact, they were a formidable duo and provided stiff competition whenever they entered a cutting arena.

Courtesy Sue Albin Magers

A cow horse with natural ability, Royal King didn't need a bridle to do his job.   **Courtesy Sue Albin Magers**

switched over to 14-3 hand, 1,150-pound Royal King and headed for the Midwestern fair circuit.

Shown at the Illinois, Minnesota and Missouri State Fairs, Royal King turned in three blue ribbon-winning efforts.

At the conclusion of this run, Albin returned to his ranch duties and Royal King continued on under the care and guidance of Andy Hensley of Pecos, Texas. Hensley headed first to the Tri-State Fair in Amarillo, Texas, and then on to the American Royal in Kansas City, Missouri. From there, it was on to the West Coast and the big San Francisco, California, Cow Palace show. There, Royal King worked his way to a first-place finish over Little Tom W., the horse who ended that year as the World Champion Cutting Horse.

Next up for Hensley and Royal King was the winter stock show circuit. Shown in January in Denver, the 10-year-old stallion finished second. From Colorado, the duo headed south to the Southwestern Exposition and Fat Stock Show in Fort Worth, Texas. There, matched once again against the best

horses the cutting industry had to offer, Royal King placed first.

From Fort Worth, Hensley and the stallion continued on to San Antonio, Texas, where they turned it yet another impressive first-place performance.

By the end of the winter run, Royal King stood firmly in the lead for NCHA World Champion Cutting Horse honors. The game competitor was $5,000 ahead of his closest competitor, but then the 1953 breeding season beckoned and he was returned to Comanche to fulfill his duties there.

In the fall of 1953, Royal King was reunited with Milt Bennett for a second trek to the West Coast. In competition at the big Cow Palace show, the veteran campaigners worked their way to a first-place tie with Phil Williams and Skeeter, the 1950 and 1951 world champion cutting horse.

In early 1954, Royal King's owner decided to give his cutting ace one more crack at the National Western Stock Show. With Albin in the saddle, the gritty stallion worked his way to a third straight second-place finish.

Although primarily known as a cutting horse sire, Royal King was capable of siring good conformation as well. In this historic shot, Major King, Kitten and Maggie represent "Royal" as the winning get-of-sire entry at the 1948 State Fair of Texas in Dallas.

Photo by Neal Lyons, courtesy Quarter Horse Journal

In the fall of 1954, yet another rider, Buck Williams of Blanket, Texas, took over the stallion's hauling and riding chores. The high point of this pairing occurred when they notched a first-place finish at the big Ak-Sar-Ben show in Omaha, Nebraska.

By 1955, Royal King's traveling schedule had been dramatically reduced. Still, he remained a competitor to be reckoned with whenever and wherever he made an appearance.

In 1960, at the age of 17, the stallion was ridden by Earl Albin's teen-aged son Billy to a pair of first-place finishes in American Junior Rodeo Association contests in San Saba and Meridian, Texas.

After those events, the stallion was permanently retired.

Royal King's final NCHA record was an exemplary one, especially given the fact that he was always required to split his time between the breeding shed and the cutting arena.

The stallion finished in the NCHA Top 10 four times. In 1953, he was the Reserve World Champion Cutting Horse, finishing second to Snipper W and placing ahead of such stand-out cutting horses as Miss Nancy Bailey, Poco Lena, Jessie James and Skeeter. In 1952, the venerable competitor was third in the standings; in 1954, he ended the year in sixth place; and in 1955, he finished ninth.

NCHA records show Royal King to have earned Bronze Award No. 42 for winning $10,000, and Silver Award No. 19 for winning $20,000. His final NCHA monetary tally, amassed over a nine-year career, stands at $24,003.

As talented an arena performer as he was, Royal King's greatest impact upon the breed was not as a cutting horse, but rather as a sire. From the stallion's first foal crop came arguably his most influential son, Major King.

"Major," a 1946 sorrel stallion out of Moon Harris, was bred by C. M. Albin. Sold while still inside his dam to Mike and Millie Leonard of Junction, Texas, and not foaled until August 4, 1946, Major developed quickly into a top show horse.

Despite the fact that he was always the youngest horse in any given halter class, the blaze-faced, stocking-legged colt still earned four grand championships at halter before the age of 12 months. Turned over to Milt Bennett for cutting training, the compact sorrel stallion was rated by the veteran trainer as the best King horse he'd ever ridden.

But, like his sire, Major King's popularity as a breeding stallion dictated that he not be campaigned heavily as a show or cutting horse. As a result, his AQHA show record lists only a performance Register of Merit and NCHA earnings of $487.

As a sire, Major King was responsible for 491 registered get. Of these, 156 performers earned 10 AQHA Championships, two Superior halter awards, one Superior performance award and 48 performance Registers of Merit.

Among the stallion's top performers were:

- Major's Maco, a 1953 sorrel gelding out of M&M's Libby—Superior cutting, NCHA earner of $16,844.
- Major Thunder, a 1955 gray stallion out of Paradise Villa Panzar—1958 and 1959 High-Point Calf Roping Stallion, AQHA Champion, Superior Halter.
- Major's Manana, a 1958 sorrel stallion out of Little Rose—AQHA Champion.
- Major's Marquay, a 1959 sorrel mare out of Little Rose—AQHA Champion, Superior Halter.

In addition, Major's Manana, a Leonard-bred stallion who stood for years alongside Major King, was the sire of three AQHA Champions and

Royal's Rose, a 1955 bay mare by Royal King and out of Jane's Flicka, qualified for her AQHA Championship in 1962.
Photo by Ray M. Watson, courtesy Quarter Horse Journal

Royal Lightning, a 1957 sorrel stallion by Royal King and out of Moss' Jackie Tobin, was also an AQHA Champion. In addition, he was the 1963 High-Point Western Pleasure Stallion, a Superior Western pleasure horse and the earner of 130 performance points.
Photo by Don Shugart, courtesy Quarter Horse Journal

Major King, a 1946 sorrel stallion by Royal King and out of Moon Harris, displayed great potential as a cutting horse. Under the ownership of Mike and Millie Leonard of Junction, Texas, he was developed into a leading sire, instead.

Photo by James Cathey, courtesy Quarter Horse Journal

Royal King Bailey, a 1951 palomino gelding by Royal King and out of Cricket Bailey, helped spread the fame of the Royal King horses to the Midwest. Trained and ridden by AQHA Hall of Fame horseman Dale Wilkinson of Findlay, Ohio, the colorful gelding was an AQHA Champion and the NCHA earner of $3,823.

Courtesy Quarter Horse Journal

the earners of four Superior awards, and was the maternal grandsire of four AQHA Champions and the earners of 28 Superior awards.

Among "Manana's" top maternal grand-get is Major Bonanza, the top show horse and leading sire.

Getting back to Royal King, his own siring career was a long and distinguished one. AQHA records reveal him to have sired 590 registered foals. Of these, 211 were performers that earned three high-point awards, 10 AQHA Championships, 15 Superior awards and 88 performance Registers of Merit.

His AQHA Champion get were: Tony Manning, MM's Moon King, Royal King Bailey, Royal's Rose, Royal Angel, Royal Lightning, Royal Rainy, Royal Cupie Doll, Royal Rosaleta and Royal D Lou.

A versatile sire, Royal King also contributed the following performers to the breed: Royal Lightning, 1963 High-Point Western Pleasure Stallion and Superior Western pleasure; Royal Angel, Superior reining; and Miss Royal Dandy, Superior reining.

But, just as Royal King's greatest personal achievements were made as a cutting horse, his greatest breeding accomplishments were made as a cutting horse sire.

Of his formidable list of cutting performers, three horses—Miss Nancy Bailey, Royal Jazzy and Royal Chess—must be recognized as the cream of the crop.

Miss Nancy Bailey, a 1946 bay mare out of Nancy Bailey, was bred by Mrs. E. A. Whiteside of Sipe Springs, Texas.

Sold first to Mike and Millie Leonard, and then to Bob Burton of Arlington, Texas, Miss Nancy Bailey went on to become an NCHA Hall of Fame Horse, four-time Top 10 finisher and the earner of $38,084. Shown in AQHA-sanctioned cutting events, she was the 1952 and 1953 High-Point Cutting Horse, a Superior cutting horse and the earner of 178 performance points.

Royal Jazzy, a 1955 sorrel mare out of Jazamu, was bred by Clyde Henderson of

Miss Nancy Bailey, a 1946 bay mare by Royal King and out of Nancy Bailey, was bred by Mrs. E. A. Whiteside of Sipe Springs, Texas. Sold to Bob Burton of Arlington, Texas, she went on to attain NCHA Hall of Fame status.
Photo by James Cathey, courtesy Quarter Horse Journal

In AQHA competition, Miss Nancy Bailey was the 1952 and 1953 High-Point Cutting Horse, a Superior cutting horse and the earner of 178 performance points. In NCHA competition, she was a five-time Top 10 finisher and the earner of $38,084.
Photo by James Cathey, courtesy Quarter Horse Journal

Royal Jazzy, a 1955 sorrel mare by Royal King and out of Jazamu, was bred by Clyde Henderson of Lubbock, Texas. Sold to C. W. "Bubba" Cascio of Tolar, Texas, she, too, became a noted arena performer.

Courtesy Quarter Horse Journal

Lubbock, Texas. Sold to C. W. "Bubba" Cascio of Tolar, Texas, she was the 1963 NCHA Finals Champion and earned $28,197. In AQHA competition, she was a Superior cutting horse and earner of 279 performance points.

Royal Chess, a 1960 sorrel gelding out of Phoebe Chess, was bred by Alvin Harper of Mason, Texas. Sold to Clyde Bauer of Victoria, Texas, he went on to become an NCHA Hall of Fame Horse, 1970 NCHA Finals Champion, four-time Top 10 finisher and earner of $71,095. In AQHA competition, he was a Superior cutting horse and the earner of 173 performance points.

In addition to the aforementioned trio, nine more of Royal King's get earned honors as AQHA Superior cutting horses. They were: Chocker, Bunner, Skeeter Conway, Buttons King, Royal Dandy, Royal Fleet, King Caperton, Royal Morris and Marilyn Twist.

Rounding out Royal King's list of outstanding cutting horse get was Royal Royale. A 1970 sorrel stallion out of Woppy Cuellar and a member of his famous sire's last foal crop, "Royale" was the 1974 High-Point Jr. Cutting Horse.

With the majority of Royal King's get competing in an era of relatively low monetary payback, it is interesting to note that he still managed to sire NCHA earners of $346,969.

Finally, as distinguished a record as the King son managed to put together as a performer and a sire, it pales in comparison to his accomplishments as a maternal grandsire.

AQHA records show Royal King to be the maternal grandsire of 1,992 foals. Of these, 481 performers earned 14 AQHA world and reserve world championships, nine high-point wins, 27 AQHA Championships, 42 Superior awards and 152 performance Registers of Merit. In NCHA-sanctioned events, to date Royal King grandsons and granddaughters have amassed $2,066,660. In NRHA competition, they have bankrolled $155,517.

Among his most-accomplished maternal grand-get are:

• Doc Wilson, a 1973 sorrel stallion by Doc Bar and out of Jazzy Socks—NCHA earner of $121,955 and sire of the earners of more than $1.2 million.

• Call Me Royal, a 1969 chestnut gelding by Leon Bars and out of Miss Royal Fleet—

Royal Chess, a 1960 sorrel gelding by Royal King and out of Phoebe Chess, was bred by Alvin Harper of Mason, Texas. Sold to Clyde Bauer of Victoria, Texas, he was developed into an NCHA Hall of Fame performer by Stanley Bush of Mason, Texas. **Photo by Jim Keeland, courtesy Quarter Horse Journal**

King Caperton, a 1959 sorrel mare by Royal King and out of Baby Hancock, was yet another top cutter. In AQHA competition, she was a Superior cutting horse and the earner of 134 performance points. In NCHA-sanctioned events, she was a four-time NCHA Finals top five finisher and the earner of $56,368.

Courtesy Quarter Horse Journal

1978 World Champion Sr. Reining, earner of three AQHA Championships, six Superior awards and 1,170 points.

- Ossun, a 1966 sorrel gelding by Chockie and out of Royal Jan—earner of four AQHA Championships, nine Superior awards and 1,342 points.
- Royal Agget, a 1965 sorrel gelding by Joe's Last and out of Royal Rita—1974 World Champion Sr. Cutting Horse.
- Royal Santana, a 1971 sorrel gelding by Peppy San and out of Royal Smart—AQHA Hall of Fame Horse and NCHA earner of $174,146.
- Sir Royal Lynx, a 1980 sorrel gelding by Doc's Lynx and out of Royal Tex Top—NCHA earner of $155,696.
- Lady Barbie Sox, a 1964 sorrel mare by Double Five and out of White Sox Lady—1968 High-Point Western Pleasure, AQHA Champion, Superior Halter, Superior Western Pleasure.

It is interesting to note that, of the above seven horses, five were geldings. A review of Royal King's sire and maternal grandsire production records vividly attests to the fact that when it came to his male offspring, true

Royal Royale was one of the last Royal Kings to enter the cutting horse fray. A 1970 sorrel stallion out of Woppy Cuellar, "Royale" was the 1974 High-Point Junior Cutting Horse.

Courtesy Quarter Horse Journal

ranching tradition was adhered to and most were gelded.

"It is true that daddy gelded most of the colts," Sue Albin Magers of Comanche said. "The one notable exception was Royal Texas. He was a 1956 roan stallion by Royal King and out of Texas Kitty. Daddy thought he was the best-looking stallion he ever raised, and he's responsible for the roan color behind the Royal Blue Boon line of cutting horses.

"But he didn't live long. He only sired 57 foals, and two of those were AQHA Champions."

Getting back to Royal King's well-deserved reputation as a broodmare sire, throughout the 1950s, J. M. Frost III of Houston, Texas, (see Chapter 6) was one of the country's foremost King P-234 proponents.

Knowing full well the worth of the line's distaff side, Frost at one time owned 21 daughters of King and 20 daughters of Royal

King. In 1957 and 1958, he contracted with Earl Albin to purchase all the Royal King fillies that were born in each of those years.

Spencer Harden of Weatherford, Texas, founded a cutting horse dynasty with the help of the Royal King line, and it was his opinion that the family's cutting style was unique.

"A lot of horses will drop their front end," he said, "but these horses will drop all over. The Royal Kings that I have had always had that drop and look, and a lot of shake and shiver to them. That's predominantly Royal King and that's what we're trying to keep coming through."

And Hardin should know. His great cutting producer Jazabelle Quixote, a Royal King great granddaughter, has produced NCHA earners of more than $1.25 million.

There are other great Royal King matrons, as well.

The blood of Royal has continued to exert a strong influence on the cutting horse world. Royal Santana, a 1971 sorrel gelding by Peppy San and out of Royal Smart by Royal King, is an AQHA Hall of Fame horse and the NCHA earner of $174,146. ***Courtesy* Quarter Horse Journal**

The Royal King story was always a family affair. In this famous photo, taken on the Albin Ranch in 1948, shows the stallion to be gentle enough to baby sit the three Albin children – Billy, Sue and Lou.

Courtesy Sue Albin Magers

Royal Blue Boon, a double-bred Royal King descendant, is the industry's all-time leading producer. To date, her foals have earned more than $2.3 million. Peptoboonsmal, her leading son, has likewise sired earners of more than $3.6 million.

That Smarts, a triple-bred Royal King mare, has produced earners of more than $875,000.

Finally, Smart Peppy, a Royal King grand-daughter, has produced earners of more than $1.1 million. Smart Little Lena, her leading son, is the industry's all-time leading sire. To date, his get have amassed more than $28 million.

Neither Royal King nor Earl Albin lived long enough to witness the amazing impact that their joint efforts had on the Quarter Horse industry.

Throughout his twilight years, Royal King was the subject of constant attention from the Albin family in general, and Mrs. Earl Albin in particular.

"My mother, Charlie Mae, was never much of a horseback rider," said Sue Magers. "But, like all of us, she was very fond of Royal King. He was just such a kind, intelligent horse to be around.

"When Royal King got old, mother made a big thing out of seeing that he always had feed and fresh water. She worried over him just like a mother hen."

By the late spring of 1971, it was apparent that 28-year-old Royal King was nearing the end of his days. He was arthritic and had trouble getting up and down. Finally, in May, the decision was made to have him put to sleep.

The renowned cutting horse stallion's kind disposition is again apparent in this photo taken in February of 1956 at the Fort Worth Stock Show. The Albin gang gathered around "Royal" is comprised of twin sisters Sue and Lou, age 11; and brother Billy, age 10.
Courtesy Sue Albin Magers

"When it came right down to it," Magers said, "Daddy just couldn't face what he knew had to be done. He did call the vet to come and put Royal down, and he, my brother Billy, and my husband, Randy, all stayed with the horse until the vet arrived.

"But then Daddy pulled Randy aside and had him drive them both off in the pickup. They left poor Billy to see that the deed was done."

Royal King was laid to rest in a grave situated under some Live Oak trees near the ranch headquarters. After witnessing a num-

ber of cattle walking over the site, Charlie Mae Albin decided that just wasn't right and had a pipe fence installed.

Earl Albin passed away in 1985. As she was arranging for the headstone to mark her late husband's final resting place, Charlie Mae also had a second marker made to place over Royal King's grave.

It was a final and fitting testimony to a member of Quarter Horse royalty who remains one of the King family's brightest stars and one of the cutting horse industry's most-enduring influences.

Chapter 10

THE HEIR APPARENT

Poco Bueno focused attention on the King line of Quarter Horses in a way it had never before seen.
Photo by John A. Stryker, courtesy Quarter Horse Journal

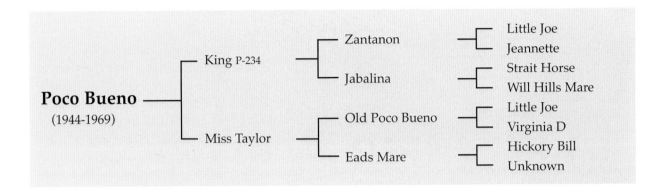

```
                                        ┌─ Little Joe
                       ┌─ Zantanon ─────┤
         ┌─ King P-234 ┤                └─ Jeannette
         │             │                ┌─ Strait Horse
         │             └─ Jabalina ─────┤
Poco Bueno ─┤                           └─ Will Hills Mare
(1944-1969) │                           ┌─ Little Joe
         │             ┌─ Old Poco Bueno┤
         └─ Miss Taylor┤                └─ Virginia D
                       │                ┌─ Hickory Bill
                       └─ Eads Mare ────┤
                                        └─ Unknown
```

Note: The Poco Bueno story is far too broad to be covered in one chapter. The renowned stallion is slated to be the subject of a separate book in the future. In advance of that effort, this chapter will serve as a brief overview of his life and legacy.

Poco Bueno.

In textbook Spanish, the words mean "little good," and that was the moniker Jess Hankins decided to hang on his King colt. That didn't mean the South Texas rancher held the foal in low esteem. On the contrary, he thought him to be of above average quality.

" 'Poco Bueno' means 'pretty good' in Spanish [slang]," Hankins said, "and he was just a pretty good colt, so that's what I named him."[1]

Poco Bueno, a 1944 brown stallion by King P-234 and out of Miss Taylor, was a member of the Hankins/King combine's first true "bumper crop."

In 1943, King had reportedly been bred to 50 mares. Of the resulting foals, 39 eventually found their way into the fledgling AQHA registry. In addition to Poco Bueno, included among them were such noteworthy sons as Lady's Black Eagle, Quarterback, L H Chock and Beaver Creek, and such noteworthy daughters as Flapper H, L H Susie, Sorrel Sue, Betty Warren and 89'er.

Each and every one of these horses went on to achieve some measure of success within the Quarter Horse industry, but none rose to stardom as fast or ascended to as lofty a height as did Poco Bueno.

As chronicled in Chapter 3, Hankins acquired King in July of 1937. Almost immediately thereafter, the Rocksprings, Texas-based rancher began scouring the countryside for Old Billy-bred mares to add to his new stallion's harem.

It didn't take Hankins long to figure out that there were certain parts of South Texas that were especially rich in Old Billy blood. The areas around Alice and Laredo were two of these, and from there, Hankins acquired such top Little Joe- and Zantanon-bred mares

Poco Bueno earned honors as the grand champion stallion at the 1951 San Antonio Livestock Exposition in San Antonio, Texas. Owner E. Paul Waggoner of Vernon, Texas, is seen at Poco Bueno's head while Rebecca Price of Ryan, Oklahoma, holds the trophy.

Courtesy Quarter Horse Journal

[1] "The Story of Poco Bueno," by Mary Ellen Harris; *The Texas Horseman.*

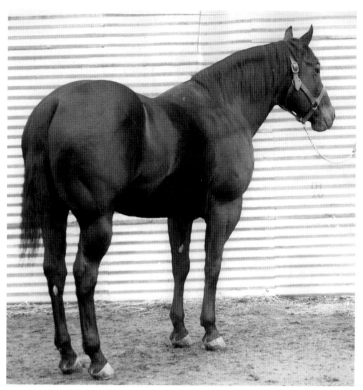

Poco Bueno was brought out of retirement to stand grand at the 1953 National Western Stock Show, Denver, Colorado.

Photo by James Cathey, courtesy Quarter Horse Journal

as Stifle, Little Pet, Maria Elena and Uncle's Pet.

In late 1941 or early 1942, Hankins was on a horse-hunting trip between Alice and Laredo when he happened on a mare that he thought might make a good addition to his herd.

She was a 1933 bay, bred and owned by Alonzo Taylor of Hebbronville. Her sire was Old Poco Bueno, a son of Little Joe, and her dam was the Eads Mare, a daughter of Hickory Bill.

Taylor was one of the great South Texas stockmen of the day. A match-racing and horse-breeding cohort of such men as Ott Adams, John Dial and Manuel Benavides Volpe, it was Taylor who had sold Ada Jones to the King Ranch (see Chapter 1), and it was on his ranch that the legendary Zantanon had died.

Jess Hankins liked Taylor's bay mare well enough to buy her and register her with

AQHA as Miss Taylor P-2636.

Prior to being purchased by Hankins, Miss Taylor was the dam of two AQHA-registered foals: Taylor's Serana, a 1940 sorrel mare, and Lotts Hazell, a 1941 sorrel mare. Both were sired by an "Adams Horse by Paul Ell."

Bred to King for the first time in 1942, she wound up producing 11 full brothers and sisters: Red Jane C, Poco Bueno, Spooks, Miss Hankins, Old Taylor, Cactus King, Old Grandad, My Mona Lisa, My Taylor Maid, King Junior and Captain Jess.

All 11 members of the cross went on to make positive contributions to the breed but, again, the accomplishments of the other 10 siblings paled in comparison to those of the eldest son—Poco Bueno.

In the spring of 1945, however, Poco Bueno was just another promising King colt, several months away from reaching any kind of bloom.

In March of that year, Hankins exhibited two King sons, Sundown and Poco Bueno, in the yearling stallions class at the Fort Worth Fat Stock Show. Sundown, a 1944 bay stallion out of Stifle, won the class and Poco Bueno placed fifth. While at the show, Hankins priced Poco Bueno for sale at $1,250. There were no takers.

Within the span of four short months, however, the fifth-place finisher began to fill out and his stock began to rise.

Exhibited over the Fourth of July weekend in Stamford, Texas, Poco Bueno placed first in his class. By this time, Hankins' opinion of his colt had also taken a turn for the better. As a result, he bumped the asking price on him to $3,500.

The amount was an exorbitant one, but did not dissuade such prominent early-day breeders as Frank Vessels of Los Alamitos, California, and Channing Peake of Lompoc, California, from expressing an interest in owning the blue ribbon-winning colt.

At the 1953 Southwestern Exposition and Livestock Show, Fort Worth, Texas, Poco Bueno earned grand champion honors and was the get-of-sire winner. Legendary trainer Pine Johnson is up on the renowned King son in this shot taken at the show. **Photo by James Cathey, courtesy Quarter Horse Journal**

1 3 7

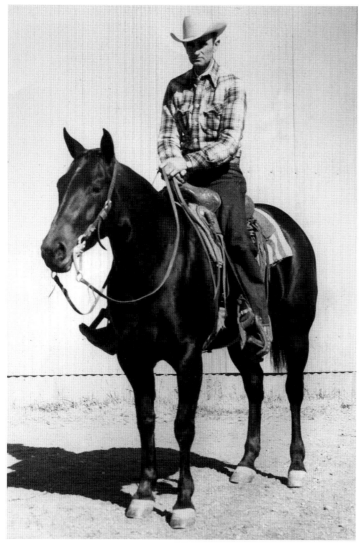

Poco Lena, a 1949 bay mare by Poco Bueno and out of Sheilwin, was one of the first of Poco Bueno's get to excel in the show ring. AQHA Hall of Fame horseman Don Dodge is seen astride the talented performer.

Photo by James Cathey, courtesy Quarter Horse Journal

sold for $5,700 to E. Paul Waggoner of Vernon, Texas.

Sundown was the sale's second-highest seller. He elicited a bid of $4,100 from none other than E. Paul Waggoner. When it came time to register the colt with AQHA, the name Sundown was already taken, so he was re-named Beaver Creek after a stream that ran through the Zacawista division of the Waggoner Ranch. Regardless of what he was named, he went on to become a top sire in his own right.[2]

Despite the fact that Waggoner now found himself the owner of not one, but two top King sons, there was never any doubt in his mind about which of the pair he intended to groom as the heir apparent.

And, as an heir himself to the huge W. T. Waggoner Estate, and owner and operator of the Three D Stock Farm of Arlington, Texas, E. Paul could do pretty much as he pleased.

The Waggoner Ranch had its beginnings in the early 1850s, when Daniel Waggoner and a 15-year-old black slave trailed 242 longhorn cattle and six horses into Wise County, Texas. In the spring of 1869, Dan Waggoner and his 16-year-old son, W. T. (Tom) Waggoner, drove 6,000 head of longhorn steers from Clay County, Texas, to Kansas City, Missouri. The drive netted the duo $55,000, and that amount formed the basis of the Waggoner Ranch fortune.

After Dan Waggoner passed away in 1904, W. T. continued to expand the ranch until it encompassed approximately 520,000 acres. Recalling his experiences with 50 "sore-backed horses" on the 1869 cattle drive, W. T. was determined to breed and own the best horses possible. With his son-in-law A. B. Wharton of Fort Worth, Texas, he raised polo ponies. Beginning in 1931, he also bred race-

At show's end, however, Poco Bueno remained in Hankins' hands.

On October 22, 1945, the three Hankins brothers—Jess, J. O. and Lowell—held their first joint production sale. Sundown, the first-place yearling stallion in Fort Worth, and Poco Bueno, the first-place yearling stallion in Stamford, were the sale headliners.

Poco Bueno topped the sale, setting the entire Quarter Horse world abuzz when he

---

[2] See Appendix A, "All the King's Men."

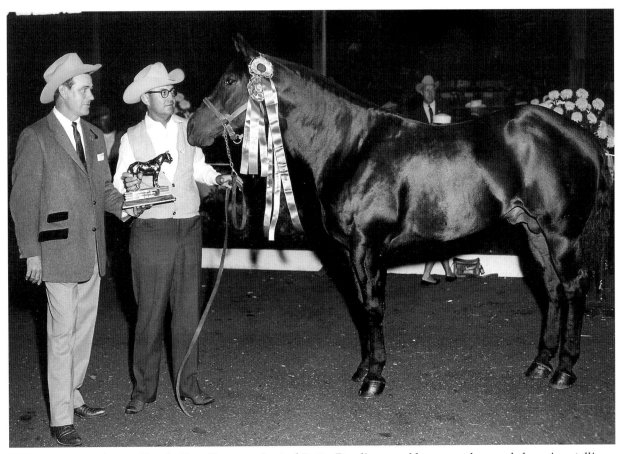

Poco Pine, a 1954 bay stallion by Poco Bueno and out of Pretty Rosalie, earned honors as the grand champion stallion at the 1959 American Royal in Kansas City, Missouri. Here, judge B. F. Phillips, Jr. presents the winning trophy to owner Paul Curtner of Jacksboro, Texas.   ***Courtesy* Quarter Horse Journal**

horses at his Arlington Downs Stables between Fort Worth and Dallas.

So driven was W. T. to own the best horseflesh in all the land that he once offered Samuel D. Riddle $500,000 for Man O' War. When Riddle turned that offer down, Waggoner upped the ante to $1,000,000. When Riddle again refused, Waggoner was purported to have handed Riddle a signed check with instructions to fill it in for whatever amount it would take.

In 1909, W. T. Waggoner divided half of his immense land and livestock holdings among his three children—Electra, Guy and E. Paul—mainly to give them training in ranching. Then, in 1923, all of the ranch's property was re-merged into the W. T. Waggoner Estate with W. T. as trustee and Electra, Guy and E. Paul as a three-member board of directors.

It was into this rich legacy of bigger-than-life Texas cattle ranchers and horsemen that Poco Bueno was thrust in October of 1945.

E. Paul Waggoner initially had Poco Bueno shipped to his Three D Stock Farm in Arlington. There, the long yearling stallion was kept up and fit for the upcoming show circuit.

Shown sparingly at halter over the next several years, Poco Bueno earned grand champion stallion honors at the 1946 Fort Worth Fat Stock Show in Fort Worth, Texas; the 1946 State Fair of Texas in Dallas; the 1946 Junction, Texas, show; the 1947 National Western Stock Show in Denver, Colorado; the 1948 American Royal in Kansas City, Missouri; the 1948 Stamford, Texas, show; and the 1951 San Antonio Livestock Exposition.

Poco Enterprise, a 1958 dun stallion by Poco Bueno and out of Lady Chock 56, was another of his sire's durable stars. He is seen here as a yearling, the year he topped a Waggoner Ranch production sale. "Enterprise" became an AQHA Champion and the maternal grandsire of NRHA icon Be Aech Enterprise.

Photo by James Cathey, courtesy Quarter Horse Journal

When he was a 2-year-old, Poco Bueno was broke to ride by Three D foreman and trainer Bob Burton.

Burton, who had also broke and trained the famed Waggoner Ranch stallions Pretty Buck and Jessie James, initially had it in his mind to turn Poco Bueno into a calf roping horse. After finding out that the 15-hand, 1,250-pound King son would "sure watch a cow," the emphasis was shifted to cutting.

Shortly after the change in venue was made, Burton left the Three Ds to go into business on his own. His successor as ranch foreman and trainer was Lewis "Pine" Johnson of Fort Worth. Under Johnson's tutelage, Poco Bueno won or placed high in the cutting events at a number of prestigious shows.

In 1948, he was third in the cuttings in Denver; Stamford; Breckenridge, Texas; and Kansas City, Missouri.

In 1949, he was first in the registered cutting in Fort Worth and Odessa, Texas; and second in the open cutting in Fort Worth. In 1951, he was the champion cutting horse at the San Antonio Fat Stock Show.

Although Poco Bueno's cutting exploits were reportedly hampered by a slight stifle joint injury, he was known to be an agile and savvy competitor.

"He was quick," Pine Johnson said. "In a turn, he would bend his knees and drop straight down – then shove himself back in the other direction.

"The first cutting I took him to was at Denver. He really turned on the job and brought the grandstand down. He lost a calf, though, and placed third, only a point and a half behind the winner."[3]

Poco Bueno was never campaigned heavily as a cutting horse. Despite that, he saw enough action to receive NCHA Certificate of Ability No. 14 on June 29, 1949.

"We didn't campaign him like you do cutting horses now," Johnson said. "We didn't have the time.

[3] "The Story of Poco Bueno," by Mary Ellen Harris; *The Texas Horseman.*

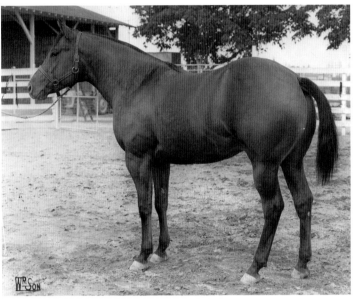

Poco Pico, a 1954 dun stallion by Poco Bueno and out of Mary D, was an AQHA Champion and the NCHA earner of $2,542.
Photo by John Williamson, courtesy Quarter Horse Journal

Poco Lynn, a 1954 dun mare by Poco Bueno and out of Lady Blackburn III, was the 1958 High Point Halter Horse. In addition, she was also an AQHA Champion and a Superior halter horse.
Photo by James Cathey, courtesy Quarter Horse Journal

Poco Ojos, a 1957 sorrel mare by Poco Bueno and out of Wimpy's Ojos, was an AQHA Champion, Superior halter horse and the earner of 157 halter points.   **Photo by Danny Santell, *courtesy* Quarter Horse Journal**

Poco Sail, a 1957 bay mare by Poco Bueno and out of Rio Rita, was a Superior halter horse and the earner of 118 halter points.
***Courtesy* Western Horseman**

"He stayed out with the broodmares from April to September. About the first or 15th of September, we'd get him in from the pasture and head to the big show at Omaha at the end of the month.

"His mares would have him poor as a snake and all skinned up, but he'd go right in there with the wolves of the world and show them what he could do. He never disappointed us."[4]

According to Johnson, Poco Bueno was not only quick on his feet but also powerful in his movement.

"One night at the rodeo at Arlington Downs," he said, "Poco Bueno made one of his fast turns and

[4] "The Story of Poco Bueno," by Mary Ellen Harris; *The Texas Horseman.*

I wound up standing on the ground. After the show, one of the boys asked me why I stepped off like that. The horse had ducked out from under me so smooth and fast that no one realized that was what he had done.

"He didn't do it a second time, though. I decided that was what the saddle horn was for, and just as he'd go into a turn, I'd pull on it for all I was worth and I'd stay on him—although I often felt like my feet were over my head."[5]

By early 1951, the Waggoner Ranch "boss hoss" had basically been retired from all show competition.

Then, in March of that year, the AQHA Executive Committee gave final approval to a national point system for show horses. Made retroactive to the beginning of the year, the new scheme had among its many features the establishment of an AQHA Champion award. To qualify for it, horses needed to earn a total of 20 points in halter, performance or racing.

In early 1953, E. Paul Waggoner decided that Poco Bueno should be given a shot at the new award. The 9-year-old King son was taken out of retirement and sent back to the show ring.

Shown at three of the four biggest shows in the nation—the National Western, Fort Worth and San Antonio Stock Shows—Poco Bueno earned grand champion honors at all three. By the end of the winter stock show run, he had accumulated 36 halter points and eight cutting points—more than enough to qualify him for his AQHA Championship.

In 1954, Waggoner moved his horse operation from Arlington to a brand new facility he had built in Vernon

Poco Lady Pep, a 1956 bay mare by Poco Bueno and out of Lady Pep Up X7, was another Waggoner Ranch-bred halter champion. That's long-time ranch manager Fagan Miller at "Lady Pep's" halter in this shot. **Courtesy Western Horseman**

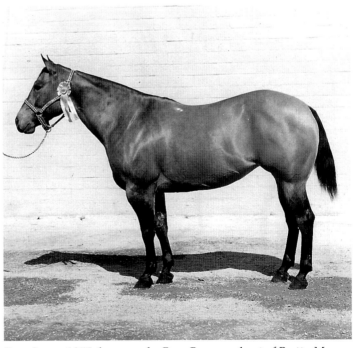

Poco Lon, a 1957 dun mare by Poco Bueno and out of Pretty Me, was also a Superior halter horse. **Courtesy Western Horseman**

[5] "The Story of Poco Bueno," by Mary Ellen Harris; *The Texas Horseman.*

Like his sire before him, Poco Bueno was a consistent get-of-sire winner.

***Courtesy* Quarter Horse Journal**

Poco Tivio, a 1947 bay stallion by Poco Bueno and out of Sheilwin, was the first of his sire's get to make his presence felt as an arena performer. A top AQHA and NCHA competitor, he went on to become an influential sire.

***Courtesy* Quarter Horse Journal**

that had been christened the Santa Rosa Fairgrounds. By this time, Poco Bueno's reputation as a sire was skyrocketing.

Poco Tivio, the first son of Poco Bueno, was a 1947 bay stallion out of Sheilwin. Broke by Willis Bennett and trained for cutting by Pine Johnson, he was shown as a 3-year-old alongside his famous sire. The sight of the Poco Bueno--Poco Tivio team cutting and turning back for each other captured the imagination of the Quarter Horse crowd and greatly enhanced the reputation of sire and son alike.

Sold first to Cliff Magers of Fort Worth, and then to Don Dodge of North Sacramento, California, Poco Tivio became one of the breed's first eight AQHA Champions, the sire of 15 AQHA Champions, and an all-time leading NCHA maternal grandsire.

Poco Lena, Poco Bueno's first AQHA Champion daughter, was a 1949 bay mare out of Sheilwin. Given first by E. Paul Waggoner as a gift to Three D ranch manager Glen Turpin, Poco Lena was later sold to Don Dodge.

Under Dodge's ownership, the Poco Tivio full sister was developed into one of the greatest cutting mares of all time.

In AQHA competition, "Lena" was the 1959, 1960 and 1961 AQHA High-Point Cutting Horse; an AQHA Champion; and the earner of 174 halter and 671 performance points. In 1991, she was inducted into the AQHA Hall of Fame.

In NCHA competition, she was the 1959, 1960 and 1961 NCHA World Champion Cutting Mare; and the 1954, 1955, 1959, 1960

Poco Lena, a 1949 bay full sister to Poco Tivio, was the greatest cutting horse of her era. An AQHA and NCHA Hall of Fame horse, her influence on the cutting industry as both a performer and producer has been enormous.

Courtesy **Quarter Horse Journal**

Poco Mona, a 1948 bay mare by Poco Bueno and out of Dolly D, was another top cutting horse competitor. In AQHA competition, she was the 1958 High Point Cutting Mare, an AQHA Champion, Superior cutting horse and the earner of 283 performance points. In NCHA competition, she was a Hall of Fame horse, a four-time Top 10 finisher and the earner of $49,654.   ***Courtesy* Quarter Horse Journal**

and 1961 NCHA Reserve World Champion Cutting Horse. In addition, she earned $99,782, was the first horse inducted into the NCHA Hall of Fame, and produced two foals—Doc O'Lena and Dry Doc.

Bolstered by the success of his first two show get, Poco Bueno went on to become one of the Quarter Horse breed's all-time leading sires. AQHA records reveal that he was the sire of 405 foals from 24 foal crops. Included in this number are 36 AQHA Champions and the earners of 18 Superior halter awards, 16 Superior performance awards and 87 Registers of Merit.

Among Poco Bueno's other noteworthy sons were:

• Pretty Boy Pokey, a 1948 dun stallion out of Pretty Girl W—1954 AQHA High-Point Calf Roping, AQHA Champion, Superior Halter.

• Poco Champ, a 1950 bay stallion out of Sheilwin—AQHA Champion, Superior Cutting.

• Poco Dell, a 1950 bay stallion out of Shady Dell—AQHA Champion, sire of 18 AQHA Champions.

• Poco Bob, a 1952 dun stallion out of Lady Blackburn III—AQHA Champion, Superior Halter, Superior Cutting.

• Poco Stampede, a 1952 dun stallion out of Pretty Rosalie—1959 NCHA World Champion Cutting Horse; NCHA Hall of Fame; 1957, 1958 and 1959 AQHA High-Point Cutting Horse; AQHA Champion; Superior Cutting.

• Poco Robin, a 1953 bay stallion out of Jeep W—AQHA Champion, Superior Cutting.

• Poco Pine, a 1954 bay stallion out of Pretty Rosalie—AQHA Champion, Superior Halter, sire of 37 AQHA Champions.

• Poco Enterprise, a 1958 dun stallion out of Lady Chock 56—AQHA Champion, maternal grandsire of Be Aech Enterprise.
• Poco Merit, a 1959 bay stallion out of Double Rita—AQHA Champion, Superior Halter.

Among Poco Bueno's other noteworthy daughters were:
• Poco Mona, a 1948 bay mare out of Dolly D—NCHA Hall of Fame horse, NCHA earner of $49,654, 1958 AQHA High-Point Cutting Mare, AQHA Champion, Superior Cutting.
• Poco Doll, a 1951 dun mare out of Dolly D—AQHA Champion, Superior Halter.
• Poco Nadine, a 1952 bay mare out of Jeep W—AQHA Champion, Superior Halter.
• Poco Lynn, a 1954 dun mare out of Lady Blackburn III—1958 AQHA High-Point Halter, AQHA Champion, Superior Halter.
• Poco Bow, a 1957 dun mare out of Miss Bow Tie—AQHA Champion, Superior Halter, Superior Western Pleasure.
• Poco Chata, a 1957 mare out of Wimpy's Chata—AQHA Champion, Superior Halter.
• Poco Ojos, a 1957 bay mare out of Wimpy's Ojos—AQHA Champion Superior Halter.
• Poco Sail, a 1957 bay mare out of Rio Rita—AQHA Champion, Superior Halter.
• Poco Panzarita, a 1960 bay mare out of Mayflower Daugherty—AQHA Champion, Superior Halter.
• Poco Miss Dinero, a 1962 mare out of Nune's Cameo—AQHA Champion, Superior Halter.

Throughout the 1950s, Poco Bueno's get reigned supreme as show horses, renowned for both their classic "bulldog" conformation and inherent working ability.

Their sire, whose personal fame grew by leaps and bounds, spent each breeding season as a pasture stallion. Turned out from

Poco Dell, a 1950 bay stallion by Poco Bueno and out of Shady Dell, was an AQHA Champion and NCHA money earner. Shown here with owner Jimmie Randals of Montoya, New Mexico, in the saddle, Poco Dell became a leading sire. **Courtesy Quarter Horse Journal**

147

Poco Bob, a 1952 dun stallion by Poco Bueno and out of Lady Blackburn III, was an AQHA Champion, Superior halter and cutting horse, and the NCHA earner of $14,608.

Courtesy **Quarter Horse Journal**

early spring to early fall with a full complement of 30 to 35 mares, he responded by becoming a remarkably consistent sire.

Represented by his offspring in 50 get of sire classes, he earned 31 firsts, 15 seconds and four thirds.

By the early 1960s, Poco Bueno was one of the most celebrated Quarter Horse stallions in all the land. During the annual Santa Rosa Roundup, people flocked to his stall just to catch a glimpse of him.

The Waggoner Ranch stallion's worth had risen from the $1,250 that Jess Hankins had been unable to get for him as a yearling, to that of the first Quarter Horse stallion to be insured for $100,000.

His stud fee was set at $5,000, an all-time high for a non-racehorse.

By the mid-1960s, thanks mainly to Poco

Bueno, E. Paul Waggoner and the Waggoner Estate of Vernon, were at the statistical top of the Quarter Horse industry.

In the May 1969 *Quarter Horse Journal's* annual performance horse issue, the Waggoner Ranch was listed as the No. 1 All-Time Leading Breeder of AQHA Champions, and the No. 1 All-Time Leading Breeder of Register of Merit Horses.

Poco Bueno was the No. 1 All-Time Leading Sire of AQHA Champions, while Poco Pine was entrenched in the No. 2 spot. Four Waggoner Ranch stallions—Blackburn, Poco Bueno, Beaver Creek and Pretty Boy— held down the top 10 spots on the All-Time Leading Maternal Grandsires of AQHA Champions list.

E. Paul Waggoner, patriarch of the Waggoner Ranch Quarter Horse program and guiding light behind the Poco Bueno era of the ranch's long and colorful history, passed away on March 3, 1967.

In his will, he left Poco Bueno not to the estate, but to his son-in-law John Biggs. Fagan Miller, long-time Waggoner Ranch manager, continued to oversee the aging stallion's day-to-day care.

It is interesting to note that, before E. Paul Waggoner's death, Poco Bueno sired 36 AQHA Champions and the earners of 34 Superiors and 87 performance Registers of Merit. After Waggoner's demise, Poco Bueno sired only the earner of one performance Register of Merit.

By the end of 1969, 25-year-old Poco Bueno was suffering from advanced arthritis. He had his own private pasture, and the gate to it was left open so he had the run of his Santa Rosa Fairgrounds home, but he experienced more and more difficulty just getting around.

No expense was spared to make Poco Bueno as comfortable as possible, but his appetite began to fail and he began having trouble getting up and down. Biggs made the decision to have him put to sleep on November 28, 1969.

In accordance with E. Paul's instructions, Poco Bueno was buried in an upright position in a grave located across the road from the main entrance to the Waggoner Ranch. A massive granite marker was placed over the grave. Under an etched likeness of the famous stallion was carved this simple epitaph: Poco Bueno AQHA P-3044 – Champion and Sire of Champions.

In recognition of his watershed contributions to the Quarter Horse industry, Poco Bueno was inducted into the AQHA Hall of Fame in 1990. Both his life-long owner, E. Paul Waggoner, and his most-famous daughter, Poco Lena, were likewise honored the following year.

In retrospect, the brown son of King P-234 and Miss Taylor might have been misnamed after all.

Maybe he should have been named Muy Bueno, or "very good," instead.

Poco Stampede, a 1952 dun stallion by Poco Bueno and out of Pretty Rosalie, was one of his sire's most-accomplished get. In AQHA competition, he was a two-time high-point cutting horse, AQHA Champion and Superior halter and cutting horse. In NCHA competition, he was a Hall of Fame horse, the 1959 World Champion Cutting Horse and the earner of $39,939. **Courtesy Quarter Horse Journal**

Chapter 11

THE POWER BROKER

Power Command, under-appreciated while he lived, still had a positive impact on the breed.
Photo by Orren Mixer, courtesy Quarter Horse Journal

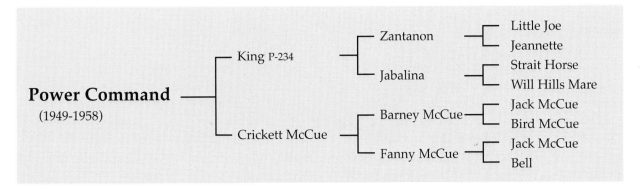

Power Command
(1949-1958)

— King P-234
  — Zantanon
    — Little Joe
    — Jeannette
  — Jabalina
    — Strait Horse
    — Will Hills Mare
— Crickett McCue
  — Barney McCue
    — Jack McCue
    — Bird McCue
  — Fanny McCue
    — Jack McCue
    — Bell

Like a Phoenix rising from the ashes, America rose from the ordeal of World War II to embark upon an age of renewal, growth and prosperity.

To be sure, the world-at-large was still in a state of flux. The vanquished threat of the Axis powers was soon to be replaced by the equally ominous specter of the Russian "Iron Curtain." Conflict in Korea loomed just over the horizon.

But, for a few precious years, all seemed right in the land of the brave and the home of the free.

The American economy, bolstered by the return of millions of service personnel eager to assimilate back into society, boomed. This homecoming horde of men and women in their prime resulted in yet another type of growth. Marriages flourished, birth rates soared and the 76 million-strong "Baby Boom" generation was born.

And American society was forever changed.

The post-war horse industry underwent a radical transformation, as well.

Before the war, horses were an integral part of the military and rural landscape. After the war, mechanization on both fronts changed the horse's role as one of a utilitarian partner to that of a recreational interest.

The Quarter Horse breed in general, and the King P-234 line in particular, were both able to adapt to the change with surprising alacrity and they prospered beyond belief.

During the first three years of its existence, AQHA registered a mere 1,301 horses. Much of this slow growth can be attributed directly to wartime restrictions placed on the entire country. Once the conflicts ended, the breed began to grow by leaps and bounds. By the end of 1948, registrations stood at 12,000.

In September of 1948, AQHA launched the *Quarter Horse Journal*, its monthly breed publication. Jess Hankins of Rocksprings, Texas, ran a half-page ad in the magazine's inaugural issue to introduce his senior herd sire as "The King of Quarter Horses." The ad further stated that King had "more registered get in the AQHA Stud Book than any other horse. He is way out in front."

After being purchased by Robert Q. Sutherland of Kansas City, Missouri, Power Command was shown by resident trainer John Ballweg to grand champion stallion honors at the 1954 Missouri State Fair in Sedalia.

Photo by L. F. Henderson, courtesy Quarter Horse Journal

King P-234 was now 16 years old and working on the second half of his life. The Hankins bay proved that his earlier breeding accomplishments were not flukes by siring an impressive string of top young stallions between 1945 and 1950. The list includes such horses as Booger H, Little Tom B, Spooks, Sunup H, Bay Bob, Bee Line, King's Joe Boy, O'Quinn's King B, Old Taylor, Roper Boy, Squeeky, Zantanon H, Brown King H, Cage's Cattle King, King A, King Sunday, Black Gold King, Fourble Joe, O'Quinn's Rialto, Old Grandad, R Joking, Scharbauer's King and Uncle Pardner.

By the end of the decade, there was no denying the fact that here was "a sire of sires."

And King proved versatile enough at stud to sire top daughters, as well. In addition to Red Bud L and Little Alice L, J. M. Frost III's two AQHA Champion mares, King con-tributed such top show and producing daughters as Asbeck's Billie, Totsey H, Carol's Ethel, O'Quinn's Breezy and O'Quinn's Queen Bee to the breed.

And then there were the geldings, both registered and unregistered.

Among the latter was "Jimmy," an unregistered sorrel gelding by King and out of an unknown mare. Imported into the Rocky Mountain region by Gus Roberson of Gunnison, Colorado, Jimmy was subsequently acquired by the Simon family of Limon, Colorado.

"My dad, 'Doc' Simon, ran across Jimmy at a rodeo in a little town near Morrison, Colorado," said Erma Jean Wayt of Longmont. "This was probably around 1946.

"Jimmy was a young horse, maybe 5 or 6. He was a little sorrel that stood 14-2 and would weigh 1,100 if he was good and fat. He had a spot on his stomach, and some of

In May of 1956, Power Command was named the reserve champion stallion at the Dallas, Texas, show.

Photo by James Cathey, courtesy Quarter Horse Journal

After switching the emphasis to performance, Ballweg campaigned Power Command to his AQHA Championship in 1956. In his last show outing at the 1957 American Royal Livestock Show in Kansas City, Missouri, the athletic stallion placed 1st in a class of 26 senior cutting horses.

Photo by Orren Mixer, courtesy Quarter Horse Journal

those rodeo boys would call him 'that little spotted horse.' But he was a Quarter Horse through and through; he wasn't a Paint."

Milton, Douglas and Erma Jean—the three oldest Simon children—were collectively known to the rodeo crowd as "the Simons from Limon." During the late 1940s and early 1950s, all three competed on Jimmy.

Milton and Douglas roped and bulldogged off the King son. In 1951 alone, $17,000 in prize money was collected roping and dogging off of the game little gelding. In 1949 and 1951, Milton was named the champion roper in Colorado.

"I roped off of Jimmy, too," Erma Jean said. "I won with him at one rodeo in Colorado Springs, and then Douglas bulldogged a steer off him in 3.2 seconds at the Boston rodeo. It set a record back then that I don't think was ever broken.

"Jimmy lived to be well past 30. He died in 1970."

In addition to siring a host of geldings like Jimmy that were never registered, King sired a number of top performers that were.

Rocky Red, a 1947 sorrel by King and out of Rocket Laning, was bred by Felton Smathers of Llano, Texas. Sold first to Earl Albin of Comanche, Texas, and later to Walter Haythorn of Ogallala, Nebraska, "Rocky" was an NCHA earner of $16,846. Shown in AQHA competition, he earned 103 performance points and a Superior cutting award.

Maybeso Joe, a 1949 black gelding by King and out of Escoba, was bred by Lowell Hankins of Rocksprings, Texas. An NCHA money-earner, the gelding was also an AQHA performer with points at halter and in cutting and reining.

In addition to the above horses, the Hankins herd sire contributed yet another great post-war stallion to the breed.

Power Command, a 1949 sorrel by King and out of Crickett McCue, was bred by J. O.

King Fritz, a 1956 bay stallion by Power Command and out of Poco Jane, is the horse most responsible for the perpetuation of the "Power Command" branch of the King family tree.

Courtesy Quarter Horse Journal

traced to Jack McCue four times, Peter McCue five times, Old Billy nine times and Piasana four times.

Jack McCue, a 1914 sorrel stallion by Peter McCue and out of Marguerite, was bred by W. J. Francis of Elida, New Mexico. Both Jack McCue and Marguerite were well-known New Mexico racehorses and both sported the streamlined, racy-looking build that spoke to their Thoroughbred heritage.

Sometime in the early 1940s, J. O. Hankins wound up in possession of both Crickett McCue and her dam, Fanny McCue.

Fanny McCue was bred to King P-234 three times, with the resulting foals being Kay H, a 1945 chestnut mare; King Black, a 1947 black stallion; and Cage's Cattle King, a 1948 black stallion.

Crickett McCue was bred to King four times and the resulting foals were Sally Blaine, a 1947 sorrel mare; Power Command; King Command, a 1955 chestnut stallion; and King's Darling, a 1956 chestnut mare. Of the four full siblings, Power Command went on to have the most impact on the breed.

John Ballweg of Olathe, Kansas, is the man most familiar with the Power Command story. A native of Mansfield, Texas, John and his wartime Irish bride, Daisy, went to work for Robert Q. Sutherland's R.S. Bar Ranch in Kansas City, Missouri, in April of 1954.

Paul A, a renowned early-day AQHA Champion, was the R.S. Bar headliner at the time, and Ballweg was placed in charge of showing both the stallion and his foals. Of Paul A's 11 AQHA Champion get, the lanky Texas cowboy showed 10.

"As I understand it," Ballweg said, "Volney Hildreth bought Power Command from J. O. Hankins as either a weanling or early yearling. Hildreth had a bunch of young cowboys working for him at the time, and they could-

Hankins of Rocksprings. Sold to V. O. Hildreth of Aledo, Texas, the stallion was initially registered as O'Meara's Command. Sold a second time to G. Simpson Johnson of Hico, Texas, he was given the name he would be known by for the rest of his life.

From the very beginning, Power Command was a King of a different cut. He was a little longer-necked, a little longer-bodied and a little leaner than the classic King–Old Billy bulldog Quarter Horse. Much of the stallion's unique build can be attributed to his dam.

Crickett McCue, a 1943 chestnut mare by Barney McCue and out of Fanny McCue, was bred by M. E. Andes of Portales, New Mexico. As an intensely line-bred mare, she

n't get along with the colt. When they started breaking him, they got into his face real bad—and he got to resenting it.

"In the fall of 1951, Hildreth sold 'Command' to G. Simpson Johnson. Johnson was in his mid-70s at the time. I knew him from my Texas days. He was a 'pure-d' cowboy and a top hand.

"Hildreth warned Johnson to be careful of Command, but the old-timer was a little cantankerous and so he took the colt straight home, saddled him up and got on him. Instead of jerking Command around, he put on a pair of big leather gloves and just cuffed him on the head and neck to get him to turn."

As Power Command matured into a 15-1, 1,150-pound adult horse, he proved to be too much for the aging Johnson to contend with.

Poco Jane, King Fritz's dam, was a 1948 bay mare by Poco Bueno and out of Mary Jane W. One of her sire's first show ring champions, she is shown here with Pine Johnson after an early halter class win.

Courtesy Quarter Horse Journal

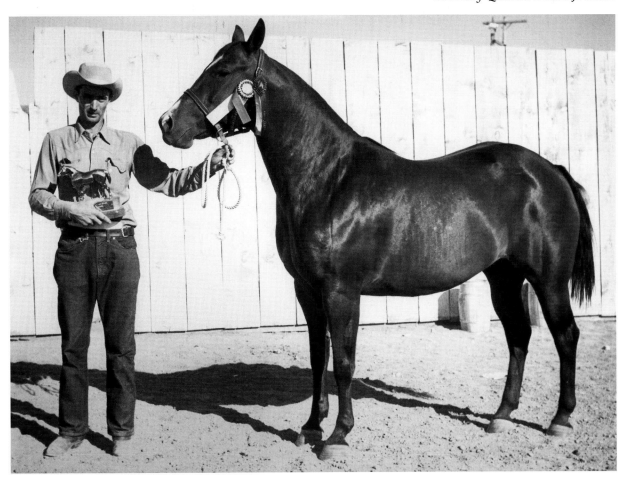

Although severely injured as a young horse, Poco Jane recovered well enough to continue her show career. Here she is after being named as the grand champion mare at a mid-1950s Emmett, Idaho, show.

Photo by Chapins Photo Show, courtesy Quarter Horse Journal

In 1955, Poco Jane was acquired, in foal to Power Command, by Ray Guthrie of Prineville, Oregon. King Fritz, the resulting foal, went on to become an AQHA Champion and leading sire.

Courtesy Quarter Horse Journal

As a result, he was turned over to a local cowboy named Garland Parker for some cutting training.

"Garland was a friend of mine," Ballweg said. "Back then, the training methods weren't near as humane as they are now. Garland got to spurring Command pretty hard on the shoulders during his training sessions, to get him in position to block a cow. Command started to get frustrated and he got to where he'd 'eat a cow.' He'd try to take a big chunk out of 'em.

"Then, when the horse was a 4-year-old, Johnson decided he'd make an all-around competitor out of him. So, Garland went to roping calves off him. On the first calf, the horse didn't know what he was supposed to do. By the second one, he'd figured it out and he slammed on the brakes so hard he turned the calf over backwards.

"Power Command had the ability to be good at anything and everything."

As noted in Chapter 8, the early to mid-1950s found much of the Southern and Great Plains lying helpless in the grip of a serious dry spell known as the Six-Year Texas Drought.

"Bob Sutherland knew of Johnson and his horses," Ballweg said. "In the fall of 1954, the old man called Sutherland and said he was in dire straits and needed to sell some horses. So Bob went down there and bought Power Command and eight or nine other horses. And then he turned Command over to me to train and show."

To begin with, Ballweg only showed the now-5-year-old King son at halter. Hauled to the 1954 Missouri State Fair in Sedalia, and the 1954 Iowa State Fair in Des Moines, he earned grand champion stallion honors at both shows and picked up three halter points.

Next up was the tough winter stock show run. Exhibited in Denver, Colorado; and Fort Worth, Houston and San Antonio, Texas; Command placed fifth or higher at each show and earned seven halter points.

Shown in May of 1956 in Dallas, Texas, the stallion placed second in a class of aged stallions and was named the reserve champion stallion. By now, his halter point total stood at 11, one more than was needed for his AQHA championship, so it was on to the performance events.

Back when Power Command was first placed under his control, Ballweg set about ridding the stallion of some of the undesirable habits he'd picked up.

"Contrary to what some people might have heard," he said, "Power Command was a very good-dispositioned horse.

"As a young horse, he had suffered through a real bad bout with distemper. Johnson had an old country vet that he used. The man never had any formal training, but he was capable and he pulled Command through. The fever settled in the stallion's chest, though, so they had to drain it. And then they treated him with penicillin and found out the hard way that he was allergic to it.

"By the time they got him over the distemper, Command had developed a solid distrust of any human who wore clean clothes and smelled good. He never did cotton to strangers.

"Then, too, he'd had some bad experiences with heavy-handed trainers," Ballweg continued. "It took us a little while to get over that. But I never did have to use anything other than a Milt Bennett cutting horse bit on him; just a little grazing bit.

"I did have to get a little serious with him over the cow-eating thing. Once we got that

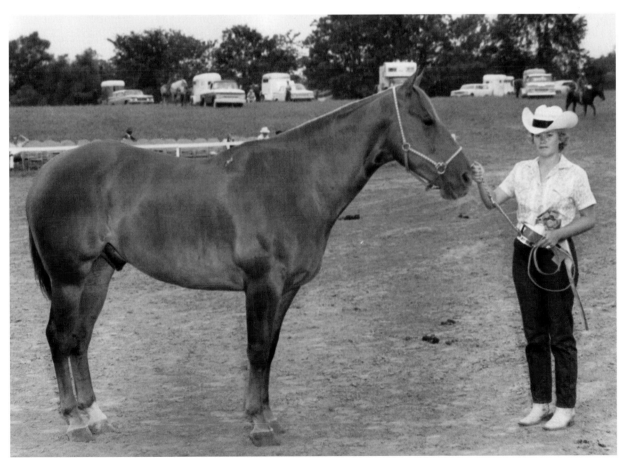

Commando King, a 1957 sorrel gelding by Power Command and out of Trixie P, was an AQHA Champion and a Superior Western pleasure horse. **Courtesy Quarter Horse Journal**

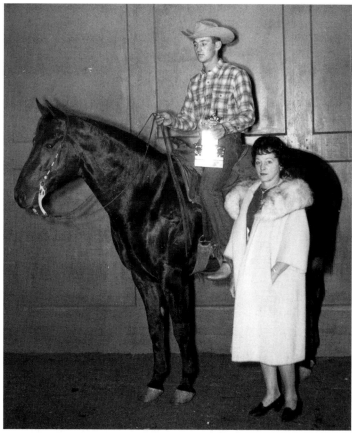

Blue Command, a 1958 grullo stallion by Power Command and out of Miss Paulette, was likewise an AQHA Champion. A top reining horse, he is shown here with Jim Willoughby in the saddle after placing first in a class of 54 junior reining horses at the 1961 Chicago International Livestock Show in Chicago, Illinois.

***Courtesy* Quarter Horse Journal**

ic ability to do anything. You could ride him in a skating rink and he'd never fall down."

As talented a performer as he was, fate decreed that Power Command would never be given the opportunity that he deserved to prove his mettle as a sire.

To begin with, G. Simpson Johnson's drought-burdened personal situation did not allow for the promotion of either the stallion or his foals. Despite this fact, several of Power Command's Texas-bred get did acquit themselves well as show horses.

Junior Command, a 1954 bay stallion out of Wonder Lady, was an NCHA earner of $4,346 and an AQHA Superior cutting horse; Power Light, a 1954 bay stallion out of Green Light G, was the 1959 high-point reining stallion; and Power Rio, a 1955 sorrel stallion out of Our Sue Bailey, was an AQHA Champion and Superior halter horse.

After being purchased by Bob Sutherland, Power Command added three more top show horses to his short but impressive production record.

King Fritz, a 1956 bay stallion out of Poco Jane, was an AQHA Champion; Commando King, a 1957 sorrel gelding out of Trixie P, was an AQHA Champion and Superior Western pleasure horse; and Blue Command, a 1958 bay stallion out of Miss Paulette, was an AQHA Champion.

In 1958, Bob Sutherland made Quarter Horse history when he sold Paul A, Power Command and 53 other horses to Edgar Brown III of Houston, Texas. Although the total price tag of the package was never revealed, it was thought to be the largest such transaction in history.

Throughout his four-year stay at Sutherland's R.S. Bar Ranch, Power Command had been forced to stand in the

problem fixed, a cow could duck underneath him and he wouldn't make a false move."

Exhibited solely by Ballweg during the summer, fall and early winter of 1956 in cutting, reining and Western pleasure, Power Command earned 18 performance points and qualified for his AQHA championship. His last show was in December at the American Royal in Kansas City, Missouri. There, he placed first in a senior cutting class of 26 horses and earned five points.

"Power Command was a once-in-a-lifetime horse," Ballweg said. "As a halter horse, he had top conformation and a neck that was better than 95 percent of the geldings that were being hauled—and he never saw a neck sweat.

"As a performance horse, he had the athlet-

shadow of the more-visible Paul A. Relocated to Brown's Pinehurst Stables, the 9-year-old stallion never even got a chance to do that.

"Power Command's distemper battle had left him with some permanent damage to his esophagus," John Ballweg said. "Apparently, after they got him down to South Texas, he got into an altercation with two other studs. At least that's what I heard.

"Somehow, he wound up being sent to Kentucky for treatment and he never made it back from there. Whether he died of complications of the esophagus problem, or as a result of the horse fight, or was just put down, I couldn't tell you. All I know is he never lived long enough to sire any colts for them."

However, included among the 55 head that Sutherland sold Brown were several mares in foal to Power Command. In 1959, the stallion's last two foals, Last Command and Power's Madam, were born.

His final production tally was a relatively paltry one. In eight foal crops, he sired 43 horses: 19 stallions, 17 mares and seven geldings. Of these, 22 performers earned four AQHA championships, one Superior halter award, two Superior performance awards, 12 performance Registers of Merit and 495.5 points.

Given the fact that he was the sire of only 17 mares, Power Command's maternal grandsire record is also relatively sparse. Fifteen of the stallion's daughters produced 111 foals. Of these, 29 performers earned two AQHA championships, one Superior performance award, eight performance ROMs and 542 points.

As far as what the ill-fated stallion's legacy to the breed would wind up being, however, there was a proverbial light at the end of the tunnel.

He sired King Fritz.

"King Fritz left here inside his mama,"

Retired to stud, Blue Command went on to become a top AQHA and NRHA sire.

Photo by James Cathey, courtesy Quarter Horse Journa

Ballweg said. "Her name was Poco Jane and she was a daughter of Poco Bueno.

"Right after I came to work for Bob Sutherland in the spring of 1954, he attended E. Paul Waggoner's Three D Horse Sale in Arlington, Texas.

"Poco Jane was in the sale. She'd been a good show mare at one time, and probably would've been a great one if she hadn't gotten hurt. One night, she and several other horses got loose in Arlington and went running down Highway 80.

"A car broadsided 'Jane' and almost killed her. I heard that, after they found her, Pine

Power Command was known both for his top conformation and athletic versatility.

Photo by Orren Mixer,
courtesy **Quarter Horse Journal**

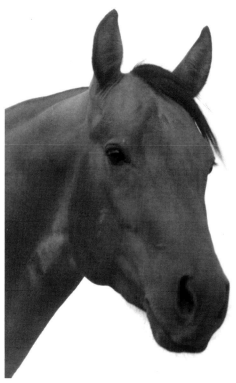

King Fritz lived up to his heritage by founding a West Coast working cow horse dynasty.

Courtesy **Quarter Horse Journal**

Johnson had to hold her together until the vet got there and sewed her up."

As serious as her injuries were, Poco Jane recovered to the point where the decision was made to start her under saddle.

"Andy Hensley was working for the Three D's at the time," Ballweg said. "They had a big old, high round pen that they broke their young horses in. So, Hensley saddled up Jane and took her down to the pen. Then he tied her stirrups together and turned her loose. The mare just about destroyed the round pen. She bucked so hard that they were afraid she'd re-injure herself. So, they made a broodmare out of her.

"Poco Jane was a 6-year-old when Bob bought her. She sold as Lot 7 in the '54 sale. They opened the bidding up on her pretty low, and the natives were bumping her price at $50 per bid. When they had her up to $400, Bob jumped in and said, 'I'll give $1,000 for her.' That scared everyone off, and he got her bought."

Bred to Power Command in 1955 and sold in a Sutherland sale that same year, Poco Jane was purchased by Raymond Guthrie of Prineville, Oregon. King Fritz, the resulting foal, was born the following spring. Sold as a 3-month-old to Fritz and Helen Watkins of Wasco, Oregon, and again as a 16-year-old to Les Vogt of Los Gatos, California, the Power Command son became a top show horse and an all-time leading sire.

As a show horse, King Fritz was an AQHA Champion and the earner of 14 halter and 23.5 performance points.

As a sire, he founded the renowned "Chex" line of performers that features four world champions, four reserve world champions, four high-point horses and 13 AQHA Champions. In addition, he sired the earners of one Superior halter award, 11 Superior performance awards, 66 performance awards and 3,536.5 points.

In NCHA competition, his get earned $34,313.

King Fritz's record as a broodmare sire is even more exemplary. AQHA records reveal him to be the maternal grandsire of 405 performers that have amassed 14 world championships, four reserve world championships, one high-point win and two AQHA championships. In addition, they have tallied 18 Superior performance awards, 156 performance ROMs and earned 5,543 points.

In NCHA competition, King Fritz grandsons and granddaughters have earned more than $1.9 million, and in NRHA competition they have earned more than $710,000.

And, as if that were not enough, two of King Fritz's AQHA Champion sons, Bueno Chex and Fritz Command, went on to become leading sires, as well.

Bueno Chex, a 1961 dun stallion out of Sutherland's Miss, was bred by Fritz and Helen Watkins. As a breeding horse, he sired one world champion, four reserve world champions and one high-point winner. In addition, he sired the earners of one Superior halter award, seven Superior performance awards, 31 performance awards and 1,775.5 points.

Like his sire King Fritz, though, Bueno Chex's lasting legacy to the breed was destined to be as a broodmare sire.

To date, the Power Command-bred stallion's grandget have earned nine world championships, eight reserve world championships and four high-point wins. They have also accumulated one AQHA championship, 29 Superior performance awards, 140 performance ROMs and 6,711 points.

In AQHA Alliance competition—NCHA, NRHA and NRCHA—they have earned more than $2.2 million.

Fritz Command, a 1967 dun full brother to Bueno Chex, has also carved out an outstanding record as a sire.

From 90 performers, he is the sire of four world champions and five reserve world champions. His get have earned two AQHA championships, 13 Superior performance

Fritz Command, a 1967 dun stallion by King Fritz and out of Sutherland's Miss, also did his part to ensure the continuity of the Power Command line.
Photo by LeRoy Weathers, courtesy Quarter Horse Journal

awards, 51 performance ROMs and 2,741 points.

In addition, the stallion's grand-get have won three world championships, three reserve world championships, one Superior halter award, 12 Superior performance awards, 49 performance ROMs and 3,181.5 points.

In AQHA Alliance competition, they have earned $516,413.

All in all, the Power Command story was one of early tragedy and ultimate triumph, paralleling the tale of the land and time into which he was born.

Power Command rose from a less-than-perfect life to attain lasting fame and glory as the founder of one of the breed's top performance lines.

Chapter 12

A STRAIGHT SHOOTER

King's Pistol, shown here with owner Jim Calhoun of Cresson, Texas, was the first stallion to be an NCHA World Champion Cutting Horse.
Photo by James Cathey, courtesy Quarter Horse Journal

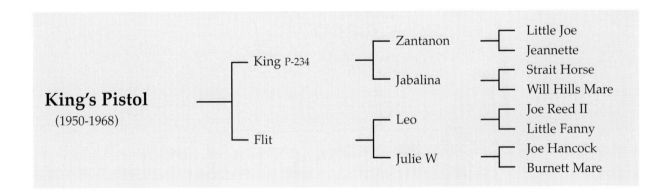

King's Pistol
(1950-1968)

```
King's Pistol ─┬─ King P-234 ─┬─ Zantanon ─┬─ Little Joe
(1950-1968)    │              │             └─ Jeannette
               │              └─ Jabalina ──┬─ Strait Horse
               │                            └─ Will Hills Mare
               └─ Flit ───────┬─ Leo ───────┬─ Joe Reed II
                              │             └─ Little Fanny
                              └─ Julie W ───┬─ Joe Hancock
                                            └─ Burnett Mare
```

The year was 1950, and America was midway through the most tumultuous century in its history.

The threat of Nazi Germany and Japan had been eliminated, only to be replaced by the menace of Communist Russia, China and North Korea. The "Red Scare" paved the way for the Joe McCarthy era of character assassination and fear mongering, and further resulted in the Cold War arms race.

In January of 1950, North Korean Communist forces invaded South Korea, the prelude to U.S. involvement in the region. Also in January, China and the Soviet Union extended diplomatic recognition to Ho Chi Minh's Democratic Republic of Viet Nam, giving Minh the resources to initiate the first Viet Nam War.

On the home front, the exodus from the inner cities to the suburbs gained momentum, and the age of the television set and the automobile was born. It was a time of unparalleled growth in the country on almost all fronts, and that expansion extended to the Western horse industry in general and the King P-234 family of Quarter Horses in particular.

Bud Warren of Perry, Oklahoma, was no stranger to either growth or the King horses. Beginning with his purchase of a King son and three King daughters in the mid-1940s, he had carved out a nitch for himself as one of the country's leading breeders (see Chapter 7).

By the early 1950s, Warren's senior stallion, Leo, was the Quarter racing industry's all-time leading sire of AA and AAA horses. The blaze-faced sorrel's get had won four of the first five Oklahoma Futurities and three Oklahoma year-end get of sire awards. In addition, Warren was achieving superior results by breeding Leo to his King-bred mares.

In 1949, however, Warren had reversed the breeding equation by taking Flit, one of his best Leo daughters, to the court of King. King's Pistol, a 1950 bay stallion, was the resulting foal.

Flit, "Pistol's" dam, was an ROM race mare who went on to become one of the breed's most noted producers.

Courtesy Quarter Horse Journal

Ceaser's Pistol, a 1944 bay gelding by Brown Ceaser and out of Hayes' Baby Doll, was Jim Calhoun's first NCHA cutting mount.
Photo by James Cathey, courtesy Western Horseman

Flit, a 1945 bay mare out of Julie W, was bred by Ed Simpkins of Pawhuska, Oklahoma. Purchased by Warren and raced as a 2-year-old, she achieved a AA rating and qualified for a race Register of Merit. Retired to the Warren broodmare band, she produced 17 foals, including:

• Leo Bar, a 1953 sorrel stallion by Three Bars (TB): SI 95 and leading sire.

• Flit Bar, a 1956 sorrel stallion by Sugar Bars: Leading show and barrel horse sire.

• Bar Flit, a 1957 bay stallion by Sugar Bars: Superior halter.

• Sugar Leo, a 1959 bay stallion by Sugar Bars: SI 95.

By the time King's Pistol was born, both sides of his family tree were being touted as legitimate sources of speed. It seemed only logical, then, to give the first representative of the King–Leo cross a chance to prove his swiftness, as well.

That chance was negated when, as a yearling, "Pistol" was sold to Jim Calhoun of Cresson, Texas. Calhoun was not a racehorse man. As a third-generation rancher, he was a using-horse man through and through. As far as he was concerned, all a horse needed speed for was to catch a calf or cut off a cow.

The Calhoun Ranch was situated on part of what had originally been a land grant issue to Davy Crockett's widow, Elizabeth, in recognition of her late husband's sacrifice at the Alamo.

Jim Calhoun, who was born in 1931, began breaking horses at the age of 13 and bought and trained his first registered Quarter Horse, Ceaser's Pistol, when he was 15. A 1944 bay gelding by Brown Ceaser and out of Hayes' Baby Doll, Ceaser's Pistol was trained and shown by the teenaged Calhoun in both AQHA and NCHA competition.

"This was the first Quarter Horse I ever trained," Calhoun said, "and he rated third in the nation [NCHA] when I sold him to A. R. Eppenauer of Marfa, Texas, when I was 17 years old."[1]

In the fall of 1952, Jim Calhoun was a 21-year-old senior in college at Oklahoma A & M in Stillwater (now known as Oklahoma State University). Still vitally interested in horses, he

---

[1] "King's Pistol and his Trainer," by Monk Lofton; *Quarter Horse Journal*; February, 1961; page 156.

paid a visit to nearby Perry, Oklahoma, to look over Bud Warren's string of horses.

There, he came across the 2-year-old King's Pistol, tied to a fence waiting to be ridden. Calhoun had been saving up to get married to his high school sweetheart, Jane Venita Saunders, that Christmas. He opted, instead, to postpone the wedding and buy the young King son.

After graduation, Calhoun did in fact get married and returned to Cresson to ply his trade as a rancher. His original plan for his new four-legged acquisition was to make a good ranch gelding out of him. H. C. Calhoun, Jim's father, reasoned that the young stallion was too well-bred not to have a chance to prove himself and urged his son to leave him intact.

Whether as a stallion or a gelding, the younger Calhoun was determined to turn Pistol into a cutting horse. To begin with, he brought the young stallion along slow and easy, and used him as a working ranch horse.

"In the summer of 1952," Calhoun said, "after I had graduated, King's Pistol began to earn his keep in regular work, showing unmistakable evidence of speed and action. He had an alert eye and an intelligent-looking head.

"By the time he had been ridden half a dozen saddles, he had evidenced a natural ability to coordinate these basic essentials for the making of a cutting horse. And he did it in a graceful and easy manner."[2]

During the next four years, from 1952 through 1956, King's Pistol was seasoned on

---

[2] "King's Pistol," by Nelson C. Nye; *The Complete Book of the Quarter Horse*; page 125.

The team of Jim Calhoun and King's Pistol was a perfect match, and one that elevated both man and horse to new heights of accomplishment. This classic shot of the pair in action served as the NCHA's logo for many years.

Courtesy Quarter Horse Journal

King's Michelle, a 1954 bay mare by King's Pistol and out of Brown Shorty, was a talented performer whose promising career was cut short when she died at the age of eight in August of 1962. Despite that fact, she still finished the year as both the AQHA High-Point Cutting Mare and the NCHA World Champion Mare.

Courtesy Quarter Horse Journal

the Calhoun Ranch and shown in AQHA competition.

In 1954, he was shown at halter and in cutting and reining in such places as Fort Worth, Dallas, Weatherford, Jacksboro, Blanco, Valley Mills and Lexington, Texas; and Omaha, Nebraska. That same year, he was named an AQHA Champion with one reining, 10 halter and 19 cutting points to his credit.

In 1955, King's Pistol was shown in cutting one time, earning two points.

In 1956, the talented performer's show schedule picked up somewhat. Exhibited in January at the Southwestern Exposition and Fat Stock Show in Fort Worth, Texas, he placed second in a class of 46 aged stallions, earning five points, and fifth in a class of 65 cutting horses, earning one point. Shown four more times during the year, he amassed

29 cutting and four halter points, and one reining point.

In early 1957, Calhoun decided that King's Pistol was ready for the next level of competition.

"It was at Odessa, Texas, where I was judging in 1957," he said, "that I decided to carry Pistol down the road in a try for [NCHA] championship honors. I realized it would be an extra-long year, as the first show starting the new year had been put on at the Cow Palace in San Francisco, and I would not be through before reaching Odessa again in 1958.

"The cutting horse that won the Odessa show was several thousand dollars in the lead, and there I was 'afoot,' with my horse back home in pasture."[3]

After making the decision to take a full-blown run at the world, Calhoun reasoned

[3] "King's Pistol," by Nelson C. Nye; *The Complete Book of the Quarter Horse*; page 127.

that he'd better get serious about getting his horse in shape.

"As soon as I got back to the ranch," he said, "I began to work Pistol on tough cattle and even a few goats that I borrowed to help tune him up. When I felt he was ready for tough competition, we took off.

"We won the two weekend shows held on January 21st and 22nd, but the big one coming up would be Fort Worth's Southwestern Exposition and Fat Stock Show, held January 26–February 3. There, King's Pistol won the cutting and was Reserve Champion at halter."[3]

From Fort Worth, the team of Jim Calhoun and King's Pistol hit the road in earnest. In the months to come, by Calhoun's own account, they were gone every weekend except one.

"King's Pistol and I traveled to shows that were weeks and, sometimes, only days apart, from one end of the United States to the other. We began to feel like gypsies moving around so much, but the satisfaction we had, we shared.

"We both liked stiff competition, and it gave us the will to win. King's Pistol never once went off his feed and only once had a cough, which I had developed, also. We both took the cough medicine a doctor had prescribed for me, and this cured us both."[3]

By the end of the 1957 NCHA season, the Cresson, Texas-based duo had reportedly logged 70,000 miles. In reminiscing about the experience years later, Calhoun admitted that it was a long, hard grind.

"I'm a homebody," he said, "and sometimes it got lonesome on the road. That's when Pistol and I got to know each other best. When we took time out to rest, it was for me, not him. He never got tired, and he learned to know the difference

[3] "King's Pistol," by Nelson C. Nye; *The Complete Book of the Quarter Horse*; page 127.

Pistol Toter, a 1957 bay stallion by King's Pistol and out of Duchess Bonnie, was an AQHA Champion and NCHA money earner.

Courtesy Quarter Horse Journal

Pistol's Machete, a 1960 bay stallion by King's Pistol and out of Jazz Band, was the 1968 and 1971 High-Point Reining Stallion. In addition, he was a Superior reining horse and the earner of 133 performance points. **Photo by Esler, courtesy Quarter Horse Journal**

Pistol's Ace, a 1963 bay stallion by King's Pistol and out of Mac's Cheryl, was an ROM performance horse. Here, he and Punch Oglesby win the junior reining at the 1967 Houston Livestock Show.

**Photo by Jim Keeland,
courtesy Quarter Horse Journal**

between winning and losing. Maybe he sensed the difference in the sound of the applause. Anyway, if he won, he pranced a little. If he lost, he went wherever I reined him, and he went in a flat-footed, ground-covering walk. He was just through with it."[4]

By year's end, King's Pistol had achieved all that Calhoun had asked of him. He was the 1957 NCHA World Champion Cutting Horse, with a record-setting $16,217 in earnings. He was the first stallion to ever be named world champion, and he finished the year ahead of such NCHA Hall of Fame competitors as Snipper W, Miss Nancy Bailey, Poco Mona, Poco Lena, Sandhill Charlie and Poco Stampede.

Pistol's last two outings came in early 1958. Shown in Odessa, Texas, he earned honors as grand champion halter stallion and the winner of both the AQHA and NCHA cutting contests. Exhibited at the Southwestern Livestock Exposition and Fat Stock Show in Fort Worth, he won the NCHA open cutting.

At the end of the Fort Worth show, he was

[4] "A Pair of Kings," by Lyn Jank, *Eastern Western Quarter Horse Journal*, April 1985, p. 52.

Pistol Mike, a 1959 bay stallion by King's Pistol and out of Lady Mike Bracke, was a AAA-rated racehorse. Here he is in the winner's circle after defeating a crack field of sprinters in a 400-yard sprint at Centennial race track in Denver, Colorado.

Courtesy Quarter Horse Journal

retired from all show and cutting competition.

Even prior to embarking on his show and cutting career, King's Pistol was utilized as a breeding animal. Bred to a handful of mares as a 3-year-old, his first foal crop hit the ground in 1954. From it came arguably his greatest performer.

King's Michelle, a 1954 bay mare out of Brown Shorty, was bred by Calhoun. Sold inside her dam, she was foaled on the Jewel Russell ranch near King, Texas. Purchased as a weanling by Dr. and Mrs. E. F. Meredith of Olney, Texas, she was broke and trained exclusively by Glen McWhorter of Throckmorton, Texas.

With McWhorter in the saddle, "Michelle" won her first cutting contest at the tender age of 30 months. Shown in AQHA cutting competition, she earned a performance Register of Merit in 1959 and a Superior cutting award in 1960. Exhibited in NCHA-sanctioned competition, she finished the 1960 season in eighth place and the 1961 campaign in third place.

The year 1962 looked to be custom-made for King's Michelle to establish herself as one of the breed's top cutting horses of all time.

Early that year, she won the big cutting in Tucson, Arizona. With a purse of $14,000, it was the richest NCHA event held to date. By mid-August, the King's Pistol daughter was firmly entrenched atop the money leader board, $4,000 ahead of the second-place horse.

Then, after winning a cutting on August 13, 1962, in Alva, Oklahoma, the 8-year-old mare began exhibiting colic-like symptoms. McWhorter left the show and headed for home. In Vernon, Texas, he stopped long enough to have the mare's illness diagnosed and treated by two veterinarians. Both assured the trainer that the mare was suffer-

Pistol's Bit, a 1960 bay mare by Pistol's Man and out of Natchez Sue, was one of the top show mares of her era. Bred and owned by Roland Stacy of Natchez, Mississippi, Pistol's Bit was a Superior halter horse and the earner of 542 halter points.
Photo by Orren Mixer, courtesy Quarter Horse Journal

ing from colic and that she would make a full recovery.

Instead, she died shortly after arriving home. A postmortem exam revealed the cause of death to be an acute case of peritonitis, or inflammation of the abdominal cavity wall.

Even though she died in the early fall, King's Michelle maintained her NCHA lead until shortly before the end of the year. She was finally overtaken by Cutter Bill for the championship, but managed to hold on to the reserve champion cutting horse and champion cutting mare titles. In AQHA com-

Smokin Pistol, a 1977 bay stallion by Mr Gun Smoke and out of Bonnie Pistol by King's Pistol, was an AQHA Superior cutting horse and the NCHA earner of $13,771. Here he is with Jim Calhoun, Jr. in the saddle after winning the senior cutting at the 1982 Texas State Fair in Dallas. **Courtesy Western Horseman**

petition, she finished the year as the high-point cutting mare.

Interviewed about the gritty mare after her death, McWhorter was lavish in his praise.

"I have never ridden a horse any more willing to do what was right before or since," he said. "She wanted to 'cow' from the very start and we cut a lot of cows in the six years I had her. She got better all the time. She didn't win every time, but she was nearly always in the money somewhere. I think this was because she was honest and did her very best every time she performed."

Getting back to King's Pistol, he followed up his earliest and most famous siring accomplishment by turning out a steady stream of top performers. AQHA records reveal him to be the sire of 236 horses. Of those, 73 were performers and they earned five AQHA championships, one Superior halter award, four Superior performance awards and 36 performance Registers of Merit. In addition, they amassed 198 halter and 1,448.5 performance points. Among the King son's top performers were such horses as:

- Janie Cal, a 1956 bay mare out of Ceaser's Bonnie: AQHA Champion, Superior cutting.
- King's Pistola, a 1956 dun mare out of Ken Ada Jane: AQHA Champion, Superior halter.
- Rock Pistol, a 1956 bay stallion out of Zantanon Babe: Superior cutting.
- Pistol Toter, a 1957 bay stallion out of Duchess Bonnie: AQHA Champion.
- Kamay, a 1959 bay mare out of Kmay Ann: AQHA Champion.
- Pistol Mike, a 1959 bay stallion out of Lady Mike Bracke: SI 95.
- Pistol's Machete, a 1960 bay stallion out of Jazz Band: 1968 and 1971 high-point reining stallion, Superior reining.
- Pistol's Lotsip, a 1964 bay mare out of Red Iler: AQHA Champion.

Like many of his half-brothers, King's Pistol also proved to be a top broodmare sire. AQHA records show him to be the maternal grandsire of 127 performers that earned six AQHA championships, one Superior halter award, 10 Superior performance awards and 45 performance ROMs. In addition, they tal-

Hollywood Smoke, a 1969 bay stallion by Mr Gun Smoke and out of Pistol's Holly by King's Pistol, was an NRHA Hall of Fame horse and top reining sire. Here, he and legendary NRHA icon Bill Horn are seen executing a sliding stop.

Photo by Harold Campton, courtesy NRHA

Miss Silver Pistol, a 1982 gray mare by Doc's Hickory and out of Pistol Lady 2 Be by King's Pistol, was the NCHA earner of more than $500,000. The flashy mare, seen here with Wes Shahan aboard, went on to become one of the cutting industry's top matrons. **Courtesy Quarter Horse Journal**

lied 334 halter and 3,809 performance points. In NCHA competition, they earned $594,332.

In terms of the perpetuation of the King's Pistol line, such second- and third-generation descendants as Pistol's Man, Smokin Pistol, Hollywood Smoke and Miss Silver Pistol are worthy of special recognition.

Pistol's Man, a 1956 bay stallion by King's Pistol and out of Jazz Band, was bred by Harold and Jim Calhoun. Sold to Roland Stacy of Natchez, Mississippi, he went on to sire such horses as:

• Pistol's Bit, a 1960 bay mare out of Natchez

Sue: Superior halter (542 points).

• Pistol's Hornet, a 1961 sorrel gelding out of Miss Topper Moore: Five-time high-point calf roping horse, AQHA Champion, Superior halter, Superior calf roping.

• Pistol's Rondo, a 1965 dun gelding out of Natchez Sue: AQHA Champion, Superior halter.

Hollywood Smoke, a 1969 bay stallion by Mr Gun Smoke and out of Pistol's Holly by Hollywood Pistol, was bred by Bud and Carol Bodell of Lima, Ohio. An NRHA Hall of Fame horse, he sired such top competitors as:

• Patch Of Smoke, a 1972 bay gelding out of Linda Suntan: 1975 World Champion Jr. Reining.

• Gunners Brawny Lad, a 1976 bay gelding out of Miz Continental: NRHA earner of $23,340.

• Gunners Rambo, a 1985 bay stallion out of Price's Start: NRHA earner of $22,033.

In addition, Hollywood Smoke is the maternal grandsire of Custom Pistol, the 2001 NRHA Futurity Reserve Champion, 2002 NRHA Derby Champion and NRHA earner of $223,343.

Smokin Pistol, a 1977 bay stallion by Mr Gun Smoke and out of Bonnie Pistol by King's Pistol, was bred by Jim Calhoun. An AQHA Superior cutting horse and NCHA earner of $13,771, he sired such top performers as:

• Smokin Pistol Rita, a 1981 sorrel mare out of Pistol's Jazzrita: Superior team penning.

• Flits Smokin Dream, a 1983 dun gelding out of Flit's Dream: 1992, 1993 and 1996 PRCA Heeling Horse of the Year.

Miss Silver Pistol, a 1982 gray mare by Doc's Hickory and out of Pistol Lady 2 Be by King's Pistol, was bred by Art Shahan of Pleasanton, Texas. The 1985 NCHA Non-Pro Cutting Futurity Champion and NCHA earner of more than $500,000, she went on to produce such top cutting competitors as:

• Smart Little Pistol, 1988 gray stallion by Smart Little Lena: sire of Chiquita Pistol, NCHA Triple Crown winner of $450,259.

• Purdy Pistol, a 1991 gray mare by Peppy San Badger: NCHA earner of $60,998.

• Playgun, a 1992 gray stallion by Freckles

Playgun, a 1992 gray stallion by Freckles Playboy and out of Miss Silver Pistol, was the NCHA earner of $168,408. Seen here being ridden by Jody Galyean, Playgun has sired the NCHA earners of more than $2.5 million.

Courtesy Western Horseman

Smart Little Pistol, a 1988 gray stallion by Smart Little Lena and out of Miss Silver Pistol, is likewise a top cutting horse sire.
Photo by John Brasseaux

Playboy: 1995 high-point jr. cutting, NCHA earner of $168,408, sire of NCHA earners of more than $2.5 million.

As far as the patriarch of the "Pistol" strain was concerned, he lived out his entire life on the Calhoun Ranch.

Jim Calhoun, who devoted much of his life to the betterment of both the Quarter Horse and cutting horse industries, was fundamentally opposed to artificial insemination and overproduction. As a result, King's Pistol sired an average of slightly less than 16 foals per year over the course of his 15 breeding seasons.

In addition to his duties as a herd sire, Pistol continued to be called on for general ranch work. By the late 1960s, the latter activities were curtailed due to the onset of arthritis in the aged stallion's front legs. By mid-1968, it became apparent to those closest to the former world champion cutting horse that the end was near.

"The time came," Calhoun said, "when only one fair call could be made. It was put him down or see the time come when he hurt too bad. I made the call to the vet.

"I went out to wait with Pistol. When I was walking toward him, he looked at me and I felt like I couldn't go through with it. I'll never know if I could have.

"Pistol kept on watching me, and then he took two or three steps toward me, and then he dropped. Quick and clean. It was over. He was gone."[4]

---

[4] "A Pair of Kings," by Lyn Jank, *Eastern Western Quarter Horse Journal*, April 1985, p. 52.

For Jim Calhoun, King's Pistol was his "once-in-a-lifetime" horse. Although the North Texas rancher continued to be deeply involved in both the Quarter Horse and cutting industries for decades after Pistol's death, he never formed a relationship with another horse that came close to the one he enjoyed with the gritty bay stallion.

Calhoun passed away of a heart attack on July 19, 1994.

Among the many treasures that he bequeathed the Quarter Horse world in general, and the cutting horse industry in particular, was an incredible photographic image of he and Pistol working their magic in a cutting arena. For years, that image served as the basis for the NCHA logo, and that was just as it should have been.

To those who were fortunate enough to have known him, King's Pistol was the epitome of what a working Quarter Horse should be. Whether on the ranch in the heat of the day, or in a crowded coliseum with the bright lights focused on him, Pistol could always be counted on to give the same, solid performance.

As his name implied, he was a straight shooter.

Chiquita Pistol, a 1999 sorrel mare by Smart Little Pistol and out of Miss Chiquita Tari, continues to advance the "Pistol" banner. The 2003 NCHA Horse of the Year, "Chiquita" is an NCHA Triple Crown winner and the earner of more than $524,000.   ***Courtesy NCHA***

Chapter 13

THE EASTER EFFECT

Easter King, seen here with Elmo Favor and an unidentified trophy presenter, was one of the reining industry's most influential early day sires.

Courtesy Quarter Horse Journal

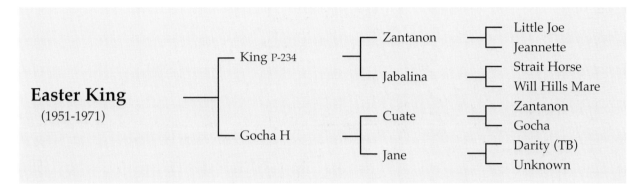

Easter King (1951-1971)	King P-234	Zantanon	Little Joe / Jeannette
		Jabalina	Strait Horse / Will Hills Mare
	Gocha H	Cuate	Zantanon / Gocha
		Jane	Darity (TB) / Unknown

As detailed in previous chapters, much of King P-234's early success as a sire was due to the exploits of his get on the racetrack and in the cutting arena.

This was due, at least partly, to the fact that, within the overall Quarter Horse industry of the 1940s and 1950s, the racing and cutting segments were the first to establish their own identities and purse structures. Put another way, throughout those early years, racing and cutting were where the money was.

For as long as there had been structured Quarter Horse competition, however, there was a third venue that the King horses excelled at—reining.

In the late 1940s, a King granddaughter named King's Doll was reputed to have won 16 blue ribbons in reining. In the mid- to late 1950s, such top King sons and daughters as L.H. Quarter Moon, Gay Widow and Martha King were showing up regularly in the reining winners' circles.

In the Far West, the "bridled-up" Vaquero style of reining had long been a part of the equine culture. Beginning in the early to mid-1960s, the King Fritz horses established themselves as a reined cow horse dynasty.

Finally, in the Midwest, the decade of the '60s saw the birth of the movement that grew into the reining industry of today. One of the first true reining horse lines to positively influence that movement was headed by a horse named Easter King.

Easter King, a 1951 sorrel stallion by King and out of Gocha H by Cuate, is listed as having been bred by Jess Hankins of Rocksprings, Texas.

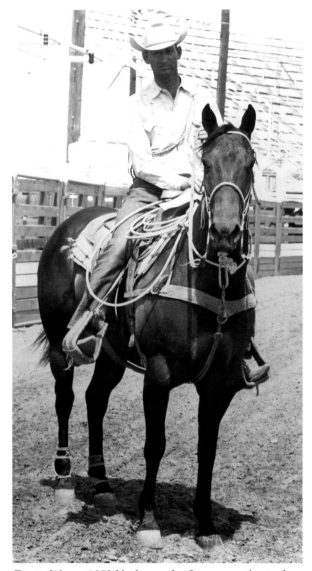

Dusty Way, a 1952 black mare by Starway and out of Gocha H, was Easter King's maternal half-sister. The 1958 High Point Calf Roping Mare, she is shown here with Jack Newton in the saddle after winning the junior reining and junior roping at the 1956 Santa Rosa Roundup in Vernon, Texas.

Photo by James Cathey,** courtesy **Quarter Horse Journal

177

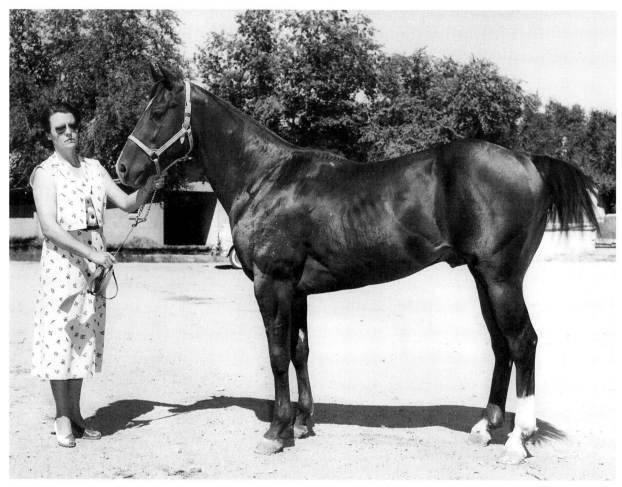

After being purchased by LaRue Gooch, Abilene, Texas, and Simla, Colorado, Easter King was put in performance training with Elmo Favor.
Courtesy Western Horseman

AQHA records regarding Gocha H's ownership are murky. As near as can be determined, she was bred by Fred Matthews, also of Rocksprings, and sold as a young horse to Garland G. Price of Roscoe, Texas.

Of Gocha H's first eight foals, Price is listed as the breeder of numbers three through eight. Official records to the contrary, it is likely that he was probably also the breeder of "Gocha's" first two foals: G Solomia, a 1950 sorrel mare by Chico P-226; and Easter King.

Dusty Way, Gocha's third foal, was definitely bred by Price. A 1952 black mare sired by Starway P-508, she was the 1958 AQHA High-Point Calf Roping Mare. Dandy Man, Gocha's fourth foal, was unquestionably bred by Price. A 1954 bay stallion sired by Easter King, he

lends further validity to the theory that Price bred Easter King and owned him for the first 12 to 18 months of the stallion's life.

In late 1953 or early 1954, Easter King was acquired by LaRue Gooch of Abilene, Texas, and Simla, Colorado. Abilene's close proximity to Roscoe, Texas, amounts to one last piece of evidence that Garland Price, and not Jess Hankins, was Easter King's breeder and first owner.

LaRue Gooch was the wife of Abilene feed lot and packing plant owner Pete Gooch. A serious horsewoman with an interest in cutting horses, she had as her primary goal the development of Easter King as a top-notch arena performer.

Toward that end, she turned him over as a long yearling or short 2-year-old to Elmo

Favor to train. Favor, who was living in Abilene at the time, had logged time as a trainer at E. Paul Waggoner's Three D Stock Farm in Arlington, Texas. While there, the lanky Texan had ridden such hallmark cutting horses as Poco Bueno and Jessie James.

By all accounts, Easter King showed considerable promise as a cutter. It has been reported that, "at the tender age of 18 months," he won the junior cutting at the Fort Worth and Houston stock shows. A search of the show results for both the 1953 and 1954 editions of those two shows does not substantiate that claim. Elmo Favor is on record, however, as saying that the young King son showed more promise as a cutting horse than any horse he'd ridden since Jessie James.

According to AQHA show records, Easter King had only four official show outings, all as a 3-year-old. On March 5, 1954, in Odessa, Texas, he placed first in the 1951 stallion class and earned two halter points. At the big Santa Rosa Roundup, held April 26–May 1 in Vernon, Texas, he placed second in junior cutting and earned two performance points.

At the San Angelo, Texas, show held May 1–2, Easter King placed third in 1951 stallions and second in junior cutting. In the latter class, he earned one performance point. Finally, on May 14, 1954, in Abilene, Texas, he placed third in 1951 stallions and split second and third places in the junior cutting. Again, he earned one performance point.

Easter King was shown at least one additional time that does not appear on his official record. On August 24, 1954, at the Colorado State Fair show in Pueblo, he placed first in the 3-year-old stallion class. (Grand Champion stallion honors at the

Easter King showed excellent promise as a cutting horse before a hock injury ended his show ring career.
Courtesy Quarter Horse Journal

show went to Spanish Nick, owned by Hank Wiescamp of Alamosa, Colorado; reserve champion honors went to Poco Bob, owned by Hilliard Miller of Eagle, Colorado.)

At some point in late 1954 or early 1955, Easter King suffered a training injury and was retired from all show competition.

During the next five years, from early 1955 to early 1959, Easter King was the herd sire for LaRue Gooch's well-thought-out breeding program. Among the blaze-faced sorrel stallion's broodmare band were a dozen or more Hollywood Gold mares and own daughters of Chubby, Rainy Day and Grey Badger II.

Among the top performers to be born during this timeframe were:

• King's Bernadine, a 1957 palomino mare out of Miss Hollywood: Earner of five halter points and 120 performance points in reining, trail, Western pleasure and Western riding.

• Easter 99 Jester, a 1959 chestnut stallion out of Miss Kingette: Superior trail; earner of 130 performance points in cutting, calf roping, reining, working cow horse, trail and Western riding.

In early 1969, Gooch decided to divest herself of the majority of her horses. Jack Brainerd, then of Rochester, Minnesota, got wind of the potential genetic goldmine and decided to check it out.

"I was attending the National Western Stock Show in Denver," he said. "The Hollywood Gold horses were all the rage as cutters. Monte Foreman and I were sitting around visiting one evening, and he told me that he knew where there was a top son of King and a set of Hollywood Gold mares that were for sale. The horses were located at Simla, Colorado, a hundred miles or so southeast of Denver. So I decided to drive out and look them over.

Pioneer Quarter Horse breeder John Bowling was destined to play an important role in Easter King's development as a sire. Here, Bowling shows John Berry to the grand champion stallion title at the 1955 Illinois State Fair in Springfield.
Photo by Lannspach, courtesy Western Horseman

180

"When I arrived at the ranch, Elmo Favor showed all the horses to me. Mrs. Gooch had Easter King priced at $4,000, and she wanted $1,500 each for the Hollywood Gold mares. I thought that was an awful lot of money, so I passed on the deal.

"The next evening," he continued, "I was visiting with John Bowling of Colorado Springs, Colorado. I knew John from back when he lived near Sycamore, Illinois. He asked me what I'd been up to, and I told him about the stud and mares.

" 'Well, you bought them, didn't you?' he asked.

" 'No, I didn't,' I said. 'They were priced a little too steep for me.'

" 'Do you mind if I go out and look them over?' he asked.

" 'Be my guest,' I said."

Here's a great shot of Easter King on the high plains east of Colorado Springs, Colorado, taken shortly after John Bowling acquired him.
Photo by Darol Dickinson, courtesy Pat Bowling Cuddy

The cross of Easter King on Hollywood Gold mares proved to be a golden one. This photo of the great cutting horse sire was taken in his youth on the Triangle Division of the Burnett Ranch in Paducah, Texas.
Courtesy Quarter Horse Journal

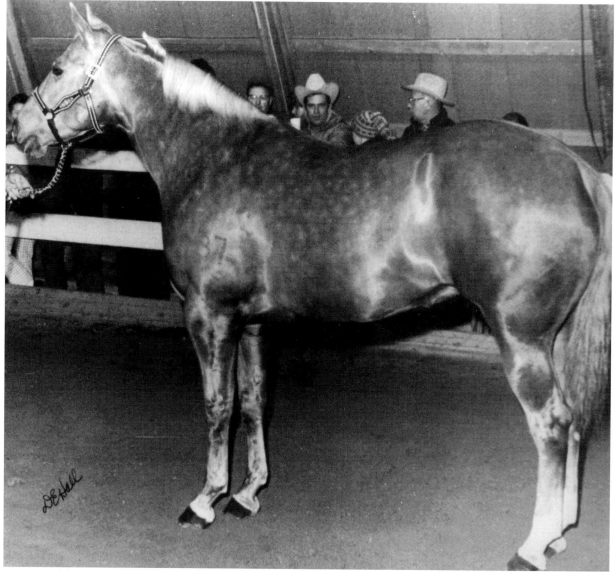

Ezee Money 37, a 1967 palomino mare by Easter King and out of Muneca 37 by Hollywood Gold, was an AQHA Champion and a Superior halter and Western pleasure horse.   **Courtesy Quarter Horse Journal**

At the time he became interested in the Gooch herd, Bowling was already a well-established horse breeder and dealer. A Maquoketa, Iowa, native, he had begun making regular horse-buying forays into the West and Southwest in the late 1940s.

An intuitive breeder, Bowling had already owned such foundation stallions as Smoky Bill James, John Berry, Dick Badger and Buck Hancock. What's more, having made numerous horse-buying trips to the Triangle Division of the Burnett Ranch, he was well-versed on the genetic strengths of LaRue Gooch's Hollywood Gold mares.

He immediately added Easter King and 12 Hollywood Gold mares to his already expansive herd.

"John came up to me the evening after he'd gone down to Simla," Jack Brainerd continued. "He told me he'd bought 13 head and asked me what he owed me.

" 'What do you mean?' I said. 'You don't owe me anything.'

" 'Well, all of the mares are in foal,' he said, 'so you come back out here this fall, and I'll let you have your choice of the colts.'

"So, I did. John was good to his word and let me choose from a pen of a half-dozen weanling colts. I chose a little palomino by Easter King and out of Holly Smoke by Hollywood Gold. I named him Holly 7 John and he went on to make a Register of Merit performance horse."

Shortly after acquiring Easter King, Bowling relocated his Quarter Horse operation to Sumner, Iowa. Placed at the head of this program, which included 250–300 mares, Easter King proved that his earlier siring accomplishments were not flukes. During the next 13 full breeding seasons—from 1960 through 1972—he sired such top performers as:

• 5 P Hancock, a 1965 chestnut mare out of Tri 7 Kitten: Superior halter, 102 halter points.

• Ezee Money 37, a 1967 palomino mare out of Muneca 37: AQHA Champion; Superior halter; Superior Western pleasure; 80 halter points; 228 performance points in Western pleasure, Western riding and trail.

• Hollywood Jac 86, a 1967 red dun stallion out of Miss Hollywood: Superior reining, 80 performance points in reining and Western riding, NRHA earnings of $6,089.

• O'Shay King 66, a 1967 sorrel gelding out of Pojon 66 Hancock: Superior Western pleasure; eight halter points; 191 performance points in Western pleasure, trail, Western riding, hunter under saddle and reining.

• King's Snoopy, a 1970 bay gelding out of Roma Long: 1975 Youth World Champion

Mr Hollywood Red, a 1971 sorrel gelding by Easter King and out of Miss Hollywood, was a six-time Superior award winner and the earner of 794 performance points.

Photo by Dick Waltenberry, courtesy Quarter Horse Journal

Holly Joan, a 1962 sorrel mare by Easter King and out of Miss Joe Tom 98, was an ROM performance horse. Shown here with Pat Bowling in the saddle, the versatile King granddaughter earned points in reining, Western pleasure, Western riding, hunter under saddle and heading.

Courtesy Pat Bowling Cuddy

Western Pleasure; Superior Western pleasure; Youth Superior Western pleasure; 20 halter points; 175 performance points in Western pleasure, hunter under saddle, trail and reining.

• Mr Hollywood Red, a 1971 sorrel gelding out of Miss Hollywood: 1976 Amateur High-Point Hunter Under Saddle Stallion, 1975 Amateur Reserve World Champion Hunter Under Saddle, Superior hunter under saddle, Amateur Superior Western horsemanship and Western pleasure, Youth Superior Western horsemanship and Western pleasure.

AQHA records show the King son to have sired 277 registered foals. Of those, 53 were performers that earned one Youth world championship, three Amateur reserve world championships, one AQHA championship, two Superior halter awards, 12 Superior performance awards (six Open, three Amateur and three Youth) and 27 performance ROMs (19 Open, three Amateur and five Youth). In NCHA competition they earned $22,989, and in NRHA events they earned $6,089.

As a maternal grandsire, Easter King was represented by 123 performers that earned one Youth world championship, one AQHA championship, eight Superior performance awards (five Open, two Amateur and one Youth), and 25 performance ROMs (18 Open, two Amateur and five Youth). In NCHA competition, they amassed $72,695, and in NRHA contests they earned $25,480.

By the time the 1970s arrived, Easter King was an established sire. Then, the distant past caught up with him.

"Back when I got my first look at Easter King," Jack Brainerd said, "I could see that he'd been hurt. I asked Elmo Favor about it and he said that one day he was working the horse on cattle, in some deep sand. 'Easter' rolled back over his hocks and damaged one or both ankles to the point where he was unsound to show."

By this time, the Bowling breeding program had grown even larger. The broodmare band now numbered in the vicinity of 500, and such popular young gray stallions as Lasso and Maybe Sixty Four had been added to the herd sire roster.

While Easter King's injuries had not interfered with his duties as a sire, they became a factor as he approached old age.

Pat Bowling Cuddy, who now lives near Santa Ynez, California, was an active participant in her parents' Quarter Horse operation throughout the Easter King era. In recalling the famous stallion's last days, she pays tribute to his disposition and heart.

"To tell you the truth," Cuddy said, "I can never remember Easter King as a lame horse. As far as what we used him for, he always seemed to get along just fine. I do recall that, as he aged, it did get harder for him to get around. But he was still the easiest horse to be around. If you didn't know better, you'd swear he was a gelding."

In the spring of 1971, the decision was made to have Easter King put to sleep.

"Injury notwithstanding," Cuddy said, "Dad never felt the need to baby Easter King. He used him as a pasture breeding horse, and that worked out just fine. The horse was never sick and never took a lame step in all the time we owned him.

"As the 1971 breeding season got underway, though, it seemed as if Easter King was just tired. He wouldn't eat or drink, so dad made the decision to put him down."

At the time of his death, the noted stallion was 21 years old. The following spring, one last Easter King foal, the aptly named Easter's Last, was born.

As had been the case with several of the top King sons that preceded him, Easter King

Hollywood Jac 86, a 1967 red dun stallion by Easter King and out of Miss Hollywood by Hollywood Gold, has seen to it that the Easter King line has been carried on. An AQHA Superior reining horse and an NRHA Hall of Fame horse, Hollywood Jac 86 is also an all-time leading reining horse sire. **Courtesy NRHA**

Custom Crome, a 1990 chestnut stallion by Chrome Plated Jac and out of Another Greyhound, traces to King through Easter King, Hollywood Jac 86 and Crome Plated Jac. Shown here with Mike Flarida, "Crome" was the 1993 NRHA Futurity Champion and earned $106,489.

Photo by Dick Waltenberry

Contemporary King's Pistol's descendants, such as Custom Pistol, have proven to be formidable reining competitors. A 1998 chestnut stallion by Custom Crome and out of Hollywood Lady Jo, Custom Pistol is the NRHA earner of $217,235.

Photo by Dick Waltenberry

Custom Mahogany, a 1999 sorrel mare by Custom Crome and out of Gay Doc Nell, traces to King nine times. She was ridden by Brent Wright to the 2003 NRHA Futurity Reserve Champion title and has earned more than $122,000.

Photo by Dick Waltenberry

sired two sons that saw to it that his branch of the family tree flourished. They were Hollywood Jac 86 and Easter Gentleman.

Hollywood Jac 86, a 1959 red dun stallion out of Miss Hollywood, is listed as being bred by John and Mary Bowling. He was actually bred by LaRue Gooch and came into the Bowlings' possession inside his dam.

Hollywood Jac 86 is an NRHA Hall of Fame Horse and the reining industry's first million-dollar sire and million-dollar maternal grandsire.

"In the late 1960s, John moved back to Iowa," recalled Jack Brainerd. "By this time, he had one of the largest herds of Quarter Horses in the country. John didn't show a lot of his horses. He made his living, instead, selling them as weanlings and yearlings.

"Burdette Johnson of Shell Rock, Iowa, was a friend and partner of mine. In 1968, Burdette was in the market for a stud prospect, so she made a trip to John's to look over some yearling colts.

"There was a little ol' lop-eared, creamy-colored palomino colt in one of the pens and John had him priced at $800. Burdette turned him down. Later on, Pat Fitzgerald of Mondovi, Wisconsin, bought him. He was Hollywood Jac 86."

Owned in succession by Fitzgerald; Spain Prestwich of Anoka, Minnesota; Richard Greenberg of Chicago, Illinois; and the partnership of Richard Greenberg and Sally Brown of Maple Plain, Minnesota, Hollywood Jac 86 went on to achieve superstar status as both a performer and a sire.

Dun Commander is the epitome of a second-generation Easter King performer. A 1968 buckskin stallion by Commander King and out of Merry King by Easter King, he earned 351 performance points in eight events.

Courtesy Quarter Horse Journal

In addition to his aforementioned AQHA show record, the Easter King son carried Greenberg to the 1974 and 1975 NRHA Non-Pro world championships and earned 12 NRHA bronze trophies.

As a reining horse sire, Hollywood Jac 86 is responsible for eight NRHA world champions, six NRHA Futurity champions, four NRHA Derby champions and the earners of more than $1.5 million. In addition, his maternal grand-get have amassed more than $1.6 million in NRHA earnings and more than $114,500 in NRCHA earnings.

Easter Gentleman, a 1970 gray stallion by Easter King and out of Bobbin Badger, also did his part to ensure that the line lived on.

Bred by John Bowling, the Easter King son was named by Pat Bowling Cuddy.

"Actually," she said, "Easter Gentleman named himself. Even as a foal, he had such a nice, easy-going disposition. But then, that was the way it was with all the Easter King horses. They were kind, willing, intelligent horses. They just wanted to please you."

By the time Easter Gentleman came along, Easter King was nearing the end of his life. Armed with that knowledge, John Bowling hand-picked "Gentleman" as his sire's replacement.

Easter Gentleman served as a Bowling herd sire for seven years. In 1979, he was sold to Ron Overstreet of Sumner, Iowa. Three years later, he was acquired by Thomas Tongyai of Gettysburg, Pennsylvania.

Like his sire and half-brother, Easter Gentleman went on to become an influential reining sire. In NRHA competition, his get earned $220,221. Among the most-accomplished are:
- Two T Whisky Royal, a 1987 gray mare out of White Whiskey: 1990 NRHA Futurity Champion, NRHA earner of $100,721.

Easter Gentleman, a 1970 gray stallion by Easter King and out of Bobbin Badger, has also made noteworthy contributions to the reining industry.

Courtesy Quarter Horse Journal

- Two T Easter King, a 1987 sorrel gelding out of Setta Badge 67: 1990 NRHA Futurity Non-Pro Champion, 1990 NRHA Futurity Limited Open Reserve Champion, NRHA earner of $32,123.
- Two T Tatiana, a 1993 gray mare out of Royal Cutters Sis: 1993 All-American Congress Junior Reining Champion, 1995 All-American Congress Senior Reining Champion.

Although, because of injury, Easter King never got the chance to live up to his potential as a performer, he did make more than his fair share of contributions to the breed. And, as the fountainhead of one of the reining industry's most-accomplished lines, the famous King son remains a highly influential genetic force to this very day.

Chapter 14

THE FUTURITY SIRE

King Glo, despite his "leggy" Thoroughbred look, lived up to his heritage as a top cow horse and sire.

Courtesy Quarter Horse Journal

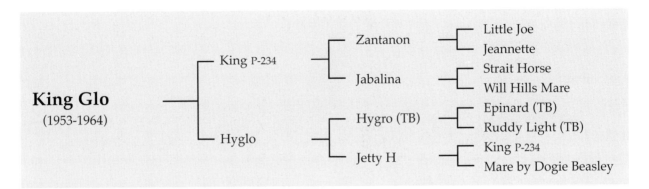

King Glo
(1953-1964)

- King P-234
  - Zantanon
    - Little Joe
    - Jeannette
  - Jabalina
    - Strait Horse
    - Will Hills Mare
- Hyglo
  - Hygro (TB)
    - Epinard (TB)
    - Ruddy Light (TB)
  - Jetty H
    - King P-234
    - Mare by Dogie Beasley

The advent of organized Quarter Horse racing and cutting in the mid- to late 1940s was the first step toward the event specialization that would one day become the industry norm.

As noted earlier, the impetus behind the creation of both the American Quarter Racing Association (AQRA) in 1945 and the National Cutting Horse Association (NCHA) in 1948 was two-fold.

To begin with, the racing and cutting interests wanted to have a more direct say in the overall regulation of their respective forms of competition. They wanted to self-determine the rules by which racing and cutting contests were held, they wanted to hire their

Hyglo, King Glo's dam, was one of the top racehorses of her era.　　　*Courtesy* **Quarter Horse Journal**

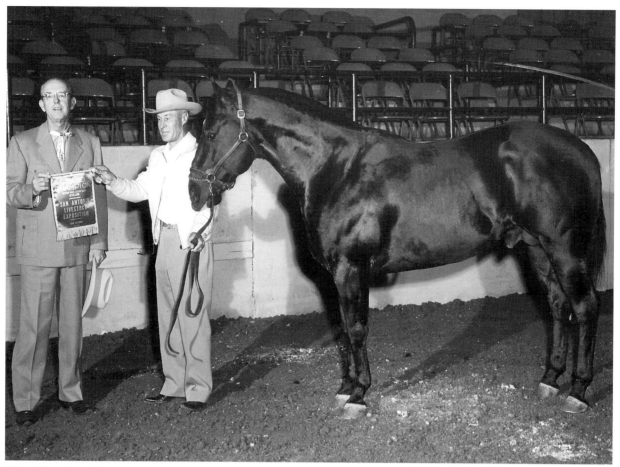

King Glo was exhibited by veteran horseman Michael Stoner of Uvalde, Texas, to the grand champion stallion title at the 1958 San Antonio Livestock Exposition and Fat Stock Show in San Antonio, Texas.

Courtesy **Quarter Horse Journal**

own stewards and judges, and they wanted to establish their own set of world champion awards.

Secondly, both factions wanted to institute a monetary payback structure that would encourage participation and fuel growth on all fronts.

In 1959, the racing brain trust conceived and implemented the All American Futurity for 2-year-olds. The purse for the inaugural running of the event at Ruidoso Downs, New Mexico, was an unheard-of $129,686. By 1978, the total payback exceeded $1 million.

Not to be outdone, the cutting horse crowd launched their own futurity for 3-year-olds in 1962. Known simply as the NCHA Futurity, it offered an initial purse of $18,375. Like the All American, it, too, eventually grew into a million dollar affair.

From the very onset of the cutting extravaganza, it was apparent that the blood of King P-234 would be a force to be reckoned with. The lion's share of the credit for this revelation can be attributed to one horse— King Glo.

King Glo, a 1953 black stallion by King P-234 and out of Hyglo, was bred by J. O. Hankins of Rocksprings, Texas. In many respects, he was a King of a different sort—a little more streamlined in his build and a little "hotter" in his mental make-up. Both traits could be directly attributed to his dam.

Hyglo, a 1944 black mare by Hygro (TB) and out of Jetty H, was bred by C. E. Miller of Mason, Texas. Both she and her dam, a 1941 bay mare by King and out of a Dogie Beasley mare, were acquired by Hankins in late 1945 and early 1946.

King Glo, with cutting horse icon Buster Welch in the saddle, was a top arena performer.

Photo by James Cathey, courtesy Quarter Horse Journa

The jet black King son, shown here with owner C. E. Boyd Jr. of Sweetwater, Texas, aboard, attained his AQHA Championship in 1962.

Courtesy Quarter Horse Journal

Leo Glo, a 1959 sorrel stallion by King Glo and out of Princess Zan, earned 37 halter points. Retired to stud, he went on to sire two AQHA Champions and one Superior halter horse.

Courtesy Quarter Horse Journal

"One time, when I was in Kerrville talking to Charlie Miller," said Hankins, "he mentioned having a filly he would like to show me. So, we went out to his place to see her. She was about 14 months old at the time and about as fat as a filly of that age could get.

"Nevertheless, I thought she showed quite a bit of quality and liked her from the moment I saw her.

"I had been wanting to get a Hygro mare to add to my broodmare band, and the fact that she was out of a King mare suited me right down to the ground. Mr. Miller priced the filly to me, but, thinking his figure a little steep, I did not buy her at that time."[1]

Several months later, Hankins reconsidered his decision.

"I bumped into Charlie in Rocksprings," he recalled, "and bought the black filly from him. When I bought her, she was unnamed. I kind of wanted to name her after her sire, Hygro. She was so black and shiny she actually glowed, so I called her Hyglo.

"I bought her under the condition that if she lowered 23 seconds, I would pay Mr. Miller another $200. She did this at Del Rio the first or second time I ran her at 440."[1]

Like her older stable mate, Squaw H, Hyglo was raced under AQRA auspices. In 1946, she qualified as a AA runner when that was

---

[1] Nelson C. Nye, "Champions of the Quarter Track," page 115

the highest rating possible. When a AAA rating was instituted in 1948, she qualified for it, as well.

Hyglo's official race record credits her with eight wins, 12 seconds and seven thirds from 30 starts. A 1948 J. O. Hankins advertisement further documents that the half-Thoroughbred mare made 15 unofficial starts, winning 14 and placing second once. The pinnacle of her racing career came in 1948, when she equaled the world record for 400 yards.

After being retired to the Hankins broodmare band, Hyglo produced such top racehorses as Hy Balmy, a 1951 brown stallion by Balmy L, S.I. 95; and Hyglobar, a 1959 sorrel mare by Three Bars (TB), S.I. 95.

It was not as a racing matron that Hyglo was destined to make her most lasting contribution to the breed, though. Beginning in

1952, she produced three straight foals by King P-234: King Glo, a 1953 black stallion; King Santa Bay, a 1954 bay stallion; and Miss Hyglo, a 1955 chestnut mare. Of these, King Glo was the cream of the crop and the horse most responsible for perpetuating the Hyglo line.

To begin with, Hankins decided to hold on to King Glo and develop him as a show horse and sire. Toward that end, he turned him over as a 3-year-old to Michael Stoner of Uvalde, Texas, to break and show at halter.

Stoner hit the show trail with King Glo in mid-1956. Exhibited four times at halter that year, the black King son tallied four firsts and two grand championships.

Between 1957 and 1959, King Glo was shown at halter nine more times. He recorded five firsts, four seconds, four grands and two reserves.

Sandy Eloise, a 1962 palomino mare by Leo Glo and out of Burke's Sandy, was a Superior halter horse and the earner of 159 halter points. Among her 80 halter class wins was a 1st place finish in a class of 95 2-year-old mares at the 1964 Southwestern Exposition and Livestock Show in Fort Worth, Texas. **Courtesy Quarter Horse Journal**

Les Glo, a 1959 sorrel stallion by King Glo and out of DJH 1, was an AQHA Champion, a Superior cutting horse and the earner of 85 performance points.

Courtesy **Quarter Horse Journal**

His two biggest victories occurred at the 1957 State Fair of Texas in Dallas and the 1958 San Antonio Livestock Exposition and Fat Stock Show in San Antonio, Texas. At the former, he placed first in a class of 10 aged stallions and was named the grand champion stallion. At the latter, he stood at the head of a class of 17 aged stallions and was again given the nod as the grand champion.

Sandwiched between these two wins was a second-place finish to King Champ in a class of 43 aged stallions at the Baton Rouge, Louisiana, show.

While under Stoner's care, King Glo was broke to ride. In later years, the veteran trainer remembered the black stallion as a horse who "wanted to run." That fact notwithstanding, the King son was started on cattle.

In the spring of 1958, Hankins brought King Glo home and his cutting training was continued under local trainers Cecil Hurley and Jerry Roach. Hurley hauled the 6-year-old to a cutting in Louisiana, where the stallion caught the eye of well-known cutting horse aficionado B. A. Skipper Jr. of Plainview, Texas.

Skipper, who owned such top cutters as Poco Lena and Poco Mona, expressed an interest in adding King Glo to his stable but was unwilling to pay what Hankins was asking for the stallion.

Several months later, a second potential buyer surfaced.

C. E. Boyd Jr. of Sweetwater, Texas, was the son of a rancher and grew up riding home-bred young horses that his father sold or traded off as soon as they were well-started. This left the younger Boyd with a healthy desire to one day own a good horse that wouldn't get sold out from under him.

In the spring of 1959, Boyd paid the Hankins Brothers a visit. He was in the market for a stallion prospect, but promptly decided that an older horse would do.

"I really wanted a young horse," said Boyd, "but they didn't have anything that suited me like King Glo did. I fell in love with the horse. We just turned him out in the arena and watched him play ... and after a few days, we traded for him.

"I had some ranch land by Limon, Colorado, and we gave that and $10,000 cash and valued him at $50,000. Then J. O. turned around and sold the ranch, and I think he figured he finally got $125,000 for King Glo. It was another horse trading deal, but I think we were fair on it. We weren't trying to inflate it."[2]

After getting "Glo" home, Boyd turned him over to Buster Welch and Leo Huff to show in cutting.

During the next three years—from the fall of 1960 to the fall of 1962—the stallion was shown in 11 AQHA-sanctioned cutting contests. He placed in the top three in all 11 and earned 15 points and a performance Register of Merit. That total, combined with his 25 halter points and two Western riding points, were enough to qualify him for his AQHA

[2] Sally Harrison, "King Glo – Father of the Futurity," *2001 NCHA World Championship Cutting Futurity*, pp. 35-37.

Money's Glo, a 1959 bay gelding by King Glo and out of Our Money, was the 1962 NCHA Futurity Champion. In addition, he earned multiple AQHA and NCHA cutting honors. **Courtesy NCHA**

197

The cross of King Glo on the daughters of Chickasha Mike was a golden one that ultimately led to King Glo's designation as "the futurity sire." Here, Chickasha Mike and Buster Welch compete in a circa early-1950s cutting contest.

Photo by James Cathey, courtesy Quarter Horse Journal

championship. During that same time, he also had NCHA earnings of $1,918.

"King Glo had so much cow it was unreal," Boyd said. "We had a little cutting at the ranch where you rode into a herd with just a little string under the [horse's] neck. No bridle. I was on King Glo and I had my eye on one cow and he had his eye on another.

"My cow went one way and his went another, and he shot me right up in the air. He had such a burst of speed, it was unreal."[2]

After attaining his AQHA championship, King Glo was retired to stud.

Even while he was being shown, however, the stallion had been utilized as a breeding horse. His first two foal crops, totaling 20 get, hit the ground in 1957 and 1958. From them came two ROM performers.

King Glo's first full crop, numbering 45, arrived in 1959. Among its members were such top performers as:

• Glo Snap, a 1959 sorrel gelding out of Tar Gal: 1969 High-Point Cutting Gelding, Superior cutting, 176 performance points.
• Les Glo, a 1959 sorrel stallion out of DJH I: AQHA Champion, Superior cutting.
• Leo Glo, a 1959 sorrel stallion out of

Princess Zan: 37 halter points.
• Prissy Glo, a 1959 bay mare out of Bay Ramona: AQHA Champion.

After Boyd's purchase of King Glo, the emphasis on the stallion's siring career was aimed specifically toward the cutting arena.

As mentioned earlier, the NCHA Futurity was inaugurated in 1962The Futurity's first three committee members were J. D. Craft, H. L. Akin and C. E. Boyd Jr.

"There were three things we were trying to accomplish in the futurity," Boyd said. "First, of course, to promote the cutting horse. Second, to improve the judging.

"Third, the only honor worth mentioning at the time was Horse of the Year, and that was a pulling contest. So we tried to set this [futurity] up so that the old boy that couldn't afford to pull all the time could take his horse and have a chance to compete against everybody on an even scale. These were maiden horses and it wasn't a pulling contest."[3]

King Glo's first crop of Boyd-bred foals hit the ground in 1960, and its members were too young to be nominated to the inaugural Futurity. Boyd rectified that situation by locating and purchasing a top prospect.

[3] Sally Harrison, "King Glo – Father of the Futurity," *2001 NCHA World Championship Cutting Futurity*, pp.35-37.

Money's Glo, a 1959 bay gelding by King Glo and out of Our Money, was bred by George Pardi of Uvalde, Texas. Leo Huff, one of four men who campaigned King Glo, discovered the young prospect at Pardi's and purchased him for $700. Boyd than acquired the gelding from Huff and sent him to Buster Welch for training.

The first NCHA Futurity was held November 23 and 24 in Sweetwater, Texas. Forty-seven horses were nominated to it and, of these, 36 actually competed. Up for grabs was a record purse of $18,375.

The legendary Peppy San, with Matlock Rose in the saddle, won the semi-finals. Money's Glo and Welch then came back to take the finals and the overall championship. The victory was worth $3,828.

Money's Glo went on to become a top show and cutting horse. In AQHA competition, he was an AQHA Champion, a Superior cutting horse and the earner of 132 performance points. In NCHA competition, he was the 1964 and 1965 World Champion Gelding and the earner of $22,553.

For his 1963 NCHA Futurity entry, Boyd was once again able to locate and buy a top King Glo-sired prospect. And this time, it was the oldest member of a five-sibling set of horses that would take the cutting horse world by storm.

Chickasha Glo, a 1960 sorrel mare by King Glo and out of Chickasha Ann by Chickasha Mike, was bred by Dr. Allen Hamilton of Big Spring, Texas. Buster Welch was well-acquainted with Chickasha Ann's sire, having owned and shown him in cutting in the early 1950s.

After being purchased by Boyd, Chickasha Glo was sent to Welch to be readied for the Futurity. One of 45 entries in the second edition of the prestigious event, she was bested

Chickasha Dan, a 1962 sorrel stallion by King Glo and out of Chickasha Ann by Chickasha Mike, won the 1965 NCHA Futurity. He followed up the prestigious victory up by being named the 1968 NCHA World Champion Cutting Horse.
Courtesy NCHA

Chickasha King, a 1964 sorrel gelding by King Glo and out of Chickasha Ann, was the NCHA earner of $70,356.

Courtesy Quarter Horse Journal

by Jose Uno in the semi-finals but came back to take the finals. Sold by Boyd to a family who planned on turning her into a barrel horse, Chickasha Glo died shortly thereafter.

Glo Doc, a 1961 brown gelding, was the next member of the King Glo—Chickasha Ann family. An AQHA Superior cutting horse, he had NCHA earnings of $8,135. Entered in the NCHA Futurity, he finished in fifth place.

Chickasha Dan, a 1962 sorrel stallion; Annie Glo, a 1963 brown mare; and Chickasha King, a 1964 sorrel gelding, were the final three members of the King Glo—Chickasha Ann cross to ply the family trade.

Chickasha Dan was retained by Hamilton, who was a West Texas optometrist, and ridden by him in the 1965 Futurity. The duo made cutting horse history when "Dan" became the first horse to win the big event

while ridden by an Amateur.

And, like his older half-brother, Money's Glo, Chickasha Dan went on to become a top show and cutting competitor. In AQHA competition, he was a Superior cutting horse and the earner of 194 performance points. In NCHA competition, he was the 1967 Reserve Non-Pro World Champion, the 1968 Open World Champion Gelding and the earner of $48,652.

Annie Glo, also owned by Hamilton, missed the 1966 NCHA Futurity finals but was a top competitor nevertheless. In NCHA competition, she was the 1979 World Champion Mare and the earner of $77,688.

Chickasha King, the last member of the family, was a finalist in the 1967 NCHA Futurity. In NCHA competition, he was a two-time top 10 finisher and the earner of $70,356.

Getting back to King Glo, who by now was widely known as "the Futurity Sire," his breeding prowess was not limited to the "Chickasha" cross. Among his other top performers were:

- Clayton Glo, a 1961 black gelding out of Miss Prenita: AQHA Champion.
- Flynt's Doll, a 1961 black mare out of Miss Flynt: AQHA Champion.
- King Glo Cody, a 1961 bay gelding out of Casey's June Twist: AQHA Champion, Superior halter.

In addition, the popular stallion sired several other ROM performance horses. Without a doubt, though, it was the golden cross of King Glo on Chickasha Ann that propelled the Boyd-owned stallion into the lofty position he enjoyed in the mid-1960s as one of the breed's top young sires.

With both entities being relatively young horses, the cross would have no doubt continued to be made had it not been for King Glo's untimely death in 1964, after a cancerous tumor was discovered in his stomach.

"I went over to see him [before the exploratory surgery]," C. E. Boyd Jr. said, "and I just couldn't stand it. He looked like a skeleton. I had him buried on the ranch."

The loss of King Glo at the relatively young age of 11 deprived the breed of one of its brightest and most-promising performance sires. Still, the King son accomplished more in half of a lifetime than most horses do given the luxury of a full life.

AQHA records reveal King Glo to be the sire of 241 horses. Of those, 81 were performers and they earned five AQHA championships, one Superior halter award, five

Hyglo Freckles was one of King Glo's most-accomplished second-generation descendants. A 1983 bay gelding by Hyglo Freckles and out of Miss Kings Hyglo, Hyglo Freckles was the 1988 NCHA World Champion Cutting Horse and the earner of $338,339. **Courtesy Quarter Horse Journal**

Superior performance awards and 26 performance ROMs. In addition, they amassed 320 halter and 1,128 performance points. In NCHA competition, despite the low purses of the day they earned $269,776.

In addition, King Glo was the maternal grandsire of 159 performers that earned eight AQHA championships (six Open and two Youth), six Superior halter awards (five Open and one Youth), 13 Superior performance awards (six Open and seven Youth) and 32 performance ROMs (26 Open, one Amateur and five Youth). In addition, they tallied 912 halter and 2,209.5 performance points. In NCHA competition, they earned $653,725.

Of King Glo's maternal grand-get, Hyglo Freckles and Mr. Joe Glo are especially noteworthy.

Hyglo Freckles, a 1983 bay gelding by Freckles Playboy and out of Miss Kings Hyglo, was bred by Bermuda Run Farm of Tioga, Texas. Sold to Faron and Sumer Hightower of Woodlake, Texas, he went on to be the 1988 NCHA World Champion Cutting Horse and earner of $338,339.

Mr Joe Glo, a 1968 black stallion by Lucky Joe Five and out of Squaw's Glo, was bred by Art Miller of Yucca Valley, California. Sold to Jack Brainerd of Rochester, Minnesota, and Burdette Johnson of Shell Rock, Iowa, he became an AQHA Champion. Retired to stud, he did much to perpetuate the King Glo line.

As a sire, Mr Joe Glo is credited with 160 performers that earned five AQHA championships (three Open and two Youth), three Superior halter awards (two Open and one Youth), 17 Superior performance awards (11 Open, one Amateur and five Youth) and 77 performance ROMs (50 Open, 15 Amateur and 12 Youth). In addition, they accumulated 388 halter and 3,950.5 performance points. In NRHA competition, they earned $183,871.

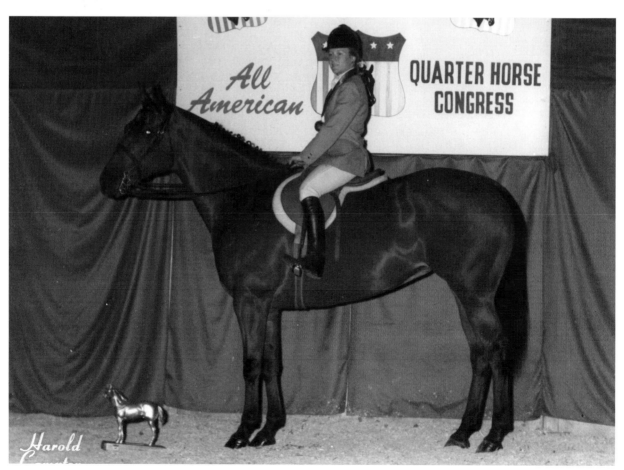

Ka Ti Be Globars, a 1969 bay mare by Driftwood Bars and out of Dora Glo by King Glo, was a top youth mount.
Photo by Harold Campton, courtesy Quarter Horse Journal

In addition to Hyglo Freckles and Mr Joe Glo, King Glo was responsible for a number of other highly accomplished maternal grand-get. Among them were:

- Ka Ti Be Globars, a 1969 bay mare by Driftwood Bars and out of Dora Glo: Open and Youth AQHA Champion; Youth AQHA Performance Champion; Youth Superior awards in Western pleasure, Western horsemanship, showmanship and hunter under saddle; earner of 66 halter (22 Open and 44 Youth) and 576 performance (68 Open and 508 Youth) points.
- Pam Par, a 1969 sorrel mare by Three Par and out of Lady Snyder Glo: Superior halter, 138 halter points.
- Blizzard Song, a 1967 roan mare by Good Excuse and out of Miss Holly Glo: Superior halter and Western pleasure; Youth AQHA Champion; Youth Superior awards in halter, Western pleasure and showmanship.
- Bay Miss Glo, a 1970 bay mare by Mocha Cutter and out of Roan Miss Glo: AQHA Champion, Superior Western pleasure.
- Miss Joe Glo, a 1969 sorrel mare by Lucky Joe Five and out of Squaw's Glo: AQHA Champion, Superior halter, 93 halter points.

In terms of his overall contributions to both the Quarter Horse breed and the King family of performers, King Glo was a one-of-a-kind horse and the vanguard sire for a cutting horse industry that stood poised to hit the big time.

As noted earlier, the coal-black stallion was a King of a different kind.

"He showed a lot of that Thoroughbred blood," C. E. Boyd Jr. said, "but he had the temperament of a Quarter Horse. He was a fantastic, intelligent horse."[4]

Mr Joe Glo, a 1968 black stallion by Lucky Joe Five and out of Squaw's Glo by King Glo, was an AQHA Champion and top sire. In addition, he and his descendants have had a positive impact on both the cutting and reining industries.

Courtesy Quarter Horse Journal

In a life cut far too short, King Glo took his bona-fide good looks, sterling disposition and superior intelligence and parlayed them into successful careers as a show horse and sire.

What more could anyone have asked of him?

---

[4] Sally Harrison, "King Glo – Father of the Futurity," *2001 NCHA World Championship Cutting Futurity,* pp. 35-37.

Chapter 15

CONTINENTAL REIGN

Continental King was the first horse inducted into the NRHA Hall of Fame. This classic photo of him, ridden by Bill Horn, was the NRHA logo for years.

Courtesy Quarter Horse Journal

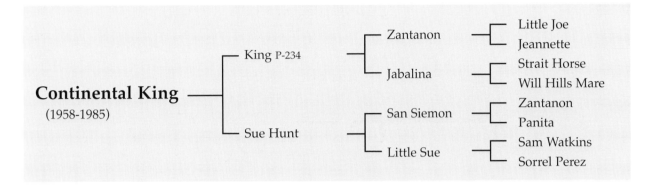

Continental King
(1958-1985)

- King P-234
  - Zantanon
    - Little Joe
    - Jeannette
  - Jabalina
    - Strait Horse
    - Will Hills Mare
- Sue Hunt
  - San Siemon
    - Zantanon
    - Panita
  - Little Sue
    - Sam Watkins
    - Sorrel Perez

The year was 1958.

Ninety-two years had elapsed from the time William Fleming happened upon Billy—the true progenitor of the modern-day Quarter Horse—tied to a tree in Southeast Texas.

The country had survived one civil war, two world wars and several smaller conflicts. It had made it through the Roaring Twenties and the Dirty Thirties, and it had progressed from a nation that ran on horse-, coal- and steam power to one that had unlocked the awesome power of the atom.

Overall, the country was in a state of comparative calm.

In the Rocksprings area of South Texas, a 26-year-old Billy-bred stallion was also in a state of relative bliss, firmly entrenched atop the Quarter Horse world.

On AQHA's list of Leading Sires of Performance Register of Merit Qualifiers–1951 through 1956, King P-234 occupied the top spot, followed by Poco Bueno and Royal King. On the Leading Sires of Horses with Halter Points–1951 through 1956 list, Poco Bueno was the leader, with King in second place. On the Leading Sires of Cutting Horses–1951 through 1956 list, King was the leader, again followed by Poco Bueno and Royal King.

And then the living legend passed away.

The death of King was big news in the Quarter Horse world, and it was reported as such in the May 1958 issue of *Quarter Horse Journal*. Beneath a photo of Jess Hankins astride King, a bold headline proclaimed, "King P-234 Dies." Following the headline, the first paragraph of a short, two-column story read:

"King P-234, patriarch of America's most famous Quarter Horse family, died March 24 at the ranch of his owners, Mr. and Mrs. Jess L. Hankins, Rocksprings, Texas. Death was attributed to a heart attack."

After presenting a brief outline of King's life, the article concluded with the following observation:

"… He proved to be so great a sire that King's stud fees went from $15 at the time Hankins purchased him, to $2,500 at the time of King's death. No other stallion now living can boast such a record as King's and only time will tell when another will equal it."

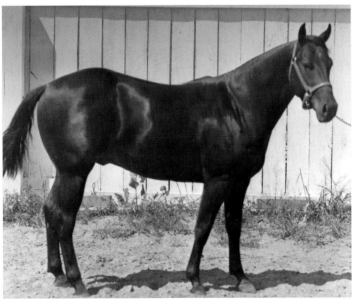

Here's a nice shot of Continental King, or "Kinger" as he was known, showing him as a 2-year-old.

Courtesy Charlie Hutton

The cross of Continental King on the daughters of Hollywood Gold was one that resulted in numerous arena champions. This classic photo shows two West Texas legends—Hollywood Gold and long-time 6666 Ranch manager George Humphreys.
Courtesy Quarter Horse Journal

King's 23rd and final foal crop numbered 43 and hit the ground in 1958. Included among that number was one stallion in particular who would play a major role in keeping the King name in the performance arena spotlight for years to come.

Continental King, a 1958 black stallion out of Sue Hunt, is listed as being bred by Ted Clymer of Hudson, Wisconsin. As attested to by Jack Brainard of Aubrey, Texas, the stallion was actually bred by Henry Boehm of La Crosse, Wisconsin.

"In the mid-1950s," said Brainard, "I was training horses in Rochester, Minnesota. Ted

Clymer and Henry Boehm were two of my customers.

"Ted Clymer passed away in 1956, and his widow asked me to help disperse the horses. We sold Sue Hunt that year to Henry Boehm, who owned and operated a clothing store called Continental Clothiers. Henry had a son of Poco Bueno named Poco Bay that I trained and showed for him. In 1956, he bred Sue Hunt to Poco Bay. Poco Boehmo, a 1957 sorrel stallion, was the resulting foal.

"Ted Clymer had another top mare that I trained and showed," continued Brainard. "Her name was Martha King, and she was a

1954 chestnut mare by King P-234 and out of Fanny H. When she was a 2-year-old, I showed her at halter at St. Paul, Minnesota. Lloyd Jinkens was the judge, and he placed her first in a class of nine head. The following year, I showed her in the junior reining at Waterloo, Iowa. James Kiser was the judge there, and he placed her first in a class of eight head.

"After Ted Clymer's death, Martha King was put on the market. In the spring of 1958, I called B. F. Phillips, who lived in Frisco, Texas, and told him I knew where there was a good King mare that was for sale.

" 'How much do they want for her?' he asked.

" 'Two thousand dollars,' I said.

" 'Well, I guess I'll take her if you'll agree to haul her down here,' he said.

"So I did. B. F. took her and paid me $100 to deliver her. Then, Matlock Rose went to reining off of her, and she was the 1958 high-point reining mare."

Getting back to Continental King and his real breeder, Jack Brainard had a hand in that, as well.

"After I cut the deal on Martha King," he said, "I called Henry Boehm up and told him that, as long as I had to haul a horse to Texas, he might as well book Sue Hunt to King. I had a two-horse trailer at the time, and couldn't see going that far south with just one horse in it.

"Henry agreed, and I loaded both mares and took off. I dropped Martha King off at the Phillips Ranch and then continued on to Rocksprings, with Sue Hunt. We got her bred to King, and Continental King was the resulting foal.

"He's named after Henry's clothing store."

Because of the distances involved, Sue Hunt was left in Jess Hankins' care to be bred and foaled out. Continental King was born on June 8, 1958.

The fact that the young King son had an exceptionally well-bred dam was a matter of fact. Sue Hunt, a 1942 dun mare by San Siemon and out of Little Sue, was bred by A. I. Hunt of Tulsa, Oklahoma. A member of one of the breed's greatest early-day "golden crosses," she was a full sister to Black Hawk, Joe Barrett, Sandy Benear, Little Sue II, Little Sue III and San Sue Darks.

Having lost King several months prior and understanding full well the potency of Sue Hunt's pedigree, Hankins called Boehm and tendered an offer for both mare and foal. Boehm declined to sell and enlisted Brainard's help in transporting the pair back north.

When Continental King was a 2-year-old, he was started under saddle. Shortly thereafter, he was sold to Dr. John and Mickey Glenn of Cincinnati, Ohio. It was at this point in the young stallion's life that a course was charted that would lead him to his spot in the history books.

Charlie Hutton of Fayetteville, Tennessee, is the one man who is most qualified to flesh out the details of the King son's life.

"I saw Continental King for the first time in 1965," he said. "After the Glenns had pur-

Dodson's Little Star, a 1950 bay mare by Hollywood Gold and out of Triangle Lady 27, parlayed her potency as a producer into a 2003 induction into the NRHA Hall of Fame.

Courtesy Quarter Horse Journal

Miz Liz Dodson, a 1965 bay mare by Continental King and out of Dodson's Little Star, was the 1968 NRHA Futurity Reserve Champion. Legendary trainer Bill Horn is seen aboard the good-looking mare.

Courtesy Quarter Horse Journal

chased him, they turned him over to Dale Wilkinson of Findlay, Ohio, for training. If they had not done that, the horse probably would have wound up being just another son of King.

"Dale had Continental King, or "Kinger" as he was known, going well in reining and he wanted to start him on cattle. At some point, though, the horse had been kicked by a mare. He'd suffered a hock fracture and the Glenns

didn't want him to be used as a cutting horse.

"Dale and Kinger were competing at the 1965 Ohio State Fair," continued Hutton. "Back then, the state fairs were where the stiffest competition was.

"Dale had showed Kinger to a first place in the senior reining. He'd also ridden Tabano Nancy, a daughter of Tabano King, to a first in the junior reining. Then they had a championship reining, with the winners of the Quarter Horse, Paint Horse and Appaloosa reining classes competing against one another. Dale and Continental King won that class, as well."

For Hutton, that first look at a horse that had greatness written all over him remains frozen in time.

"I can still remember my first glimpse of Continental King," he said. "Here was this big black horse. He had a breast collar on, and Dale had been galloping him so hard that his chest was covered with white foam.

"I was in my 20s at the time and the new assistant professor of horse management at Ohio State University (OSU), in Columbus. I'd never seen a horse sit down, stop hard and spin as fast as Kinger did that day. And then, after each of his runs, he'd just stand in the middle of the arena like a statue. He made

an impression on me that day that changed the way I looked at performance horses."

At the same time Hutton got his first glimpse of Continental King, Dale Wilkinson had a promising young trainer named Bill Horn in his employ. With Horn as his primary rider, Continental King went on to become one of the top reining horses of his era. AQHA records reveal that, between July of 1964 and September of 1968, the King son was shown in 33 reining classes. Of those, he won 14, placed second 13 times and third six times, earning a Superior reining award and amassing 72.5 performance points (69 reining, two working cow horse and 1.5 Western pleasure).

Among his top wins were the 1965 Indiana State Fair, the 1965 and 1966 Illinois State Fairs, the 1965 and 1966 Ohio State Fairs, and the 1967 Kentucky and Michigan State Fairs.

Continental Ace, a 1966 black full brother to Miz Liz Dodson, was a Superior reining horse and placed third in the 1969 NRHA Futurity. **Courtesy Charlie Hutton**

Continental Mira, a 1973 chestnut mare by Continental King and out of Poco Red Ant, was another top "Kinger" performer.
Photo by Harold Campton, courtesy Quarter Horse Journal

At the conclusion of the 1967 Midwestern fair season, Kinger was retired to stud.

As noted in previous chapters, the age of specialization within the Quarter Horse industry was spawned with the formation of the American Quarter Racing Association (AQRA) in 1945 and the National Cutting Horse Association (NCHA) in 1948.

After years of slow, steady growth, both the racing and cutting factions launched their own prestigious futurities.

The National Reining Horse Association (NRHA) was born in 1966. With the successes of its specialized predecessors available as blueprints, NRHA immediately launched its own 3-year-old hallmark event. Like both the racing and cutting futurities, the NRHA extravaganza eventually mushroomed into a $1 million event.

Appropriately enough, Bill Horn and Continental King were instrumental in the birth of the modern-day reining industry.

On October 31, 1965, the team competed in an Open reining held at an AQHA show in Dayton, Ohio. Carroll Brumley was the judge and, after seeing the quality of the men and horses entered in the class, he devised a more-difficult pattern for them to perform.

Horn and Kinger won the event, and the excitement it generated among owners, riders and spectators alike is credited with setting the wheels in motion that led to the formation of NRHA.

Four years after Continental King was retired from competition, his life became inexorably joined with that of Charlie Hutton.

"By 1971," Hutton said, "Dr. Glenn's health had begun to deteriorate and he decided to cut back on his involvement with the horses. Mrs. Glenn called me up one day and said, 'I'm thinking of donating Continental King to the OSU horse program. What do you think of that?'

" 'Do you want me to pick him up today, or wait until tomorrow?' I asked.

"I didn't even discuss it with my bosses. I just hopped in a university station wagon, hooked onto a two-horse trailer, and went and got the horse."

With Hutton as his primary handler, Continental King stood to outside mares at the university for the next three years. Then, the man and horse were separated.

"The University of Georgia hired me to start up their horse program," said Hutton. "Looking back, I can honestly say that the hardest part about leaving Columbus, Ohio, and relocating to Athens, Georgia, was saying goodbye to that good, black horse."

The separation was not for long, however. Two years later, Hutton orchestrated a reunion.

"In 1976," he said, "I called Bob Kline, the man who had succeeded me at Ohio State. I told him I was interested in bringing Continental King down to Georgia. After we

High Cards In A High Stakes Game ———

Continental King
ridden by Bill Horn

Continental Ace
ridden by Charlie Hutton

By the late 1970s, both Continental King and his son Continental Ace were under the control of Charlie Hutton and the University of Georgia at Athens. As this Hutton-designed brochure cover illustrates, the jet black duo were thought to be "top cards" as both performers and sires. **Courtesy Charlie Hutton**

discussed the matter, he said that he didn't want to try to sell the horse because of the politics and the paperwork.

" 'What if I find you a "modern" horse, and we set up a lease-swap arrangement?' I asked.

" 'That'll work,' he said.

"So I called Dale Rose, an accountant friend of mine in Ohio, and asked him if he knew of any modern horses that might be available as a donation for tax purposes.

" 'I sure do,' he said.

"The horse Dale had in mind was Go Mobile, a AAA AQHA Champion son of Go Man Go. He was 9 years old at the time and totally blind.

"My man in Ohio agreed to the swap, so, once again, I hopped in a university station wagon and drove up to get Continental King."

Dating back to when he was owned by Henry Boehm, Continental King had been used as a breeding horse. From the very onset, it was apparent that he was going to be a pre-potent sire.

King C Reed, a 1963 brown stallion by Continental King and out of Dimples Reed, was the ex-reining star's first noteworthy performer. Bred by Boehm's Continental Farms in La Crosse, he earned 94 performance points in cutting, Western pleasure, Western riding, trail, hunter under saddle, barrel racing and pole bending

And, just as LaRue Gooch had discovered years earlier with Easter King, Dr. and Mrs. Glenn were quick to realize that Continental King nicked exceptionally well with the daughters of Hollywood Gold. Among the top performers to result from this cross were:

• Miz Liz Dodson, a 1965 bay mare out of Dodson's Little Star: earner of 42.5 performance points (26 reining, 14 cutting and 2.5 Western pleasure); 1968 NRHA Futurity Reserve Champion; NCHA earner of $2,126.
• Continental Ace, a 1966 black stallion out of Dodson's Little Star: Superior reining; third

Although primarily known for his prowess as a reining horse, Continental King was an NCHA Certificate of Achievement horse. What's more, he qualified for that award as a 21-year-old.

Courtesy Charlie Hutton

in the 1969 NRHA Futurity and winner of 23 of 30 AQHA reining classes.
- Continental Buff, a 1966 dun gelding out of Miss Gold 01: Youth Superior reining, NRHA earner of $1,063.

While under the control of Ohio State University, Continental King continued to establish himself as one of the Midwest's top performance horse sires. Among his top performers during this era were:
- Continental Charo, a 1970 black mare out of Dodson's Little Star: 1973 NRHA Futurity Reserve Champion.
- Clene Continental, a 1972 black gelding out of Mona Weimer: 1975 NRHA Futurity Champion.

After being reunited with Hutton at the University of Georgia, Continental King finished off his sterling breeding career by siring the likes of:
- Continental Pistol, a 1979 sorrel gelding out of Gunsmoke Ann: Superior reining; 1989 Youth high-point working cow horse; 1990 Youth high-point reining; Youth Superior reining; earner of 207.5 performance points (75.5 Open, 2.5 Amateur and 129.5 Youth).
- Continental Nancy, a 1982 chestnut mare out of Beauty Bird Kate: 1987 high-point reining and high-point reining mare, Superior reining, earner of 83 performance points.
- King Of Four Mac, a 1985 black stallion out of Nita Joe Wimpy: 1990 high-point reining and high-point senior reining, Superior reining, earner of 124 performance points (116.5 Open and 7.5 Amateur).

All three of these horses were trained and shown by Hutton.

"In 1982," he said, "I decided to say goodbye to the academic world and become a full-time horse breeder and trainer.

"Continental Pistol might have been the best Continental King horse I ever rode. We

Like his sire, Continental Ace was an NCHA money earner.
Courtesy Charlie Hutton

bred him at the University of Georgia, and he was out of a Mr Gunsmoke/Wimpy III-bred mare.

"I showed 'Pistol' to a Superior in reining in 1986. He wasn't a particularly good-looking horse, but he was honest. I could slide him to a stop at the same spot on the track 20 straight times and he wouldn't set up or short-stride. He just seemed to have the attitude that said, 'OK ... this is fun; let's just go do it.

"I bred Continental Nancy," Hutton continued. "She was out of a King/King Ranch-bred mare and she was one of my all-time favorites. I only got to show her as a 5-year-old in 1987. We made 52 reinings that year and won 43 of them. In the remaining nine contests, we placed second. By late September, 'Nancy' was so far ahead for the High Point title that I decided to use her to put on a reining clinic in Virginia. We got into a trailer wreck, and she and another horse were killed."

King Of Four Mac, a 1985 black stallion by Continental King and out of Nita Joe Wimpy, was endowed with his sire's beautiful head and big, intelligent-looking eye.

Photo by Cindy Coke, courtesy Charlie Hutton

King Of Four Mac, the final member of the Georgia-era Continental King stars, was bred by Cliff McGaughey Jr. of College Park, Georgia.

"King Of Four Mac had kind of a funny name," Hutton said. "Cliff's family was comprised of him, his wife and their two children. That made four 'Macs,' and that's why he named the horse the way he did.

"I sold King Of Four Mac to Henry Lee of Alma, Georgia, and showed him to the 1990 honor roll reining title. Then, later, I showed him for two subsequent owners, Eric Storey of Henagar, Alabama, and Jerry Stover of Ellijay, Georgia.

"Of all the Continental Kings that I was associated with, King Of Four Mac was probably the most like his sire. Color-wise, they were both non-fading blacks; they didn't turn brown when they were out on pasture.

"And both horses had the same big, intelligent-looking eye and were kind-dispositioned. They even both turned out a little on their right front leg; not enough to hurt them

or cause them to break down, but turned out never-the-less.

"I thought enough of King Of Four Mac to eventually add two of his daughters—SF Kings First Lady and SF Skidboots—to our broodmare band," continued Hutton. "I showed 'First Lady' to the 1993 high-point reining horse title and, at one point, won 18 reinings in a row with her. 'Skidboots' was also a top show horse and earned 74 points in six events."

Continental King's final siring record was one to be proud of. According to AQHA records, he was the sire of 272 horses. Of these, 59 were performers and they earned two high-point titles, four Superior performance awards and 22 performance ROMs (19 Open and three youth). In addition, they tallied 28 halter and 1,078 performance points (810 Open, 21.5 Amateur and 246.5 Youth). In NCHA and NRHA competition, in an era of low purses they still earned $7,675 and $13,478, respectively.

Continental King was also the maternal grandsire of 181 performers that earned one Amateur world championship, two Amateur high-point titles; 16 Superior performance awards (seven Open, five Amateur and four Youth); and 44 performance ROMs (24 Open, 12 Amateur and eight Youth). In addition, they tallied 27.5 halter and 4,003.5 performance points. In NCHA competition, they earned $266,661, and in NRHA competition, they earned $268,212.

Several years after getting Kinger back under his control at the University of Georgia, Hutton decided to give the aged stallion one last crack at arena competition.

"Back when Bill Horn was showing Kinger," said Hutton, "he used him as a cutting turnback horse. The horse had tons of 'cow' and, at some point, Bill managed to convince the Glenns to let him show in some NCHA contests. In fact, when Kinger was 11, he was the Ohio State Champion Novice Horse.

"One day in 1979, I got to studying Kinger's show record and realized that he only lacked a few dollars in earnings to qualify for his NCHA Certificate of Achievement (COA) award. So, I started cutting on him, took him to a few contests and finished off his COA. He was 21 years old at the time.

"If he'd been given the chance," he continued, "Kinger would have made a great cutting horse. He would turn as hard on a running cow as any horse I ever rode; and he wouldn't come up. He'd keep his head dead-level with the cow."

Several years after procuring Continental King for the University of Georgia, Hutton managed to also add one of his top sons to the college's equine program.

"We ran the horse program as a self-sus-taining business," he said. "We took in income, and we paid our own bills. By early 1979, Continental King had made us so much stud fee money that I was able to purchase Continental Ace for the program.

"At the time we bought him from Chelsea Rodeffer of Lewisburg, Ohio, he had earned seven reining points. I put him back in training and then showed him to his Superior reining award."

In 1980, Hutton decided to use his famous father/son equine duo in an impromptu college demonstration.

"When Kinger was 22," he said, "I gave a cutting demonstration to some of my college students. First, I cut a few head with Continental Ace. Then I told the students, 'Now I'll show you what the old man can do.'

King Of Four Mac was the 1990 High Point Reining Horse. Shown by Charlie Hutton, he was also a Superior reining horse and the earner of 124 performance points. **Photo by Dick Waltenberry, courtesy Charlie Hutton**

The blood of Continental King has continued to impact the reining industry. Aces Command, a 1978 bay gelding by Continental Ace and out of Sweet Command, was the 1981 NRHA Futurity Champion.

Courtesy NRHA

"Kinger flat out-performed 'Ace.' After I got off, I told the class that was the last time I'd ever show the horse a cow. He still had so much 'try' in him that I was afraid he'd hurt himself going after one."

By the mid-1980s, Continental King was approaching the end of his tenure at the University of Georgia.

"When I left the university," Hutton said, "I told the people that I worked for to let me know when Kinger was of no further use to them. I told them that, if they'd just call me, I'd come up and get him one last time and see to it that he lived out his life in comfort.

"In the summer of 1984, they did just that. They told me that Kinger had gone sterile. Well, I knew that old horse better than anyone. He'd been a pasture-breeder, and he'd been used in an A.I. program. I suspected that he just didn't want to be collected anymore.

"I was living at Paradise Manor Farm in Albany, Georgia, at the time. I went up and got him and, after we arrived home, I turned him out with the only two open mares I had. He got them both in foal."

Over the course of the summer, fall and early winter, Continental King enjoyed his life of total retirement. He spent the bulk of the winter months with an old palomino granddaughter of Otoe as a companion.

In the spring of 1985, he managed to get yet another mare in foal. By mid-summer, it was apparent that Continental King was nearing the end of his days.

"Even at age 27," Hutton said, "Kinger was remarkably sound on his legs. His teeth were pretty much all gone, though, and he just seemed tired.

"We brought him in and put him in a box stall every night. On the evening of July 24, 1985, he laid down on his side. I knew the end was near, so I stayed with him until around 11 o'clock. Then, my son David, said, 'You go to bed, dad. I'll stay with him and let you know if anything happens.'

"At 2 a.m., David woke me and said, 'He just went to sleep. He never rolled, he never kicked, he just went to sleep and never woke up.'

"So, we had him buried on a little hill overlooking our arena."

In 1988, Continental King was accorded the singular honor of being the first horse inducted into the NRHA Hall of Fame.

"If I had to sum up Continental King in just a few words," Hutton said, "I would say that he was a horse that lived his entire life with 'quiet dignity.' He was never any problem to be around, he was one of the most intelligent and kind horses imaginable, and he was honest to a fault.

"Honesty—in horses and people—is a trait that cannot be valued too highly.

"And, Continental King was a true representative of the family of horses he came from. He, like all of the King horses I ever had anything to do with, was a good-minded, trainable horse that retained what he was taught. And he passed those critical characteristics on to his descendants, three and four generations down the line."

As a member of King P-234's last foal crop, Continental King's life amounted to something of a swan song. He was his legendary sire's last show ring superstar, and he helped write a fitting final chapter to one of the greatest Quarter Horse stories of all time.

Spirit of Five, a 1984 bay mare by Brinks Hickory Joe and out of Continental Stormy, was the 1987 NRHA Futurity Champion. Like Aces Command, "Spirit" was ridden to her big win by Bill Horn.

Photo by Dick Waltenberry, courtesy NRHA

Chapter 16

THE KING'S COURT

Gay Widow was the first of the noteworthy King show mares. Owned by Julia Reed of Meridian, Texas, the 1950 sorrel mare was an AQHA Champion, a Superior halter horse and the earner of 105 halter points.

Photo by James Cathey, courtesy Quarter Horse Journal

King's Francis, a 1956 bay mare by King and out of Wimpess, qualified as an AQHA Champion in 1960.
Photo by James Cathey, courtesy Quarter Horse Journal

From the very onset of his breeding career, King P-234 proved himself to be a "sire of sires." His eldest sons, such as Hank H, Royal King and Poco Bueno, were instrumental in creating the AQHA foundation gene pool. And subsequent sons, such as Power Command, King's Pistol, Easter King, King Glo and Continental King, played important roles in supplying the specialized cutting and reining industries' with many of their early-day horses.

But King was more than just a sire of sons; he was also undeniably one of the breed's first great show mare and broodmare sires.

Gay Widow, a 1950 sorrel mare out of Happy Gal, was the standard-bearer of the show mares.

Bred by Jess Hankins of Rocksprings, Texas, Gay Widow made news when she was purchased for $5,000 by teenaged Julia Reed of Meridian, Texas. The athletic mare added to her fame when, in 1953, she became King's first AQHA Champion daughter, and then permanently secured her spot in Quarter Horse history when she gave birth to a son named Gay Bar King in 1958.

Among King's other top AQHA Champion daughters were J. M. Frost III's Red Bud L, Little Alice L and Rose King (see Chapter 6). And such outstanding performers as King's Francis and King's Madam joined them on the AQHA Champion rolls.

Asbeck's Billie, a 1948 bay mare out of Billy Jack, was one of her era's top cutting horses. In AQHA competition, she earned 47 performance points. In NCHA competition, she earned $23,069. Olga Fay, a 1950 bay mare out of Bo Dell 9, earned 57 performance points and a Superior in cutting.

In reining competition, Martha King, a 1954 chestnut mare out of Fanny H, finished the 1958 show season as the high-point reining mare.

King's Madam, a 1950 sorrel mare by King and out of Turner's Honky Tonk, was an AQHA Champion and the NCHA earner of $1,173.

Photo by James Cathey, courtesy Quarter Horse Journal

As noted as they were as show horses though, the main contribution of the King mares was as producers of both race- and show horses.

AQHA records show King to have been the maternal grandsire of 206 race starters. They accumulated one world championship, three Superior race awards, 94 race Registers of Merit and earned $22,288.

On the show horse side, King was the maternal grandsire of 280 halter point earners and 375 performance point earners. They amassed six world championships (three Open, one Amateur and two Youth), five reserve world championships (two Amateur and three Youth) and nine high-point wins (seven Open, one Amateur and one Youth).

They also qualified for 51 AQHA championships (50 Open and one Youth); 19 Superior halter awards; 35 Superior performance awards (26 Open, one Amateur and six Youth); 235 performance ROMs (210 Open, two Amateur and 23 Youth); and tallied 4,633 halter and 8,298 performance points. In NCHA competition, they earned $281,013.

Heading the list of vaunted King producers has to be O'Quinn Midget, Red Bud L and Totsey H.

O'Quinn Midget, a 1943 sorrel mare out of Midget's Mother, was bred by Harry Brigham of Houston, Texas. Sold to O. C. "Preacher" O'Quinn of Houston, Texas, she produced:

- Super Charge, a 1951 sorrel stallion by Depth Charge (TB): 1953 World Champion Quarter Running 2-Year-Old Colt, Superior racehorse, S.I. 100.
- Leo's Midget, a 1956 sorrel mare by Leo: S.I. 95.
- Barbara Leo, a 1959 sorrel mare by Leo: S.I. 95.
- Midget O'Quinn, a 1962 sorrel mare by Three Bars (TB): S.I. 95.
- O'Quinn's Bar, a 1964 sorrel stallion by Three Bars (TB): S.I. 95.

Red Bud L, a 1945 roan mare by King and out of Roan Alice L, was bred by Suel Lanning of Rocksprings, Texas. Sold to J. M. Frost III of Houston, Texas, she produced:

- Red Rueben, a 1956 bay stallion by Bay Bob: AQHA Champion.
- Red Bars, a 1957 sorrel mare by Three Bars (TB): AQHA Champion, Superior halter and earner of 126 halter points.
- Little Rayleen, a 1958 bay mare by Leon Bars: 1962 high-point calf roping mare and AQHA Champion.
- Eyes Of Texas, a 1962 brown stallion by Three Bars (TB): AQHA Champion.

King Lucky Bar, a 1961 sorrel stallion by Lucky Bar and out of King's Madam, was an AQHA Champion and a Superior halter horse. **Photo by Dick Harman, courtesy Quarter Horse Journal**

Totsey H, a 1947 sorrel mare by King and out of Little Britches H, was bred by Jess Hankins of Rocksprings, Texas. Sold to the Grafe-Callahan Construction Company of Santa Paula, California, she produced:
• Jimeny Jumpup, a 1955 dun stallion by Pretty Pokey: AQHA Champion.
• King Leo Bar, a 1957 sorrel stallion by Leo Bar: S.I. 95, AQHA Champion.
• Breeze Bar Lady, a 1964 sorrel mare by Breeze Bar: AQHA Champion.

Numerous other King daughters proved to be excellent producers, as well.

Brownie Hargrove, Carol's Ethel, King's May Day, King's Trinket, L H Susie, May King, Mayme H, Willful Miss and Winnetka were all high-point and/or world champion producers.

Bitsy, Clyde Sis, King's Fleet, King's Madam, Lady H King, Molly Dolly, Red Jane C, Rocky Pearce and Sonora Honey Kay were multiple AQHA Champion and/or Superior award producers.

And the power of the distaff side of the King line has endured. Of the current top 10 all-time leading dams of NRHA money earners, all 10 trace to King from one to nine times. Of the current top 10 all-time leading dams of NCHA money earners, nine trace to King from one to four times.

Moreover, the daughters of King proved time after time that they could be crossed on virtually any other line of horses and consistently produce offspring that were a marked improvement over both sire and dam.

Finally, the King mares became renowned as "stud's mothers." Among the next-generation sires they contributed to the breed were Okie Leo, Leo Bob, Joe Cody, Aledo Bar, Blondy's Dude, Gay Bar King, Smooth Herman, Super Charge, Speedy Peake, King Lauro, Poco Dondi and Wallaby.

As show horses, performers and producers, King's "Court" served its family well and helped assure that it prospered for generations to come.

Martha King, a 1954 chestnut mare by King and out of Fanny H, was the 1958 high-point reining mare. She is seen here with Matlock Rose in the saddle after winning the junior reining at the 1958 Houston Fat Stock Show.

Photo by James Cathey, courtesy Quarter Horse Journal

Asbeck's Billie, a 1948 bay mare by King and out of Billy Jack, was one of her sire's top NCHA performers.
Photo by James Cathey, courtesy Quarter Horse Journal

Olga Fay, a 1950 bay mare by King and out of Bo Dell 9, earned a Superior cutting award.

**Courtesy
Quarter Horse Journal**

Super Charge, a 1951 sorrel stallion by Depth Charge (TB) and out of O'Quinn Midget by King, was a typical example of the reproductive power of the King mares. The 1953 Champion Quarter Running 2-Year-Old Colt, Super Charge was also a two-time stakes winner and a track record holder.

Photo by John Williamson, courtesy Quarter Horse Journal

Red Bars, a 1957 sorrel mare by Three Bars (TB) and out of Red Bud L by King, was one of the top show mares of her era. She is shown here with Ford Frost and J. M. Frost III after being named grand champion mare at the 1964 Houston Livestock Show in Houston, Texas. ***Photo by Jim Keeland, courtesy Quarter Horse Journal***

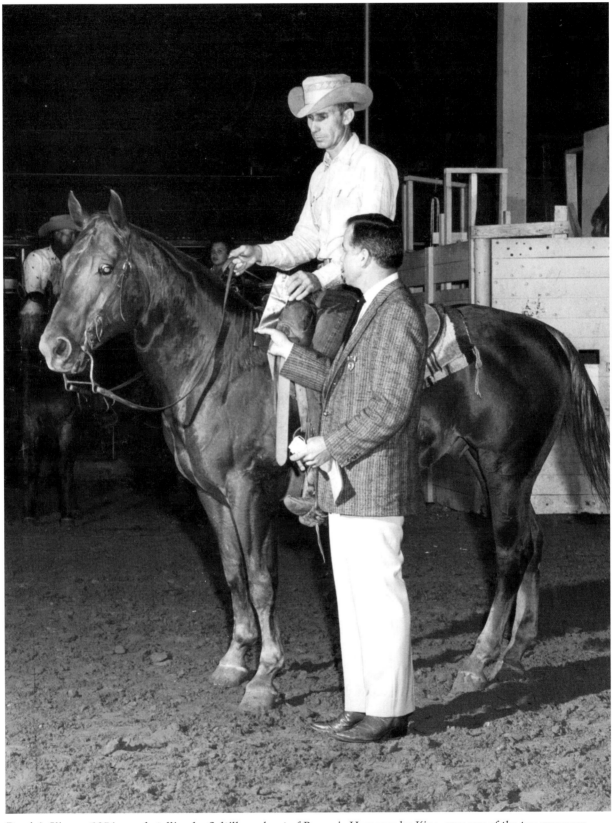

Rondo's King, a 1954 sorrel stallion by Saltillo and out of Brownie Hargrove by King, was one of the top arena performers of his era. Ridden by NRHA Hall of Fame horseman Dale Wilkinson, Rondo's King was the 1958 high-point reining horse.

Photo by Squire Haskins, courtesy Quarter Horse Journal

Sonora Sorrel, a 1957 sorrel gelding by Lauro and out of L H Susie by King, was also one of the top halter horses of his era. The 1964 high-point halter horse, he was an AQHA Champion and the earner of 672 halter points.

Photo by Darol Dickinson, courtesy Quarter Horse Journal

Alf, a 1958 sorrel gelding by Leon Bars and out of King's Fleet by King, was an AQHA Champion and a Superior halter, Western pleasure and reining horse.   **Courtesy Quarter Horse Journal**

King Leo Bar, a 1957 sorrel stallion by Leo Bar and out of Totsey H by King, was an AQHA Champion show horse. Retired to stud, he became one of the Northwest region's top sires.

Photo by J. F. Malony, *courtesy* **Quarter Horse Journal**

Janie Bar, a 1960 sorrel mare by Doc Bar and out of Red Jane C by King, was a talented two-way performer. In the show ring, she was an AQHA Champion, Superior halter horse and the earner of 113 halter points. In the cutting arena, she was a Superior cutting horse and the NCHA earner of $10,560.

Photo by Western Livestock Journal, *courtesy* **Quarter Horse Journal**

Poco Dondi, a 1956 sorrel stallion by Poco Dell and out of Miss Lady by King, was an AQHA Champion, Superior halter horse and the earner of 135 halter points. Seen here with his breeder and owner, Jimmie Randals of Montoya, New Mexico, the double-bred King descendant became a top sire. **Courtesy Quarter Horse Journal**

Phantom Bar, a 1965 black stallion by Three Chicks and out of King's Sukey by King, was a Superior halter horse and the earner of 139 halter points. **Photo by H. D. Dolcater, courtesy Quarter Horse Journal**

Chapter 17

A ROYAL LEGACY

King P-234, shown here in a circa early 1950s photo, has positively influenced the Quarter Horse breed as few other foundation horses have. **Courtesy American Quarter Horse Heritage Center & Museum**

Likewise, the Hankins brothers—Jess, Lowell and J. O.—helped lay the foundation for one of the industry's most enduring lines. **Photo by Jim Jennings, courtesy Quarter Horse Journal**

King P-234 was, at the time of his death, the most prominent Quarter Horse stallion in the world. While at first glance that statement might seem a little strong, the facts bear it out.

To begin with, King and his two best-known sons—Royal King and Poco Bueno—were prolific sires. King sired a total of 658 AQHA-registered get from 23 foal crops. Royal King sired 590 registered get, and Poco Bueno sired 405. These figures might pale in comparison to those put up by today's stallions, bolstered as they are by the advantages of artificial insemination and shipped semen. But in the horse breeding world that existed in the 1940s and 1950s, the King trio's reproductive numbers were huge.

Then, too, King P-234's final tally as a sire was an exemplary one, and one that no stallion up to that point had ever achieved.

In show and performance competition, King was represented by 234 performers that amassed 20 AQHA championships, three Superior halter awards, 10 Superior perform-ance awards and 84 Registers of Merit. In addition, they earned 1,088 halter points and 2,061 performance points (2,030 Open and 31 Youth). In race competition, the legendary stallion had 35 starters that earned 12 ROMs.

Finally, one of the most prestigious barometers by which the worth of an individual horse and his contributions is measured is whether or not he (or she) is of Hall of Fame caliber.

The inaugural AQHA Hall of Fame class was inducted in 1989. King was among the four horses to make it in on that initial ballot. Leo, Three Bars and Wimpy P-1 were the remaining three. In due time, five more of King's get and grandget were enshrined: Poco Bueno (1990), Poco Lena (1991), Joe Cody (1995), Royal King (1997) and Blondy's Dude (2001).

The NCHA Hall of Fame was instituted in 1962. Its initial class of inductees was comprised of nine horses, all of whom were King grandget: Poco Lena, Poco Mona, Poco Stampede and Miss Nancy Bailey. This quartet was followed in short order by five more King grandget: Miss Elite (1962), Hoppen (1965), Alice Star (1969), Chickasha Dan (1970) and Annie Glo (1979).

The NRHA Hall of Fame was instituted in 1988. As detailed previously, its sole inaugural inductee was Continental King. He was followed in short order by six additional King descendants: Joe Cody (1989), Enterprise Lady (1990), Glenda Echols (1990), High Proof (1991), Hollywood Smoke (1992) and Hollywood Jac 86 (1993).

The statement bears repeating: King P-234 was, at the time of his death, the most prominent Quarter Horse stallion in the world.

As detailed throughout this book, King and his first-generation offspring were instrumental in taking the original Billy blood of South Texas, refining it and then dispersing it throughout the country. Their influence was of particular import as AQHA and its offshoot organizations—AQRA, NCHA and NRHA—were founded and nurtured into the multi-million dollar organizations that they are today.

After King's death, his sons and daughters were quick to pick up his banner and carry it forward.

Poco Bueno, buoyed by the vast resources of the Waggoner Ranch, was especially

Jazzote, a 1977 sorrel stallion by Doc Quixote and out of Queen Vicky, traces to King four times and Royal King twice. An NCHA Hall of Fame horse, he was the 1986 NCHA Open World Champion and the earner of $504,286.

Photo by Don Shugart, courtesy Quarter Horse Journal

Bob Acre Doc, a 1981 chestnut stallion by Son Ofa Doc and out of Sapp's Sandy, traces to King once through Royal King. An NCHA Hall of Fame horse, he was the 1991 NCHA Open World Champion and the earner of $381,703.

Photo by Dalco, courtesy Quarter Horse Journal

instrumental. His sons and daughters, in turn, went on to exert a tremendous positive influence on the halter, cutting and reining segments of the Quarter Horse industry in the 1950s and 1960s.

Royal King, without the benefit of a million-dollar bank account, also exerted a tremendous impact on the industry. More so than even his famous sire and half-brother, his genetic potency is still reverberating throughout the cutting industry.

In today's cutting horse world, bloodlines are of paramount importance and are studied by both aspiring and veteran breeders alike to a degree never before seen. On the paternal side, the blood of the "Peppy," "Freckles" and "Doc Bar" horses dominate. On the

maternal side, the blood of Royal King holds sway. Among the top modern-day cutting horse competitors who trace one or more times to Royal King are:

- Royal Blue Boon—$381,764 and dam of the earners of more than $2.3 million.
- Jazabell Quixote—dam of the earners of more than $1.2 million.
- Smart Peppy—dam of the earners of more than $1.1 million.
- That Smarts—dam of the earners of more than $875,000.
- Little Pepto Girl—2002 NCHA Horse of the Year, $349,308.
- Justa Smart Peanut—2001 NCHA Horse of the Year, $353,414.

Jae Bar Fletch, a 1980 sorrel stallion by Doc's Jack Sprat and out of Jae Bar Lena, traces to King four times and Royal King once. An NCHA Hall of Fame horse, he was the 1989 NCHA Open World Champion and earned $454,416.

***Courtesy* Quarter Horse Journal**

- Shania Cee—2000 NCHA Horse of the Year, 1999 Futurity Open Champion, $399,028.
- Shakin Flo—1998 NCHA Horse of the Year, $417,109.
- Not Quite An Acre—1997 NCHA Horse of the Year, $153,256.
- Hollywood Nus Bar—2003 NCHA Open World Champion, $102,472.
- Rosies Lena—2001 NCHA Open World Champion, $281,116.
- Go Little Lena—1998 NCHA Open World Champion, $136,144.
- Boon San Lena—1994 NCHA Open World Champion, $118,782.
- Bet Yer Blue Boons—2000 NCHA Open World Champion, $350,615.
- Bob Acre Doc—1991 NCHA Open World Champion, NCHA Hall of Fame, $381,703.
- Jae Bar Fletch—1989 NCHA Open World Champion, NCHA Hall of Fame, $422,935.
- Jazzote—1986 NCHA Open World Champion, NCHA Hall of Fame, $586,212.
- Doc Wilson—NCHA Hall of Fame, $124,614.
- Red White and Boon—$839,464 and counting (see opposite page).
- Royal Blue Boon—$381,764 and dam of the earners of more than $2.3 million.
- Pappion Cat—$362,466.
- One Smart Lookin Cat—2003 Futurity Open Champion, $225,310.
- Royal Fletch—2000 Futurity Open Champion, $206,059.• Dainty Playgirl—1998 Futurity Open Champion, $269,122.

- Some Kinda Memories—1997 Futurity Open Champion, $363,546.
- Peptoboonsmal—1995 Futurity Open Champion, $165,308.
- Bobs Smokin Joe—1993 Futurity Open Champion, $267,257.
- July Jazz—1989 Futurity Open Champion, $289,540.
- Smart Little Senor—1988 Futurity Open Champion, $329,351.
- Smart Date—1987 Futurity Open Champion, $142,511.
- Royal Silver King—1986 Futurity Open Champion, $164,065.
- Smart Little Lena—1982 Futurity Open Champion, $743,275.
- Mis Royal Mahogany—1980 Futurity Open Champion, $147,999.
- Lynx Melody—1978 Futurity Open Champion, $113,681.

Poco Bueno is often portrayed as the one horse that was most responsible for King P-234's meteoric rise as a sire. In retrospect, that designation must be at least be shared with Royal King. As noted previously, the AQHA Hall of Fame trio of King, Poco Bueno and Royal King passed away in 1958, 1969 and 1971 respectively

By the early part of the new millennium, the pioneering trio of Hankins brothers had likewise passed from the scene. Jess, the oldest of the three, passed away on October 16, 1994. Lowell, the middle brother, passed away on October 28, 2000, and J.O passed away on May 11, 2002.

Royal Fletch, a 1997 sorrel stallion by Jae Bar Fletch and out of Royal Blue Dually, traces to King eight times and Royal King three times. The 2000 Futurity Open Champion, he earned $235,098.

Photo by Don Shugart, courtesy Quarter Horse Journal

Red White And Boon,
a 1988 red roan gelding by Smart Little Lena and out of Royal Blue Boon, traces to King P-234 seven times, Royal King three times and Poco Bueno twice. Bred by Larry Hall of Weatherford, Texas, and owned by Jim and Mary Jo Milner of Southlake, Texas, "Red" was the 1992 NCHA Derby Reserve Champion.

The durable campaigner has helped Mary Jo win four straight NCHA Non-Pro World Championships (2000-2003) and is on track to add a fifth title.

Red White And Boon is ranked second on NCHA's list of all-time leading money earners with $841,885 (as of November 1, 2004). He remains hale and hearty at age 16, and an odds-on favorite to eventually become the number one money-earning cutting horse of all time.

Red White And Boon and Mary Jo Milner have established themselves as one of the top Non-Pro cutting duos of all time.
Photo by Ross Hecox, courtesy NCHA

As of November 1, 2004, the colorful, line-bred King descendant has amassed more than $841,000 in NCHA earnings.
Photo by Don Shugart, courtesy NCHA

Alisa Lark, a 1969 brown mare by Leolark and out of Aliso Gill 3, was a Billy/King descendant through Sorrel Sue and Queen Ann. One of the top Youth horses of her era, she earned five Youth world titles.

Photo by Jill Landers, courtesy Quarter Horse Journal

Rugged Lark, a 1981 bay stallion by Really Rugged (TB) and out of Alisa Lark, was the 1985 and 1987 AQHA World Show Superhorse. The charismatic show and breeding superstar, who passed away in October of 2004, represented yet another milestone in the evolution of a Quarter Horse line that can trace its roots to post-Civil War South Texas.

Photo by Mary Phelps, courtesy Lynn Salvatori Palm

The seeds that the Hankins clan planted in a South Texas horse climate that is far removed from the Quarter Horse world of today were sown in the late 1930s and 1940s. They sprouted and took hold in the 1950s and 1960s, and have continued to blossom and bear fruit in the ensuing years.

In today's Quarter Horse environment, from halter to cutting to reining, and from Western pleasure to barrel racing to rodeo competition at all levels, the blood of the King horses continues to flow.

It's doubtful that those who were involved with the legendary South Texas "Billy" horse during his early years could comprehend the eventual impact that their contributions would have on the history of the Western horse.

The involvement of each and every one of those early-day Quarter Horse pioneers played an integral part in fashioning the King P-234 life story.

One of the most significant events in that long and colorful tale might have occurred in the mid-1930s, when Mrs. Byrne James of Encinal, Texas, decided that she didn't like the name of the young mahogany bay Quarter Horse stallion that her husband had just acquired. The breed owes the insightful young rancher's wife a debt of gratitude for that revelation and subsequent name change.

As do I. …

After all, Buttons P-234…Cornerstone of an Industry just wouldn't have cut it as a book title.

Little Town, a 1964 chestnut stallion by Buzz Bar and out of Custus Liz, was a Billy/King descendant whose genetic make-up was enriched by the blood of Leo, Three Bars (TB) and Custus Rastus (TB). He was an AQHA Supreme Champion, AAA-rated racehorse and the earner of 230 points in racing, halter, Western pleasure, calf roping, reining, Western riding, working cow horse, hunter under saddle and pole bending. What more could anyone ask of a Western horse?
Photo by Darol Dickinson, courtesy Quarter Horse Journal

Appendix A

ALL THE KING'S MEN

King P-234 – as portrayed in a 1951 Orren Mixer painting.

King P-234 was truly a "sire of sires," and his many sons played key roles in the early development and spread of the Quarter Horse breed. While a number of the more prominent King sons have been featured in the preceding pages, 17 additional ones deserve attention and are profiled in the pages that follow.

There were still other King stallions that made solid contributions as performers and/or sires. Time and space constraints preclude covering them in this book. Suffice it to say that, without the contributions of these "unsung sons," the King story would not be nearly as long or colorful. We salute them, as well.

Beaver Creek *P-3038*

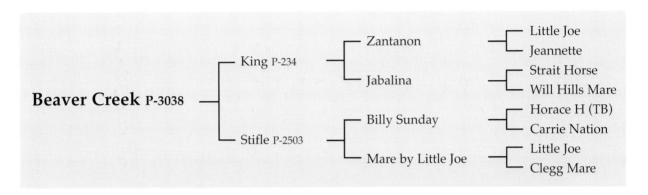

Beaver Creek P-3038

King P-234
— Zantanon
— Little Joe
— Jeannette
— Jabalina
— Strait Horse
— Will Hills Mare

Stifle P-2503
— Billy Sunday
— Horace H (TB)
— Carrie Nation
— Mare by Little Joe
— Little Joe
— Clegg Mare

Bay stallion, foaled 1944; bred by Jess L. Hankins, Rocksprings, Texas.

Beaver Creek (a.k.a. "Sundown") was purchased by E. Paul Waggoner at the Hankins Brothers 1st Production Sale, Oct. 22, 1945, San Angelo, Texas. After breaking his left front pastern, he was sold in the mid-1950s to Hoss Inman, Lamar, Colorado. He spent his last years at the Reed Hill/Mitchell Ranch, Canadian, Texas, where he died in 1961.

The sire of 236 registered foals – six AQHA Champions: Beaverette, My Beaver, Kitty Bee Creek, Starlita Creek, Beaver Bell Boy and Lucky Roan King. He also sired the earners of two Superior halter awards and 10 performance ROMs. Other notable get: Bear Creek, NCHA earner of $3,251; and Little Electra, 12-time Produce of Dam winner.

Beaver Creek was the maternal grandsire of 26 AQHA Champions (20 open, one amateur and five youth).

Bimbo Hank   P-107,691

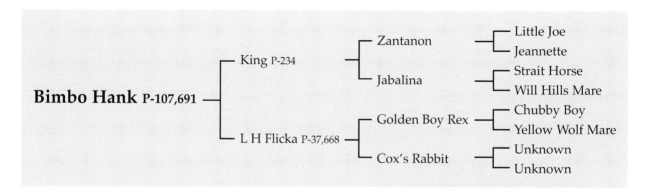

				Little Joe
			Zantanon	Jeannette
	King P-234			Strait Horse
Bimbo Hank P-107,691		Jabalina		Will Hills Mare
		Golden Boy Rex		Chubby Boy
	L H Flicka P-37,668			Yellow Wolf Mare
		Cox's Rabbit		Unknown
				Unknown

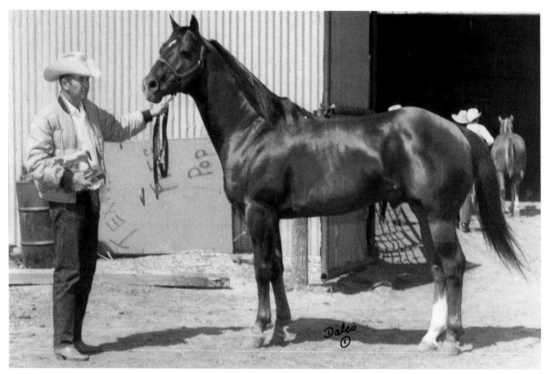

Sorrel stallion, foaled 1957; bred by Lowell F. Hankins, Rocksprings, Texas.

Bimbo Hank was owned for most of his breeding career by the partnership of F. E. Anderson and Weldon McConnell, Dublin, Texas. McConnell became the sole owner in 1969. "Bimbo" was an AQHA Champion – the last one sired by King. He also had NCHA earnings of $1,919.

The sire of 93 registered foals, including the earners of two performance ROMs. Other notable get (all NCHA money earners): King Bim, $9,497; Miss McConnell, $4,507; Old Bim, $2,307; Bimbo's Adair, $1,688; Bimbo Flash, $1,297; Cowtender King, $1,167; and Katy M King, $1,053.

Brown King H   P-20,521

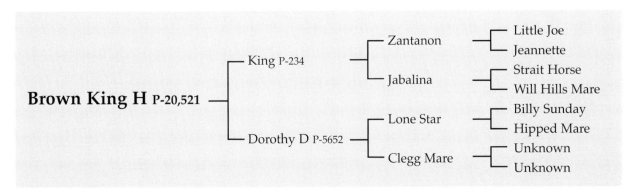

Brown King H P-20,521
- King P-234
  - Zantanon
    - Little Joe
    - Jeannette
  - Jabalina
    - Strait Horse
    - Will Hills Mare
- Dorothy D P-5652
  - Lone Star
    - Billy Sunday
    - Hipped Mare
  - Clegg Mare
    - Unknown
    - Unknown

Brown stallion, foaled 1948; bred by Jess L. Hankins, Rocksprings, Texas.

Brown King H was one of the few Kings sons to stand in California in the early 1950s. Owned by several different California breeders, he was sold in 1961 to the Double D Hereford Ranch, Eagle Point, Oregon. A Register of Merit racehorse with a AA+ rating, he set a track record for 350 yards and earned $4,711. In addition, he earned GCS honors at the Pacific Coast Quarter Horse Association Bay Meadows show.

The sire of 84 registered foals – one AQHA Champion: Top State Gold (17 open halter and 38 open performance points, 12 youth halter and 116 youth performance points). He also sired four racing ROM get: Mobile's Mite (AAA), earner of $7,288; Royal Pan (AA), earner of $4,359; Black Sapphire (AA), earner of $2,119; and King's Trudy (AA), earner of $2,373.

Captain Jess P-47,476

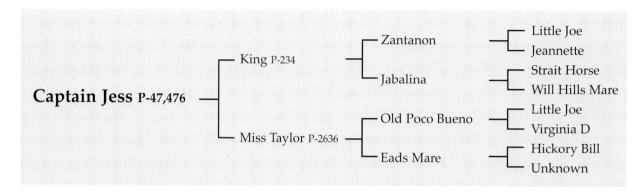

King P-234
— Zantanon
— Little Joe
— Jeannette
— Jabalina
— Strait Horse
— Will Hills Mare

Captain Jess P-47,476

Miss Taylor P-2636
— Old Poco Bueno
— Little Joe
— Virginia D
— Eads Mare
— Hickory Bill
— Unknown

Bay stallion, foaled 1953; bred by Jess L. Hankins, Rocksprings, Texas.

Captain Jess was bred and owned by Jess L. Hankins and stood at stud along side his sire. He later sold to Glenn Neans, Round Rock, Texas. He accumulated 29 performance points and had NCHA earnings of $1,404.

The sire of 224 registered foals – four AQHA Champions: Captain Joker (Superior cutting, 45 halter points, 355 performance points and NCHA earnings of $12,952);

Caliche King (Superior cutting, 25 halter points, 63 performance points and NCHA Earnings of $1,316), India Ruby (NCHA earnings of $2,495) and Captain's Bobbin (48 performance points). He also sired the earners of three 3 Superior performance awards and 16 performance ROMs. Other notable get: Captain's Bonita, NCHA earnings of $1,630; and Captain's Crest, 53.5 performance points.

Cuellar P-1821

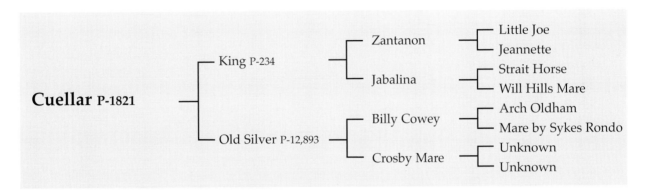

Cuellar P-1821
- King P-234
  - Zantanon
    - Little Joe
    - Jeannette
  - Jabalina
    - Strait Horse
    - Will Hills Mare
- Old Silver P-12,893
  - Billy Cowey
    - Arch Oldham
    - Mare by Sykes Rondo
  - Crosby Mare
    - Unknown
    - Unknown

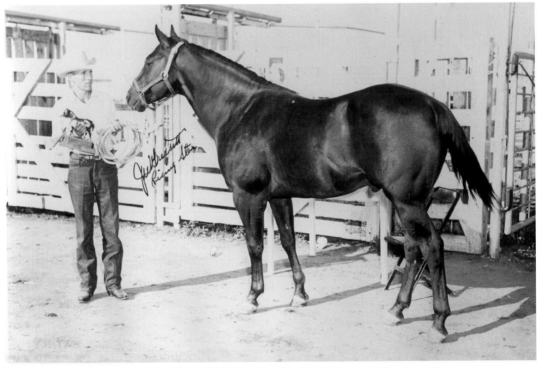

Chestnut stallion, foaled 1942; bred by Jess L. Hankins, Rocksprings, Texas.

Cuellar was owned in the 1950s by eventual AQHA President, Ed Honnen, Quincy Farms, Denver, Colorado. Cuellar suffered a heart attack and died at Quincy Farms in March, 1959.

The sire of 141 registered foals – five AQHA Champions: Quincy Lee (177 halter points), Brady Lady (136 halter points), Hill Queen, Vaquero King and Apache Quill. He also sired the earners of three Superior halter awards and 12 performance ROMs. Other notable get: Cuellar Pet, King Quilo and Cuellar Ann.

Fred B Clymer   P-58,016

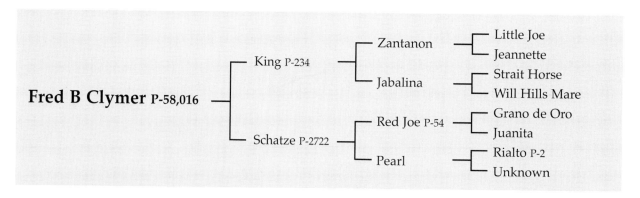

Fred B Clymer P-58,016

- King P-234
  - Zantanon
    - Little Joe
    - Jeannette
  - Jabalina
    - Strait Horse
    - Will Hills Mare
- Schatze P-2722
  - Red Joe P-54
    - Grano de Oro
    - Juanita
  - Pearl
    - Rialto P-2
    - Unknown

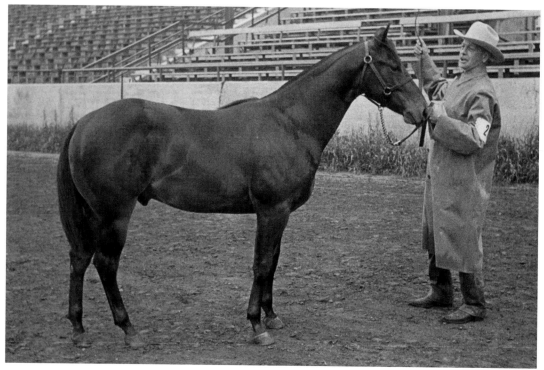

Brown stallion, foaled 1956; bred by Jess L. Hankins, Rocksprings, Texas.
(Shown here as a yearling.)

Fred B Clymer was owned first by Ted Clymer, Hudson, Wisconsin, and then by George W. Golden, Golden Ranches, Alberta, Canada. AQHA Superior cutting horse and earner of 101 open performance points. NCHA earner of $15,404, NCHA Bronze Award earner and finished in 6th place, World Champion Cutting Horses of 1966.

The sire of 101 registered foals – two AQHA Champions: Princess Pep, Franklie Freddy (Superior awards in halter, reining, western pleasure and western riding). He also sired the earners of three Superior halter awards, three Superior performance awards and 12 performance ROMs (11 open and one youth). Other notable get: Rex Clymer, NCHA earnings of $2,335.

Hill King P-51,289

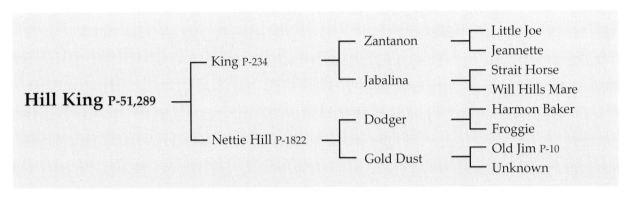

Hill King P-51,289
- King P-234
  - Zantanon
    - Little Joe
    - Jeannette
  - Jabalina
    - Strait Horse
    - Will Hills Mare
- Nettie Hill P-1822
  - Dodger
    - Harmon Baker
    - Froggie
  - Gold Dust
    - Old Jim P-10
    - Unknown

Chestnut stallion, foaled 1955; bred by J.O. Hankins, Rocksprings, Texas.

Hill King was owned during the later 1950s and early 1960s by Rhoades Bros. & Meek, Lovington, New Mexico (J.L. "Dusty Rhoades, 16th AQHA President). He was later owned by the Perry Shankle Ranch, Boerne, Texas. He was a three-time GCS and a ROM cutting horse.

The sire of 136 registered foals – six AQHA Champions (five open and one youth): Jerome King (Superiors in halter and western pleas-ure), RBM Miss Hill (Superior western pleasure, 72 performance points), Hardrock King (open and youth Champion, open and youth Superior western pleasure, 157 youth performance points), Hill King's Gal and Fiesty Nettie. He also sired the earners of six Superior awards (two halter and four performance) and 17 performance ROMs. Other notable get: Lady Capri (Superior halter) and King Burnett (55 youth performance points).

King Burke P-61,557

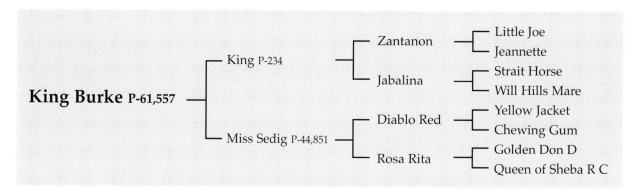

King Burke P-61,557
- King P-234
  - Zantanon
    - Little Joe
    - Jeannette
  - Jabalina
    - Strait Horse
    - Will Hills Mare
- Miss Sedig P-44,851
  - Diablo Red
    - Yellow Jacket
    - Chewing Gum
  - Rosa Rita
    - Golden Don D
    - Queen of Sheba R C

Sorrel stallion, foaled 1956; bred by E. J. Burke, Laredo, Texas.

King Burke was purchased in 1959 by Ed Honnen, Quincy Farm, Denver, Colorado, following the death of his famous King son, Cuellar.

The sire of 114 registered foals – four AQHA Champions: Quincy Dee King (52.5 performance points, NCHA earnings of $4,290); Quincy Leola (Superior halter, 75 halter points); Quincy Leora (Superior halter, 80 halter points); and Shanty Scarlet (21 halter points and 45 performance points). He also sired the earners of 10 performance ROMs (six open and four youth). Other notable get: Spanish Sun, 155 youth performance points and three youth ROMs; Kings Debbie, 66 youth performance points; and Burkie King, 39 youth performance points.

King Joe Jet P-77,349

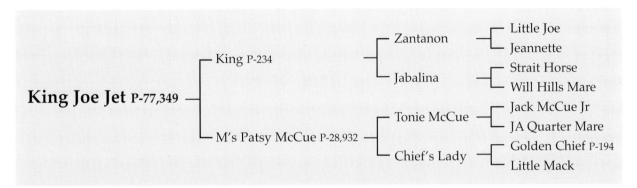

King Joe Jet P-77,349
- King P-234
  - Zantanon
    - Little Joe
    - Jeannette
  - Jabalina
    - Strait Horse
    - Will Hills Mare
- M's Patsy McCue P-28,932
  - Tonie McCue
    - Jack McCue Jr
    - JA Quarter Mare
  - Chief's Lady
    - Golden Chief P-194
    - Little Mack

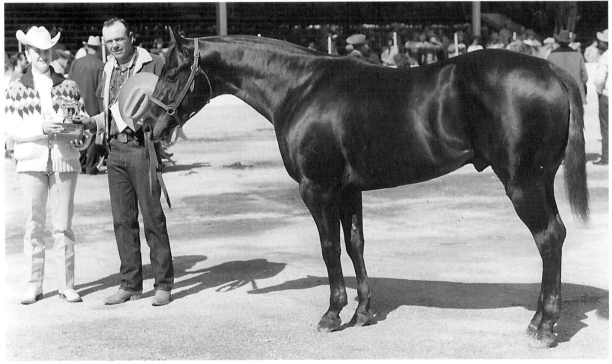

Sorrel stallion, foaled 1958; bred by Mrs. Pete Martin, Ponder, Texas.
(Shown here after being named as the reserve champion stallion at the 1961 Houston Livestock Show.)

King Joe Jet was last owned by Ralph King Jr., Winnsboro, Louisiana. He was an AQHA Champion, Superior halter horse and earned 57 halter and 64.5 performance points.

The sire of 120 registered foals – one AQHA Champion: Rock Eagle Jet (15 halter and 24 performance points). He also sired the earners of five performance ROMs (four open and one youth). Other notable get: Tioga Joe, 11 halter and 24.5 performance points, 10 halter and 12 performance points in Palomino Horse Breeders Association competition.

King Paul   P-58,697

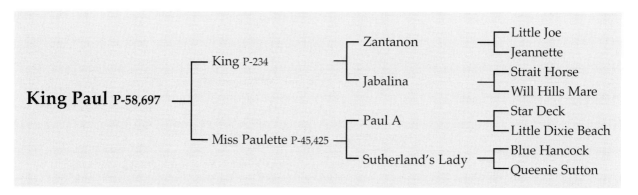

King Paul P-58,697 ┬ King P-234 ┬ Zantanon ┬ Little Joe
                   │   │   └ Jeannette
                   │   └ Jabalina ┬ Strait Horse
                   │   └ Will Hills Mare
                   └ Miss Paulette P-45,425 ┬ Paul A ┬ Star Deck
                                            │   └ Little Dixie Beach
                                            └ Sutherland's Lady ┬ Blue Hancock
                                                                └ Queenie Sutton

Grullo stallion, foaled 1956; bred by Robert Q. Sutherland, Overland Park, Kansas.

King Paul was owned first by Blue Bonnet Farms, Indianapolis, Indiana, and then for 15 years by King Brothers, Marion, Illinois. He was an ROM cutting horse.

The sire of 174 registered foals – seven AQHA Champions: Miss King Paul (231 halter points and 85 performance points), King's Bo Ka (154 open performance points and 114 youth performance points), King's Ci Bo (135 halter points), King's Blue Chip, King's Paulette, King Paulisle and Paul's Jefro. He also sired the earners of three Superior halter awards; 28 Superior performance awards (16 open, one amateur and 11 youth); and 63 performance ROMs (51 open, two amateur and 10 youth). Other notable get: Hollywood Ibby, 1975 High Point Reining Mare; Paul Bita Pleasure, 685 youth performance points; Paul's Leo Kings, 505 youth performance points; Paulite King, 267 youth performance points; and King's Kickapoo, Superior western pleasure and 90 youth performance points.

King So Big P-73,764

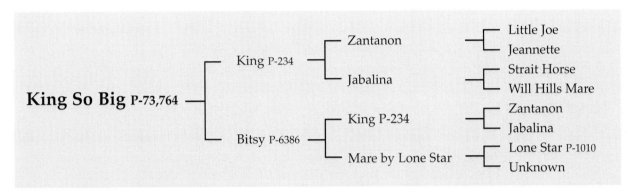

King So Big P-73,764
- King P-234
  - Zantanon
    - Little Joe
    - Jeannette
  - Jabalina
    - Strait Horse
    - Will Hills Mare
- Bitsy P-6386
  - King P-234
    - Zantanon
    - Jabalina
  - Mare by Lone Star
    - Lone Star P-1010
    - Unknown

Brown stallion, foaled 1956; bred by J. O. Hankins, Rocksprings, Texas.
(Photo not available; above painting is of King P-234)

King So Big was owned and campaigned for most of his career by Dr. Cecil and Robert Lorio, Port Allen, Louisiana. He was an AQHA Champion, Superior Cutting Horse, earned 15 halter points, 75.5 performance points and had NCHA earnings of $1,784. As a junior cutting horse, he placed first at Birmingham, Alabama; Natchez, Mississippi; Bryan, Texas; Brenham, Texas; and Orange, Texas.

The sire of 86 registered foals including So Big's Fancy, Open and Youth AQHA Champion, Superior youth showmanship, 92.5 youth performance points; and So Big's Cat, 51.5 youth performance points. He also sired the earners of 10 performance ROMs (8 open and 2 youth).

King Wimp P-81,019

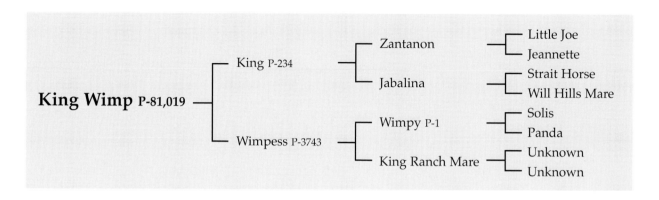

King Wimp P-81,019 ── King P-234 ──┬── Zantanon ──┬── Little Joe
                                    │   └── Jeannette
                                    └── Jabalina ──┬── Strait Horse
                                                   └── Will Hills Mare

                  └── Wimpess P-3743 ──┬── Wimpy P-1 ──┬── Solis
                                       │   └── Panda
                                       └── King Ranch Mare ──┬── Unknown
                                                             └── Unknown

Sorrel stallion, foaled 1956; bred by Jess L. Hankins, Rocksprings, Texas.
(Photo not available; above painting is of King P-234.)

King Wimp was owned by F. E. Anderson, Dallas, Texas. He was an AQHA Champion.

The sire of 191 registered foals – three AQHA Champions: Cody Wimp (30 halter and 45 performance points); King Wimp Redman (Superior western pleasure, 90 open and 43 youth performance points); and King Wimp Mr (Superior western pleasure and 71.5 performance points). He also sired the earners of four Superior awards and 12 performance ROMs (10 open and 2 youth). Other notable get: Wimp Eight, Superior reining; King Wimp Twist, Superior cutting and NCHA earnings of $2,789; and Skippers Wimp, 1983 and 1984 Palomino Horse Breeders Association Reserve world Champion Performance Horse, 2,320 PHBA points.

Little Tom B   P-9259

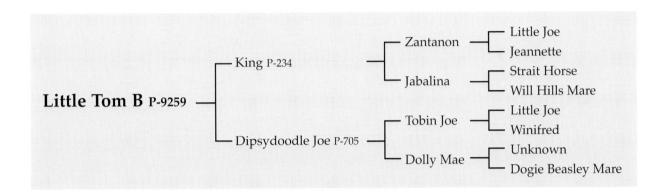

Little Tom B P-9259 ─┬─ King P-234 ─┬─ Zantanon ─┬─ Little Joe
                     │   │   └─ Jeannette
                     │   └─ Jabalina ──┬─ Strait Horse
                     │   └─ Will Hills Mare
                     └─ Dipsydoodle Joe P-705 ─┬─ Tobin Joe ─┬─ Little Joe
                                               │   └─ Winifred
                                               └─ Dolly Mae ─┬─ Unknown
                                                             └─ Dogie Beasley Mare

Bay stallion, foaled 1945; bred by H. W. Bierschwale, Rocksprings, Texas.

Little Tom B was purchased in October 1947 by his second and final owner, C. E. Hobgood, Lubbock, Texas.

The sire of 212 registered foals – five AQHA Champions: Stage Bird Tom (Superior halter, 77 halter points and 54 performance points), Little Tom Rose (42 performance points and NCHA earnings of $1,498), Tom B Man (Superior halter and 65 halter points), Little Tom B Traveler and Beste's Tom. He also sired the earners of two Superior halter awards and 13 performance ROMs. Other notable get: With Respect, $1,181 race earnings; Rocky Tom Bee, 34 halter points and performance ROM; and Miss Baker Hobgood, 32 halter points.

Mr Harmon P-42,705

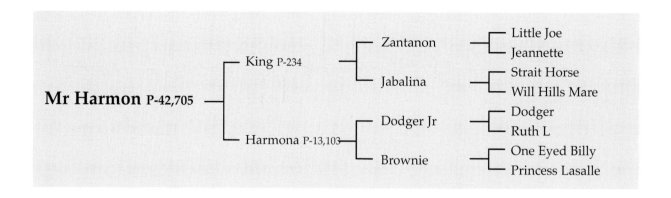

Mr Harmon P-42,705 ─┬─ King P-234 ─┬─ Zantanon ─┬─ Little Joe
                    │   │   └─ Jeannette
                    │   └─ Jabalina ─┬─ Strait Horse
                    │   └─ Will Hills Mare
                    └─ Harmona P-13,103 ─┬─ Dodger Jr ─┬─ Dodger
                                         │   └─ Ruth L
                                         └─ Brownie ─┬─ One Eyed Billy
                                                     └─ Princess Lasalle

Bay stallion, foaled 1950; bred by Jess L. Hankins, Rocksprings, Texas.

Mr Harmon was owned and shown to most of his cutting accolades by his last owner, Percy W. Bailey, Beaumont, Texas. He was an AQHA Champion, Superior cutting horse and the earner of 15 halter points and 103.5 performance points. In NCHA competition, he earned $12,631. He finished the 1961 NCHA World Champion Cutting Horse competition in 16th place, ahead of such notables as Poco Stampede, Vegas Boy and Hoppen.

The sire of 68 registered foals and the earners of four performance ROMs.

Scharbauer's King P-29,406

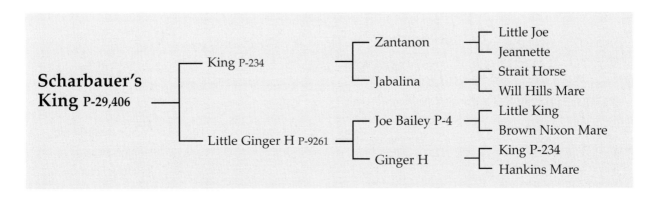

			Little Joe
		Zantanon	Jeannette
	King P-234		Strait Horse
		Jabalina	Will Hills Mare
Scharbauer's King P-29,406			Little King
		Joe Bailey P-4	Brown Nixon Mare
	Little Ginger H P-9261		King P-234
		Ginger H	Hankins Mare

Black stallion, foaled 1949; bred by Jess L. Hankins, Rocksprings, Texas.
(Photo not available; above painting is of King P-234)

Scharbauer's King was purchased as a weanling by Clarence Scharbauer Jr., Midland, Texas (AQHA 25th President). He spent his entire life as a Scharbauer Ranch working horse and sire.

The sire of 130 registered foals – seven AQHA Champions: Kid Five (NCHA earnings of $5,103); Pardner Five (80 open and 115 youth performance points); Liz Five (Superior halter and western pleasure); Betsy Cee (Superior halter, 91 halter points); Fifi King (44 halter points); Fortunate Five and Little Bit Five. He also sired the earners of three Superior awards (two halter and one performance) and 17 performance ROMs (15 open and 2 youth).

Tabano King   P-84,928

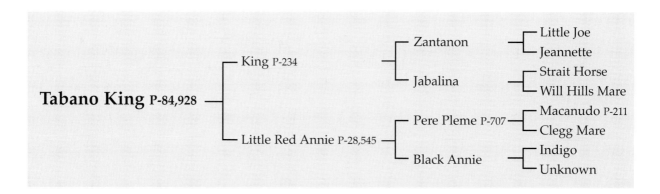

Tabano King **P-84,928** ─┬─ King P-234 ─┬─ Zantanon ─┬─ Little Joe
│   │   └─ Jeannette
│   └─ Jabalina ─┬─ Strait Horse
│   └─ Will Hills Mare
└─ Little Red Annie P-28,545 ─┬─ Pere Pleme P-707 ─┬─ Macanudo P-211
                              │   └─ Clegg Mare
                              └─ Black Annie ─┬─ Indigo
                                             └─ Unknown

Bay stallion, foaled 1956; bred by Emmett Donegan, Sequin, Texas.

Tabano King was owned by two farms for most of his breeding career – Circle 5 Quarter Horses, Defiance, Ohio; and North Wales Quarter Horse Farm, Warrenton, Virginia. Although not shown extensively, he was a five-time GCS as a 2-year-old. Later, as a sire, he ranked fourth as a Leading Sire of Register of Merit horses.

The sire of 208 registered foals – 13 AQHA Champions: Tabano Command, Tabano Star Jr, Tabano Mollie, Tabano Star, Tabano Bay, Tabano Nancy, Tabano Pam, Tabano Rosa, Tabano Bobbie, Tabano Knight, Tabano Reno, Tabano Panther and Tabano Robin. He also sired the earners of seven Superior performance awards (five open and two youth).

Zantanon H P-18,679

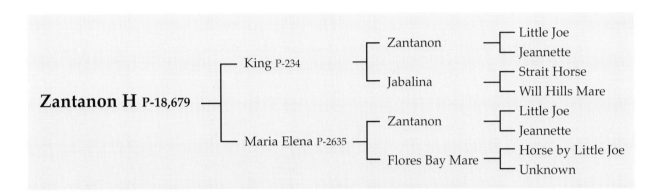

				Little Joe
			Zantanon	Jeannette
		King P-234		Strait Horse
			Jabalina	Will Hills Mare
Zantanon H P-18,679				Little Joe
			Zantanon	Jeannette
		Maria Elena P-2635		Horse by Little Joe
			Flores Bay Mare	Unknown

Bay stallion, foaled 1947; bred by Jess L. Hankins, Rocksprings, Texas.

Zantanon H was bred and owned by Jess L. Hankins and stood at stud along side his sire. He sold in 1965 to Joe Earnest, Rhome, Texas, and was still under his ownership when he died.

The sire of 171 registered foals – five AQHA Champions: Zan Sun (1964 NCHA Futurity Co-Champion; NCHA earnings of $6,582) Poco Zantanon, Traveler Sam, Zan Hankins and Georgie Zan (youth Champion). He also sired the earners of one Superior halter award, four Superior performance awards (two open and two youth); 20 performance ROMs (15 open and five youth); and the NCHA earners of $22,577. Other notable get: Black Gold Zan, 140 performance points and NCHA earnings of $4,397; Zantanon Charley, 163 youth performance points; and Zanto's Buster, 111 youth performance points.

Appendix B

King
Was Not
a
Quarter Horse

by

FRANKLIN REYNOLDS

King and the Saddlebred Controversy

By Robert A. Lapp

King's rise to fame was not without controversy. By the late 1950s, historian and pedigree researcher Franklin Reynolds began to suspect that part, if not all, of King's pedigree was incorrect. His subsequent research resulted in the 1960 publication of a 44-page booklet titled *King Was Not a Quarter Horse* and gave rise to the "Saddlebred controversy."

Because this now very rare booklet was of sufficient historical import to be noted in Don Hedgpeth's book *They Rode Good Horses: The First Fifty Years of the American Quarter Horse Association*, it deserves comment in this treatise on King's life.

By his own account, as noted on the inside cover page of the booklet, Reynolds was a "Sometime (1948–1950 and 1956–1959) historian for the American Quarter Horse Association." He further described himself as a "regularly employed historian, devoting all of my time to this work [historical research] and deriving the whole of my income from funds belonging to the members of the American Quarter Horse Association."

He was, in his own words, "a lawyer by profession and an historian by preference."

Prior to the start of his King investigation, Reynolds had published highly detailed and well-documented stories in the *Quarter Horse Journal*. Though his writing style was cumbersome, difficult to read and perhaps more suited for academic journals, it revealed a man highly passionate about his work and dedicated to reporting the truth. He was not to be taken lightly, nor was he.

King Was Not a Quarter Horse not only gave the legendary stallion an entirely new pedigree; it attacked AQHA's hierarchy and accused various people and the association's executive committee of covering up efforts to set the record straight. Though Reynolds believed he had found the truth and was obliged to report it, the issues he raised were never resolved and they ended his career as a Quarter Horse historian.

What, then, was this "Saddlebred controversy"?

Reynolds hinted at an impending storm by publishing an article about King in the September 1957 issue of *The Cattleman*. He wrote on page 56: "This historian does not believe that the correct pedigree of Jabalina (King's dam) has ever been published, and that when finally authenticated it may be quite different from anything so far offered. A search for it is now underway."

His search must have reached a satisfactory ending, for *King Was Not a Quarter Horse* described, in considerable detail, five major claims, the substance of which are as follows:

1) The AQHA studbook contains many errors: "It is well known ... that there is a vast multiplicity of errors ... in the stud books of the American Quarter Horse Association."

2) These errors "are presently being ignored, if not actually concealed. ..."

3) "But now it has been developed that the dam of King was not by the Strait Horse; that her entire breeding as given in the Stud Book was, and is, wrong, and that a completely new pedigree, one never offered before, is in order."

4) Jabalina's paternal and maternal grand-sires were one and the same—a registered American Saddlebred named Barrington: "What is presented here is sufficient to show King as a part-bred Quarter Horse, not a full-bred one, he being one-quarter American Saddle (five-gaited) Horse."

5) King's sire was not Zantanon: "This historian has done a great deal of research ... and it is his personal opinion, based on accu-

mulated evidence, that King's sire should be designated as 'unknown.' "

As would be expected, these claims—first suggested in 1957 while King was still alive and subsequently detailed a short two years after the famous stallion's death—did not go unnoticed.

Roy Davis, then editor of the *Quarter Horse Journal*, responded to Reynolds, challenging the "evidence" in a September 1960 *Journal* editorial titled, "The Breeding of King." Davis offered counter-evidence, arguing that Barrington, for many different reasons, could not possibly have been Jabalina's ancestor.

Is King's official pedigree incorrect? Did Reynolds make an indisputable case for a revised pedigree? Did AQHA intentionally cover up the truth because of King's already legendary status in the annals of Quarter Horse history? Should the entire issue have received greater attention?

Reynolds believed he had discovered the truth of King's pedigree and was convinced the available evidence warranted correcting the record. Others were not so sure and remained unconvinced.

In the end, the official pedigree remained unchanged, Reynolds and AQHA went their separate ways, and the controversy found its proper place—an interesting sidebar in the epic story of the life and times of King P-234.

Whatever the stallion's pedigree, even Reynolds could not and did not deny King his role as a cornerstone of the Quarter Horse industry. Davis probably put the issue to rest in the most appropriate way when he wrote: "I figure the arguments mean very little to the offspring of King. They are what they are by matter of heritage. They have made their own way and won their own laurels."

PHOTO INDEX

King P-234 & Jess Hankins

AUTHOR'S PROFILE

FRANK HOLMES has been penning horse-related feature articles and historical books since 1965. His interests have always been centered on the historical aspects of the western horse breeds, and his broad-based knowledge of the origins of the Quarter Horse, Paint, Appaloosa and Palomino registries have established him as one of the pre-eminent equine historians of all-time.

As a former staff writer for *Western Horseman* magazine, Frank co-authored volumes 2 through 6 of the immensely popular Quarter Horse Legends book series and authored *The Hank Wiescamp Story*.

As the award-winning Features Editor of *The Paint Horse Journal* he contributed a steady stream of top-notch personality profiles, genetic studies, and historical overviews.

In early 2001, Frank launched LOFT Enterprises, LLC – his own publishing company. Since that time he has devoted the lion's share of his journalistic efforts to the research and writing of historical books designed to capture the West's rich history and pass it on in a way that both enlightens and entertains. Among the books to be authored under LOFT's banner are *Wire to Wire – the Walter Merrick Story* (2001), *More Than Color* (2002) and *Spotted Pride* (2003).

Now living in Falcon, Colorado, Frank and his wife Loyce have three sons – Eric, Craig and Morgan; three daughters-in-law – Carrie, Roxanne and Renee; and three grandchildren – Steven, Mitch and Sydnie.

Production continues on the grandchild front…

For more information on the American Quarter Horse, contact:

American Quarter Horse Association
1600 Quarter Horse Drive, Amarillo, TX 79104
P.O. Box 200, Amarillo, TX 79168
Customer Service (806) 376-4811
Records Research (806) 376-7415
AQHA Web Site: www.aqha.com

The American Quarter Horse Heritage Center & Museum
2601 I-40 East, Amarillo, TX 79104
(806) 376-5181

The American Quarter Horse Journal
1600 Quarter Horse Drive, Amarillo, TX 79104
P.O. Box 32470, Amarillo, TX 79120
(806) 376-4888   FAX (806) 349-6400
E-mail: aqhajrnl@aqha.org

TO BE CONTINUED...

Harlan

Joe Cody

Gay Bar King

Blondy's Dude

THE LINES...

KING P-234   Vol. 2

Hollywood Dun It

Royal Blue Boon

Smart Little Lena

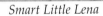

Smart Chic Olena

Shining Spark

...OF SUCCESSION